The Miriam Tradition

TEACHING EMBODIED TORAH

UNIVERSITY OF ILLINOIS PRESS

URBANA, CHICAGO, AND SPRINGFIELD

Library of Congress Cataloging-in-Publication Data
Sautter, Cia.
The Miriam tradition : teaching embodied Torah /
Cia Sautter.
p.   cm.
Includes bibliographical references and index.
ISBN 978-0-252-03577-7 (cloth : alk. paper)
ISBN 978-0-252-07762-3 (pbk. : alk. paper)
1. Dance—Religious aspects—Judaism. 2. Miriam (Biblical
figure) 3. Jewish women—Religious life. 4. Women in Judaism.
5. Sephardim. I. Title.
BM729.D35S28   2010
296.4'6—dc22   2010024454

Contents

Preface

WHY MOVEMENT MATTERS

This is a tale about women's leadership of important Jewish rituals that conveyed Torah truth, following in the tradition of Miriam the prophetess. In many ways it is a forgotten story, perhaps because it involves dance and women, two things that Western intellectual tradition tends to deem inconsequential. Yet a high point of the Exodus story is Miriam leading women in dance and music, after Israel crosses through *Yam Suf*, the Red or Reed Sea.[1] This image has always intrigued me, because Torah says that Miriam was a *naviah*—a female prophet. For that reason, her performance seemed especially important.

It is possible to argue that Miriam's celebratory leadership was indeed significant. The same might be said of the leadership of the Jewish women of the past who followed in her tradition, leading life celebration rituals for their communities. Some scholars maintain that their rituals are "cultural" and "entertainment," implying that they were not a part of religious life. Yet religion is a part of culture that deals with deepest beliefs and values. With this view, the dance of Miriam and her descendants may be considered part of Torah tradition, as an enactment of Jewish values.

The Jewish women in this study were Sephardic, meaning that they were of Spanish Jewish origin. Following in the tradition of Miriam, they brought their culture of dance, drumming, and song to their Judaism. They also brought their Judaism to their culture, performing dance and music rituals for specific Jewish holidays and special occasions. I explore this history as significant embodied text through a detailed cultural analysis involving written and visual records, along with evidence from dance and musical traditions.

Called *tanyaderas*, these women "taught" Torah values by leading appropriate behavior for major life events. At first this may seem an odd idea, but I purposely chose it to challenge limited definitions of Torah. Through their dance performances, the *tanyaderas* taught their community how to enact Torah through symbolic movement. By recognizing their "teaching," we can more fully include these women in Jewish history, and write them back into the records as important leaders of the community. Much research and many publications in the past ten years have dealt with this kind of recovery of women's history. My study is slightly different, however, as I seek more than the details of history. My emphasis is on practices of women outside the synagogue as a significant part of Jewish religious life. Rather than featuring exceptional Jewish women who entered the realm of rabbinic scholarship, I seriously consider what more ordinary women accomplished in an extraordinary activity.

Sephardic women were teachers of Jewish Torah through their rituals for celebrations marking holidays and life passages. My inclusion of studies on dance as a form of communication, cultural encoding, and teaching shows how I am here establishing this point. In fact, the dance studies are vital for understanding *how* Sephardic women's rituals might serve as a means of gathering evidence for the recording of religious history. Movement creates meaning. Jewish women's dance created and encoded specific meanings of, and for, Judaism. Therefore, the overall purpose of this book is to examine how embodied movement creates our deepest values, which cannot be expressed through words alone: they must be performed.

Religious values are imparted to a community in many ways, but perhaps especially through ritual and symbolic movement. Sephardic women's dance and music were simple in structure, and usually similar to the dances and music of the surrounding culture. But the focal point for their performances was often a time of life passage. If this type of ritual activity was a basis for Victor Turner's influential *The Ritual Process*, should it not be significant enough to examine in more detail here?

In our present multicultural society, while we may recognize and appreciate the many spiritually rich movement traditions in Eastern religions, we seem to have forgotten that Judaism and other Western religions have them as well. I want to correct this inaccuracy. Along with current theories of embodiment and performance, Judith Plaskow's concept of Torah as something lived provides me with a means of including the rituals of *Sephardiyot* (Sephardic women) as part of Jewish tradition, and of overcoming objections to Torah as more than written text. The concept also allows me to expand the definition of religion, rather than limiting it to philosophy or theology. There is nothing wrong with philosophy or theology. Yet to confine religion to a thought process alone siphons the spirit and culture out of the practice. So I join Plaskow's idea of Torah with the dynamic concepts of modern Jewish thinker Franz Rosenzweig. Although his work is from the early twentieth century, his ideas on the importance of ritual movement and revelation in Judaism still have much relevance, and relate well to more recent ritual theories.

To better examine ritual performance, I have also incorporated the ideas of ritual scholars Ronald Grimes, Catherine Bell, and especially Tom Driver as they have outlined in detail the primacy of the body in creating meaning. Critically, I have included the work of George Lakoff and Mark Johnson on the body basis of language, and in the process redefined postmodernist views of dance as "text." Rather then viewing dance as a reflection of spoken and written language, I view the symbolic movement of dance as a means of creating language.

I greatly appreciate the lessons I have learned from study of dance about movement as primary; without movement, there is no life. This is true especially in religious life. Movement is not tangential to religion, for religious life is about performance. Unfortunately, much of the dance history that I have studied in academic classes and personal research has concentrated on stage dance or non-Western cultures. Some scholars even complain that Western religion is antithetical to dance. However, dance anthropology and dance therapy studies have provided me with rich resources on the social and psychological impact of dance, and even a few studies on dance and religion. Ethnomusicologists supplied even more specific knowledge of dance in Judaism.

Studies on dance in religion are few, however, and in my research it seemed that only ritual scholars pay attention to the body and movement. I found that while postmodern thought produced some studies on thinking about the body, they had little to say about lived, physical reality. My intent is to begin to fill this gap in religious scholarship, providing a case study on the performance of religion. I look at dance as ritual that prepares individuals to act out their beliefs in culture. If anything, then, this is a study that examines "internal dimensions of performance, symbolism, and intention" to "allow for an understanding of major metaphors employed in . . . ritual activity."[2]

My study maintains that people live out their beliefs in action as well as in words. In Judaism specifically, Torah is a prime example of teaching that is deeper than can be expressed in words alone. Of course, there is a physical Torah, composed of words and written in a scroll. But because the Torah is a teacher of how one is to live life, it may also be expressed without words. This might be seen in the visual, musical, and movement history of the *Sephardiyot*. When the many reports about the lives and culture of these Jewish women are collected and compared, their leadership might help us create inclusive rituals of deep significance for our own lives.

Much more research on the history of Jewish women is required before any clear conclusions can be drawn, and at best this will still be historical interpretation. Yet by learning about Sephardic women's performance traditions, we may gain some insight into their lives as well as our own.

Acknowledgments

Since the writing of this book, both my father and my doctoral advisor died. Both assisted me greatly. My father was my initial proofreader, advisor, and writing mentor. Doug Adams guided me through the doctoral program at the Graduate Theological Union, and with his great grace and humor made it a fabulous adventure. Thanks also go to my family, my friend and fellow scholar Emily Silverman, as well as those who assisted me at United Theological Seminary of the Twin Cities, Richard Weis, Mary Farrell Bednarowski, and Carolyn Pressler. Finally, thanks to all my dance friends, teachers, and students—you make the world a better place.

THE MIRIAM TRADITION

1 Women and Sacred Power

Rambam (1135–1205) mentions in his writing the
adoption of alien dance-customs by the Jews in Egypt,
when he describes a bride taking a sword or rapier in
hand and executing a sword-dance before her wedding
guests. He of course prohibits this sort of dance as
opposed to Jewish morals and altogether alien to the
spirit of Jewish tradition.

—Zvi Friedhaber, "Dance among the Jews in the
   Middle Ages and the Renaissance"

When scholars say that women are more concerned with
ritual than with theology, the implication often is that
ritual is somehow less noble, important, or sophisticated
than theology. While men sit and ponder and write about
complex metaphysical problems, women jump up and
down and ask the spirits to cure their children of the flu.
This sort of dichotomous and androcentric thinking is of
little use in grappling with women's religions.

—Susan Starr Sered, *Priestess, Mother, Sacred Sister*

Women's Texts and Rituals

When I tell people that I study "religion and dance," the response almost always makes me wince. I often hear, "David danced before
the ark and all that, but what else is there?" Apparently no one remem-
bers Miriam: a prophet and leader of Israel, she is the icon for dance in
the Torah. Of the many overt passages on dance in the Bible, most refer
specifically to women's role as leaders of ritual for the community of
Israel. The supreme example is the prophetess Miriam, who led women
in dance and song after the crossing of the sea.

So what happened to Miriam and these dancing women? And why do people remember David rather than Miriam? Those questions became a starting point for my investigation into the relationship between women, dance, and ritual around the world, especially in the West. Through my investigation, I concluded that Miriam not only danced, but she danced a Torah lesson. And even though the many Jewish female ritual leaders who followed her tradition seldom received credit for their important leadership, they were also teaching Torah values to their community through their dance and music.

My conclusion is meant to be a bit jarring, although it is not a simplistic idea. It considers the complexity of Torah interpretation, the range of Torah meaning, and the limits set on acknowledging Jewish women as transmitters of Torah tradition. The questions I ask along the way involve historiography, ritual, and culture in the study of Judaism. But first there is the issue of dance itself. In the Western world, study of dance has often been removed from its base in religious ritual. It has frequently been feminized into a realm for the Anna Pavlovas, Isadora Duncans, and Martha Grahams among us. Yet the Eastern world has the *devadasi* temple dancers of Juggernaut, the ritual dancing of Thai girls, and Balinese sacred dancers. When the world dances, women are often the dancers. In most of the world, dance is also commonly a part of religious ritual. For instance, African warriors' rites of passage, Native American Sun Dance ceremonies, and Hopi Kachina dance practices are the subject of numerous fascinating studies in the fields of anthropology and sociology. Significantly, it seems, these are dances performed by males.

But what of *women's* dance rituals? What happened to the biblical tradition of women leading the community in celebration? And from a broader perspective, where are the dance rituals of Western society? It is not that this material is absent from scholarship; there are, for example, anthropological studies of European dance rituals. But this is not a subject that is likely to be included in a religious textbook. With the exception of Carole Meyers's "The Drum-Dance-Song Ensemble," there has been scant attention to this role of women in biblical and Jewish traditions.

There are many reasons for the absence of information. One is the post-Enlightenment rational approach to religion and Judaism, which stresses philosophy and written text over performance. As Susan Sered indicates, women were not always recognized as *religious* ritual leaders because of their use of movement, dance, and music rather than doctrine. Their emphasis on ritual and ritual movement is somehow interpreted as primitive, or less developed. Or their activities are called "cultural" rather than religious because they do not take place in a temple, church, or synagogue. In Judaism, however, there is no break between the "religious" and the secular. All of life is a part of being Jewish. Rituals occur at home on the Sabbath, on holidays, and even through blessings said when observing natural phenomena. Furthermore, dance has been a part of Jewish ritual since biblical times, and continued to play a role in community life in the Diaspora.

Judaism, Dance, and Women

In the Bible, the Talmud, and rabbinic writings (*responsa*), dance is portrayed not only as an activity connected with Jewish worship and celebration, but in fact as a necessity. Some may be surprised to learn that dance was endorsed by the rabbis of the Talmud. However, in Mediterranean cultures, including Israel, there were many dances for rituals and celebrations. Women were part of this activity, and at times the leaders of these events, although documentation of their leadership is sparse. Yet there is enough evidence to demonstrate that Jewish women performed stylized and specific actions during significant times in significant places using symbolic gestures, motions, and dance.

In the Hebrew Bible, there are ten primary words used to describe the activity of dancing in general, and its use for celebration, worship, and mourning. Significantly, one term, *machol*, refers specifically to women's dance. Biblical passages that use this word include Exodus 15:20, Judges 11:34, and 1 Samuel 18:16, 21:12b, and 29:5. The word could mean to whirl or to writhe.[1] There are also "countless passages of biblical and post-biblical literature" about dance. Post-biblical rabbinic material contains so many words for dance that Alfred Sendrey declared, "no other ancient language possesses this wealth of expressions describing the various aspects of dancing."[2] European medieval and Renaissance Jewish reports also note that dance was a part of Jewish festivities. Every Jewish community in the medieval period had a dance hall, and dance was a favorite activity.[3]

Some of the dances mentioned in the Bible were led by women and were used for worship-specific activities. Parallel archeological evidence from the Eastern Mediterranean region even suggests that a special women's chorus led the dance and music of the ancient Temple in Jerusalem. Carol Meyers's article "The Drum-Dance-Song Ensemble" explores this activity and its implications for understanding women's leadership in the ancient Near East.

Written evidence of women's leadership includes passages in the

Psalms (30, 149, 150), the story of Miriam leading women in a victory dance, the account of the victory dance by Jepthah's daughter, and similar passages in the book of Judges, all using the term *machol*. These texts report on times during the period prior to or during the First Temple. Biblical and archeological evidence from the Second Temple period is more tenuous on women's musical leadership. Written rabbinic evidence suggests that as the synagogue service developed, women ceased to function as ritual leaders.

During the rabbinic period, it appears that Jewish women were not initially excluded from performing Jewish synagogue ritual, and that they could participate in worship services.[4] However, their musical leadership of sanctioned ritual eventually became an impossibility. At first, the rabbis determined that women were not obligated to fulfill all ritual commands. Time-bound positive commandments were the obligation of only the men. There was an understanding that "women may observe them if they so choose," but limiting factors existed.[5]

Women were sometimes excluded from services, and were even silenced. For instance, a *minyan* of ten men was required for group prayer; women could not participate. A *minyan* was also required for "reading . . . the *haftarah* (Prophets) . . . recitation of *Kaddish* (mourner's prayer) and sanctification prayers (*Kedushah* and *Barekhu*), consolation of mourners, and the seven blessings of marriage."[6] Another limitation on women's involvement in worship involved the laws of *niddah*. A *niddah*—a menstruating woman—was often excluded from services in the synagogue. In *Women and Jewish Law*, Rachel Biale points out that this was not actually *halakhah* (law), and there were many interpretations of when and how a *niddah* could participate in a synagogue service. Yet the custom of excluding a *niddah* persisted.[7] Finally, according to rabbinic interpretation of the Talmud, hearing a woman's voice was abhorrent, because it distracted men from worship.[8] This interpretation eliminated the possibility of women's musical leadership in the synagogue, and of any associated dance practices.

Other sources of information provide a picture of a dynamic Jewish community in medieval southern Spain, offering a different picture of synagogue life. For example, secular poetry by notable Spanish Jews such as Abraham Ibn Ezra and Judah Halevi was set to music and sung responsively within the synagogue.[9] This interesting slice of medieval Jewish life in Spain suggests that rabbinic ruling may not have been actively employed, and what became written text was not necessarily the reality of embodied text. Accounts suggest that congregations were lenient about rulings, as rabbis objected to the use of secular music in synagogue worship.[10] This probably means that secular music was used in synagogue services. Still, there is little doubt that if women led Jewish ritual, their performance occurred outside the synagogue.

SEPHARDIC SPAIN IN MUSIC AND DANCE

Dance might have provided a ritual activity for women, even though it was not necessarily done in fulfillment of Jewish law. However, rabbinic and biblical records indicate that women's dances have long been a part of Jewish custom. Dance as a part of Jewish ritual celebration did not end when the Second Temple was destroyed, but the connection to Jewish worship practices then became more peripheral. Perhaps one reason for the lack of dance was new strictures on the use of music. According to the Talmud, after the destruction of the Second Temple, Israel was to mourn; playing of musical instruments on the Sabbath would no longer be permitted. In conjunction, "when the Jews were sent into exile the dancing associated with the normal activities of a nation in its own country ceased." Women did not cease to dance, however; "some vestige of the women's dances may have remained in the female singers and drummers who accompany the joyful dancing of women in many of the ethnic groups."[11]

By the time of Raba B. Hanin (c. 350 C.E.), the elimination of dancing from the Sabbath and from festivals was explained by arguing that dancing might lead to the repairing of instruments, as labor was forbidden on such occasions (Mishnah Sotah 48a; Mishnah Bezah 36b and 30a; Mo'ed VI). But the rabbis were also specific in stating that one was to "rejoice" during weddings, and this was interpreted to mean "dance." According to Doug Adams, "rabbis are reported to have even led dancing with the brides after the fall of the Sanhedrin." He refers to the Talmud (Kethuboth 17a, Nashim III, Pe'ah 15d), in addition to other early rabbinic materials.[12] Significantly, then, in the Mediterranean world, weddings became the focal point for women's dance and music connected with Jewish practice.[13]

Despite regulations concerning music, and by association dance, we know from the Talmud, rabbinic *responsa*, artwork, and travelogues that weddings were not the only occasions on which women danced. These materials record dance of a more purely entertaining nature performed for social occasions, as well as dance associated with more obviously sacred occasions. Records on social dances note the activity of Jews in the higher echelons of Spanish society, indicating that participation in mixed-couples dances was part of their education and social life.[14] Other material shows that Jewish women in pre-expulsion Spain used dance for the celebration of the New Moon (*Rosh Chodesh*), holidays, and funerals, in addition to weddings.[15]

SOCIAL DANCE AND JEWISH WOMEN IN SPAIN

There is a relative abundance of material concerning the practice of mixed-couples social dance in medieval Spain, in which Jewish women participated. Mixed-couples courtly dance was a precursor of Renaissance dance, so the records of Jewish dance masters contain evidence on women's involvement. Part of the reason for the documentation is that the rabbis generally did not approve of men dancing with women, and they wrote about their dissatisfaction in *responsa*. Some *responsa* comment on this new, tradition-breaking behavior. According to Amnon Shiloah, "R. Abraham, son of Maimonides (1135–1205)," objected to "women who imitate the dances of Gentiles" engaging in the "deplorable behavior" of "dance before men." He believed that they would be "completely excluded from the world to come." Rabbi Shlomo Ben Aderet (1270–1343) complained that it was "overstepping all moral bounds" to let young people dance together on the Sabbath as they did in Spain. Shiloah also reports an interesting dance custom that was popular in Spain, involving the wearing of a horse figure around the neck called a *kurraj* (an Arabic word): "Girl dancers . . . would decorate themselves by hanging the models on their bosoms when they appeared at parties."[16]

These comments are not surprising, given that Jews were fully integrated into the Islamic society of medieval Spain and lived in all strata of society.[17] The *responsa* statements also tell us something about the social status of Jewish women, which appears to have been rather dynamic. Also worth noting is that the *responsa* cited above do not object to women dancing. The objection is to their dancing in mixed company, and their adapting offensive local customs.

Women's performance in front of men does not seem to have been an issue for the rabbis of medieval Spain. There remains a question, however, of when women were permitted to dance in public. A case in point is the *zambra* celebration. *Zambras* were grand parties given by the Moorish rulers of Andalusia. Jews actively participated in these events, which literally involved wine, women, and song. Islamic law bans all three, yet a great deal of wine was served at a *zambra*, while the guests listened to talented instrumentalists. While the music played, women danced behind a transparent veil. Raymond P. Scheindlin reports that "revelers passed the night drinking, nodding, waking, and drinking again," and "enjoy[ing] the performances of dancers and singers . . . [who were] usually women who performed behind a curtain."[18] It is possible that Jewish women danced at these celebrations.

The musicians and poets at these events were often Jews. Judah Halevi and Ibn Ezra frequently described *zambras* in their poems, and their works were performed at the parties. Who the dancers were is not clear. They were perhaps slaves from Persia, professional entertainers, or women of the courts.[19] Evidence exists for all three possibilities, and all three possibilities could have involved Jewish women. Judging from what is known about the period, the only thing that is safe to assume is that the dance style was strongly Middle Eastern.

According to Richard Schechner, performance may be edifying, entertaining, or a mixture of the two. While the "belly dance" style of the *zambra* was in an entertaining secular performance mode, the style itself was probably common to the women of southern Spain, and used for a wide variety of dance events.[20] In her classic work *The Dance in Spain*, Anna Ivanova cites very old Roman historical records indicating that Spanish women swung and trembled their hips when they danced, and that they also played a castanet-type instrument made out of shells.[21] Wendy Buonaventura mentions that Romans noted this type of dance in Spain during the time of Ovid, who commented on a dancer from Cadiz. The dance sounds very sensuous in his description: "graceful her arms, moving in subtle measure; insinuating she sways her hips." Juvenal "described dancers who 'sink to the ground and quiver with applause' . . . while the poet Martial recorded seeing them 'swing lascivious loins in practised writhings.'"[22]

Most likely, Jewish women in Spain also practiced this style of dance, as it was part of the culture. And despite the objections from those such as Maimonides, there was nothing in Jewish law that prevented the possibility. In contrast to Christian and Islamic doctrine on dance, this is a significant point.[23] However, calling a dance style "Jewish" is problematic, suggesting that there were common or unique characteristics of movement, and perhaps a symbolic expression of a set of values.

Records describing Jews in processionals mention a characteristic "national" dance that they were "forced" to present for Corpus Christi processionals in the late fifteenth century, and as "Saracenic" (Arabic) in style.[24] This same label was applied to a dance used by Jewish women for a processional in Italy around this period, which according to Dvora Lapson perhaps indicates what the "national" style looked like.[25] How

Jewish women danced is not the major issue for recovering their history, as "according to the custom of the land" seems to be the usual answer.[26] But questions of when, where, and why they danced do start to involve religious significance.

Dance scholar Judith Brin Ingber indicates that a broad variety of times and places for dance existed, according to evidence in *responsa* comments, manuscripts, illuminations, and public records. Her research focused on dancing at *zambra* parties in an exploration of the history of dance among the Sephardim.[27] While these courtly parties of music, dance, and poetry were a cultural activity of Jews in Moorish Spain, held for entertainment and enjoyment, there may have been a theological dimension to some degree as well, especially in terms of recreation as celebrating creation, and mention of God in the poetry at *zambra* parties. But *zambras* were not rituals for religious celebration.

Because rabbis defined the time, place, and purpose of official Jewish worship, rituals conducted in Spanish synagogues might indicate unique Jewish movement patterns. These movements may also have influenced or modified movement in the dances of Spanish Jews. Some records of medieval Spanish liturgical practices provide fascinating insights into this possibility. For instance, a "Dance of Death" (*Danza de la muerta*) in fourteenth-century Spain is attributed to a Rabbi Santob de Carron, and a Rabbi Hacen ben Salomo reportedly taught Christians a chancel dance for performance around an altar in Saragossa.[28] Yet synagogue worship was primarily the realm of men; and women's ritual leadership within the synagogue did not exist.

Information about synagogue worship allows for a greater understanding of the kinds of encoding that occurred in movement for Judaism of the period, and suggests why there are references to a Jewish style. Yet for women, their nonverbal text of dance existed outside the realm of the synagogue. The *zambra* parties and reports of social dance provide clues about the dances that were done by Jewish women in Spain. But beyond the *responsa*, and beyond the poetry and records of the *zambras*, there are other sources that can provide insight into dancing by Sephardic women for, and among, women. This material consists of images from the time period and "oral" history of dance in the Sephardic communities of the Diaspora. Jewish travelers' reports and folkloric records that note times when women gathered with drums and song are also helpful. All written and visual sources of evidence indicate that weddings, births, and deaths were times for women's dance, involving rituals for these events of life passage.[29]

Critical Perspectives

In *Ritual Medical Lore of Sephardic Women,* Isaac Lévy and Rosemary Lévy Zumwalt describe Jewish women's rituals that involved herbs and healing. Rather than label this activity "cultural," they borrow Barbara Myerhoff's use of Robert Redfield's concept of a "Greater Tradition" and a "Little Tradition." They conclude that Jewish women's domestic ritual practices are a "Little Tradition" that exists alongside official Judaism.[30]

Evaluations of local traditions existing alongside official religious practices are common in Hindu studies, with village Goddess worship considered a "Little Tradition" paradoxical to Orthodoxy. While such assessments work relatively well for the complex system that is Hinduism, they can reduce the value of women's practices as part of an official, larger religious tradition. As a result, the patriarchal "orthodox" structure becomes the official religion as the "Greater Tradition." Such an evaluation may often be overly simplistic. For instance, Roxanne Gupta suggests that the *devadasis,* the women temple dancers of India, may well have been the feminine side of yoga. While officially unorthodox, ascetic male yogis practiced outside the official temple system, the erotic *devadasi* served as the feminine *yoganini* "mirror" in the temple.[31]

Gupta's research is noteworthy, and her conjecture underlines the complexity of referring to unofficial traditions as standing outside the total complex of a religion. Of course, the *devadasis* did not practice a domestic tradition, although their inclusion in temple practices may reflect the "Little Tradition" of domestic village Goddess worship. Hinduism itself is perhaps best described as a collection of Indian practices held together through a foundation in the Vedas. Paradoxical practices within Hinduism, then, are not so surprising. Yet Judaism might also be viewed as a complex tradition held together through a foundation in Torah. *Minhag* or custom has frequently been part of the practice of this religion.[32]

It is possible, then, to view Sephardic women's dance leadership as significant and as part of the larger, official tradition of Judaism, rather than as *minhag* or a lesser practice. Susan Sered's research on women's dominant religions and ritual practices explains this point. Sered finds that with "an emphasis on ritual," women-dominant religions are not "simplistic," as is apparently assumed by some in modern religious study. Rather, their practices are holistic, involving the body and mind through ritual. She surmises that "if we abandon a dichotomy between ritual" as "magical, superstitious, ignorant" and "theology" as "philosophical, abstract, unselfish, moral," we begin to see that ritual can express very complex belief systems.[33] Likewise, Sephardic women's dance rituals might be viewed as a complex and active encoding of Torah tradition. Practiced outside the synagogue, it was a tradition they owned, not subject to the dictates of male hierarchy.

In postmodernist thought, there is perhaps more acceptance of the significance of performance and ritual in a society, especially as alternative texts to the written word. Yet because of the perceived dichotomy between religion and culture that developed after the Enlightenment, often we still do not have a clear understanding of the connection between beliefs, culture, and embodied practices. For instance, the popularity of Argentinean tango dancing might have something to do with what people perceive as proper social behavior. The tango may demonstrate religious morals that respect a male-female partnership, with clear gender identity in community or the merit of cooperation. These values are reflected and embodied in the dance, with stress on a strong male lead and the interconnection of partners.

As the product of a culture, dance can function as a form of symbolic communication, translating and even creating important values, and conveying religious standards of socially acceptable behavior. For, of course, religion itself is a product of culture, even though it may maintain a separate identity. Muslim religious scholar Talal Asad sheds light on this relationship, explaining that a dialogue exists between religion and culture. A culture's total pattern of thinking and doing is part of religious and social existence. "Religious symbols" of all types are created in conjunction with their "historical relations with nonreligious symbols," and how they are used in a society.

Asad explains that religion is a part of culture and develops as a part of history. Understanding a religion may mean that it is necessary to first examine the culture in which it exists.[34] A dance may not be part of a religious ritual, for example, but its movement patterns might reflect ritual practices. Or a sacred ritual may borrow an appropriate style of movement from a culture's social dance customs. Additionally, what is considered appropriate movement might be set by religious values, creating and reflecting metaphors of deeply held principles about what is most important in life. Those metaphors may be stated in actual words and scripture, or they may be embodied in forms of art.

Asad's view is as a Muslim critiquing the academic study of religion. But he echoes the Jewish concern for understanding religion as a way of life. Many postcolonialist scholars agree with him, including Richard King. In *Orientalism and Religion* King concludes that a focus on theology can blind religious scholars to the integrated view of religion and culture in most of the world. The result has been a disembodied construction of religious history, with little insight into how people performed their religion.

The importance of perceiving a dialogue between religion and culture is certainly not a new insight. Prior to postcolonialist critique, theologian Paul Tillich recognized that it is not necessary for an obvious religious form to be present in order for art to express religious values. Discussing "existentialist aspects of modern art," he explained that sacred symbolic value may be ascribed to secular art.[35] Tillich dealt primarily with visual art, yet his insights highlight how religious thought can be expressed in physical symbols, and how those symbols can also help form religious thought. Rather than simply reflecting culture, the arts might help shape religious understandings through physical reality.

Dance can be thought of as a highly embodied art form, conveying values through the body. Study of dance and movement might allow for recognition of how our highest values are enacted through movement, and how the parameters of our movement shape our understanding of the world. More recent feminist scholars such as Judith Butler and Gayatri Chakravorty Spivak seem to call for such scholarship. They identify a need for study that recognizes the "lived body" of women, "interwoven with and constitutive of systems of meaning, signification, and representation."[36] However, the tendency in this criticism is to see the body as socially constructed, reflecting cultural and often patriarchal ideas. While this view allows for women's lives to enter history, women's practices are frequently seen as the product of an inscribed social norm. Society constructs the individual in this view, and "is the sole source of meaning; our bodies . . . are inert repositories for the meaning structures produced by the collective mind" of culture.[37] Similarly, even women-led rituals might be construed as an oppressive pattern of behavior forced on unwilling participants.

Postcolonialist feminist scholarship has corrected this problem to some degree, and there are many fine studies that show women interpreting and acting independently of their social norms. These studies allow for the possibility of women's performance not only as a response to an inscribed system, but as a means of independent thought. For instance, in an essay on postcolonialism and religious discourse, Kwok Pui-lan shows that Chinese women's foot-binding was not a given, but an option that involved attaining social status for some.[38] Such attention to women's performance—what they did do—also corrects the postmodernist tendency to view actions as a literary text, reflecting the language of a culture. "Metaphors of 'authorship' and 'text' as the building blocks of human reality are still quite thick on the ground," Edward Slingerland notes in his critique of social constructionist theories, even though heavy-hitting theorists such as Jacques Derrida have distanced themselves from this position.[39] The body and performance are lost in the process.

In *Philosophy in the Flesh*, George Lakoff and Mark Johnson write about the body as the base of language and thought, providing a more physically oriented view of "lived bodies" creating meaning. This is a highly physical view of culture, suggesting that rather than acting only within given social structures, individuals create and respond to them through the body. The body is elementary, whereas spoken language is a secondary, abstract reflection of lived reality. Lakoff and Johnson say this occurs through the creation of conceptual metaphors that are based on bodily performance. In fact, they use religion as an example of a system that is thoroughly grounded in body-based metaphor. This is because religion deals with the noncognitive, almost inexpressible experiences of life. Therefore ritual action and spatial and body-based metaphors serve as the best means of relating such experience.

For Slingerland, examining religion with this type of grounding in physical reality is exactly what is required to overcome dualistic, disembodied, and ultimately incomplete views of religion.[40] Although he is concerned with science and religion, his point is that it is important not to overlook physical reality. With respect to women's history, then, women's activities must not be overlooked as "untheological" or simply as prescribed and patterned cultural custom. Sephardic women's dance and music was cultural custom, to be sure, but it was also much more than that. It may also be viewed as a reflection of Torah text, and as a generator of lived Torah tradition.

Dance as Embodied Religious Text

Recognition of movement and its meaning in a culture offers a way of actually deciphering the life, if not the creation, of values. Study of dance, then, might prove extremely important, as the activity is a concentrated, often sophisticated form of expression that offers insight into a given culture's symbol system. For example, a hip grind may be seductive and lewd in one culture but part of a sacred dance of life in another. It depends on the limits set by the values of the culture, and also on the culture's ability to accept and incorporate new movement patterns.

While this may seem a bit abstract, there are many examples from religious history to make the idea concrete. In fact, dance has played a significant role in religion and cultural history in the Western world as a symbolic performance of beliefs. Dance in Western religions has sometimes been acknowledged as something out of the distant past, as in such classic dance histories as Curt Sachs's *A World History of the Dance* or Lincoln Kirstein's *Dance: A Short History of Classical Theatrical Dancing*.[41] Yet in Judaism and Christianity, there were and are special times of religious dance celebration that are outside the worship setting yet associated with it in time and theme.[42]

In Judaism, examples include Purim feasts and *Lag B'Omer* bonfire dances. In Eastern and Western Christianity, there were dances for Pentecost, St. John's Day, and Sunday gatherings; some are still performed today. These occasions provide rich examples of how a religion can influence a culture, as the culture met the religion in specialized forms of music and dance. Still, it would be easy to argue that dance is a topic of culture, as a form of entertainment rather than edification, and that dancing seldom appears in Western religious life. Again, if dance is to be a topic of religious study, consideration of the importance of *performing* belief must be recognized. Movement might be viewed as nonverbal communication responding to or interpreting written text as a type of *midrash*.

When considering dance in religion, specific movements are not at issue. Concentrating on this one aspect of dance often results in missing the total complex of meaning, and focusing too narrowly on the production of signed and signified meaning. For instance, after presenting a paper on movement as a generator of language and thought at a literature conference, I performed a flamenco dance. One extremely vocal participant was obsessed with the meaning of every hand spin and arm move. Even though I explained that the dance was not story-driven like some parts of Indian *bharatanatyam* dance, he persisted in his attempt to turn my dance into a signifier of specific words. In this approach dance becomes a performance of language, rather than a preverbal initiator of meaning or a reflection on values and life experience.

It is a postmodern linguistic methodology that sets spoken and written language as the standard for communication. Dance is embodied communication, however, and it is highly effective in relating patterns of movement that display values. For example, bowing, lifting arms up, moving in circles, taking slow, deliberate steps, and making hand gestures are all typical examples of actions in a worship service. These movements might convey reverence, joy, wholeness, dignity, or peace.

Dances that are associated with, but not central to, religious worship services might still be viewed as a form of ritual practice, communicating beliefs through the body. Ritual theorists help explain how this happens.

Catherine Bell describes the practice as one where *"ritual exists as an implicit variety of schemes whose deployment works to produce socio-cultural situations that the ritual body can dominate."* Her point is that ritual occurs in the body, through the actions of the body, as a way of re-acting to what happens in a given setting. But body-reactive movement also changes what happens in that setting.[43] By employing movement, we conduct a conversation with the actions and events around us. Our highest values tell us which movements are proper and good for a ritual and which need to be added, and this movement also sets boundaries for how we act in society.

A very simple example of what Bell means would be shaking a neighbor's hand during a religious service to "pass the peace." Valuing this gesture in a ritual elevates its meaning outside the ritual setting, and in fact may encourage the behavior and the use of words that express the embodied values. Additions to set ritual movement might also encourage changed behavior in other settings. People in a small, intimate congregation, for example, might also hug one another at the passing of the peace, even though this action is not officially part of the ritual. As a result, the members might then be more prone to greet people in a social setting with a hug.

Like ritual movement, dance is expressed through the body, communicating that which is beyond words. It is preverbal expression as well as nonverbal expression. Religious scholars who considered this idea include Geradius Van der Leeuw. He examined the role of dance in the development of religion, equating dance with a feeling of power. Power being associated with transcendent reality, dance then connects the spiritual world with lived reality, as it "is not merely an esthetic pursuit existing side by side with other more practical activities." Rather, this extraordinary activity is "the service of the god," and through it "life is ordered to some powerful rhythm and reverts to its potent primeval motion." He concludes that experiencing such primal rhythm leads to a sense that one can "attain to all manner of things by 'dancing.'"[44]

The amount of energy that people feel when they are dancing at a rock concert might be the closest modern example of what Van der Leeuw means by power generated through dance and rhythm. Participants often report experiencing a surprising spiritual uplift; they find sacredness amid the supposed secular. Judging by some of Van der Leeuw's comments in his book *Sacred and Profane Beauty*, he might describe such a dance experience as inspiring because of the existence of sacred moments in what is supposedly a secular activity. Only when "dance diminishes" from worship, he maintains, does the notion of the sacred and profane arise.[45]

Emile Durkheim also described dance as a primary factor in the formation of religion, saying that, along with music, it is foundational to religion because it exhilarates participants. He paints a scene of a nighttime procession with dance and song, imagining that "smoke" and "blazing torches," and "showers of sparks falling in all directions," resulted in "effervescent social environments." From this experience, "the religious idea seems to be born."[46]

Both Durkheim and Van der Leeuw speak of the primordial stages of religious formation, and of how a sense of spirituality and experience of the transcendent might arise through dance. Philosopher Susanne Langer also described dance as primary to the formation of religious consciousness, as it makes concrete an imagined reality of greater beings: "the prehistoric evolution of dancing . . . is the very process of religious thinking, which begets the conception of 'Powers' as it symbolizes them." For Langer, then, dancing produces the concept of transcendent "Powers" because it has the ability to change consciousness. For example, even watching lively movement might lift one out of depression, or a group dance might generate a sense of community for those participating. Langer also ties dance to what she calls "mythic consciousness." Like verbal or written mythology, nonverbal ritual movement and dance raises one's awareness of realities beyond everyday existence. She calls this the "balletic realm of forces," which "is the world, and dancing is the human spirit's participation in it . . . the dancer's world is a world transfigured, wakened to a special kind of life."[47]

Langer wrote about stage performances such as *Swan Lake*. However, her use of "mythic consciousness" is rich, suggesting that dance and ritual actions produce not just metaphors in motion, but also mythic truth in motion. Her comments regarding dance and ritual are significant, and her remarks are particularly applicable to Jewish women. But what was their mythic consciousness if they could not read Torah, but only heard its stories? And how was their mythic consciousness of Torah and Judaism embodied and developed through a nonverbal process of ritual movement?

As members of a patriarchal religion, Jewish women were usually excluded from official ritual leadership within the synagogue. But Judaism is a way of life, as a religion that is practiced beyond sanctuary walls. So even in rabbinic Judaism, women did have ritual roles to play. Their traditionally acknowledged role was home-based, and involved ritual actions, motions, and gestures for blessing the Sabbath candles or baking challah loaves.[48] Even, or especially, in Jewish communities where women were denied access to traditional education and did not read, they still practiced Judaism through home ritual, as Sered describes in *Women as Ritual Experts*.

Rabbinic Jewish written liturgical practices for the synagogue might be recognized as official Jewish ritual. Yet this is an extremely limiting notion, even in regard to rabbinic Judaism. The words of blessings and prayers are extremely important to Jewish ritual, but actions are equally important. In fact, the Talmud tells us that the rabbis considered the performance of an action to be essential for completing a prayer. One was even to "bend the spine" in saying the eighteen benedictions (*Brachot* 28b). Torah teaching thus becomes a *living* reality through the accompanying gestures of blessings. Although the actions are for ritual, they set the Torah teaching into the body. This concept has almost always been important to the practice of Judaism. As Lawrence Hoffman points out in *Beyond the Text*, within rabbinic liturgies and prayers, one was "to do" the words rather than simply recite them.[49]

Women, however, were not obligated to perform Judaism as men were. Yet they too were Jews with a "mythic consciousness" as they practiced their Judaism. Dancing and dance rituals were part of Jewish women's experience in Sephardic communities, including almost every Jewish community that originated in Spain. Like Miriam and the other biblical women who danced, they danced mainly at celebrations, especially weddings, with often elaborate week-long proceedings consisting of ritual processions, songs, dances for the bride, and dances for the couple.[50]

When the *Sephardiyot* danced, they did not dance with men. Separation of men and women for dance was the custom in the Mediterranean communities where the Sephardim lived. Dances done by the women might be considered secular or cultural in style and nature, meaning that they were intended purely for entertainment. The women did dance in a pattern familiar to the culture, with secular music and steps. When and why they danced is equally important to consider. For instance, Hasidic men's dance has received attention as a special expression of Jewish spirituality. The traditional Hasidic dances look almost exactly like dances specific to northern and northeastern Europe, but they are recognized as theologically significant and as a particular expression of Jewish prayer. These dances are not labeled "cultural" because the intent is recognized as one of religious reverence and fervor.[51]

Studies of Yemenite music and dance provide another example of Jewish men's dance that is labeled as more significant than women's. The men utilized dance for part of their Sabbath ritual. But here, too, there was an interplay between religion and culture. When and where they danced depended on whether the lyrics were in Hebrew or Arabic, with dances specific to Yemenite culture rather than Jewish religious practices.[52]

Rather than cultural entertainment, Sephardic women's dance rituals might be seen as a form of expressive religious text utilizing local cultural tradition. Religious expression as a product of culture is, of course, what Clifford Geertz discussed in *The Interpretation of Cultures*, where he talks about religion as a model for, and a model of, a culture. Applying this to ritual, he suggests that it is a form of "cultural performances" of diverse meaning and purpose. Therefore rituals offer a special view of belief, in thought and action. "All cultural performances are not religious performances," yet it is not easy to tell the difference between the "artistic" and "religious." For "in practice . . . *symbolic forms can serve multiple purposes.*"[53]

Dance and ritual movement are symbolic, and may convey social or religious values or both; therefore, it is significant that Sephardic women were separated from men when they danced for times of life passage relevant to their existence, specifically for weddings, births, and deaths. Such occasions were social in nature, but they were marked by religious traditions. It is also important to question what dance at these life-cycle events might have meant to their sense of religious identity. Given the times and purpose for their dancing, there is at least an indication that in separation from men, they were able to express personal beliefs as Jewish women, free of oppressive restrictions. We do have some information in this regard, as they sang as well as danced, with their lyrics suggesting their understandings.

The musical legacies that we have from Sephardic women are poignant, relating their often difficult lives under patriarchal oppression. But music is only one side of the story. The silent language of dance that accompanied the music is as much an encoding of religious ideals as are lyrics and liturgical texts.[54] To delve into the possible meaning and history of these dances, examining the place of dance and women in Judaism, is revealing. A focus on the dance culture of Judaism, especially from Spain, also reveals much about how Jews involved themselves in culture. Along with textual information, the surviving dance traditions of these Sephardic women can serve as a means of recovering Jewish women's history.

Women and Dance: Gender Issues

Jewish dance history reveals a colorful view of Jewish life. If anything, the frequent use of dance in Jewish communities underscores that it was an activity in use by the Jewish community. This dance history also provides some insight into women's history in the Sephardic community, while raising familiar issues concerning gender and culture. Underlying issues include *when* and *how* women attain status and power within a society. Did establishing their own ritual leadership give women a means of coping with their exclusion from sanctioned ritual? Was dancing then a means of seeking power over oppression? It certainly may appear so, considering women's dance traditions in the Mediterranean and Near Eastern world.

Performance of ritual might have been a vehicle for women to assert their strength and leadership. "If discourse is power and ritual is discourse," writes Lesley Northup, "logic leads to the inescapable conclusion that ritual is . . . power."[55] Sered indicates how women's religions make use of movement, and Northup's study of modern women's creation of new worship experiences indicates that dance is frequently utilized. Yet women do not inherently use dance as a means of ritual expression.

Studies show that Jewish women's rituals for rites of passage frequently involved dance. It was an activity that was open to them for ritual expression. Yet saying that all women's rituals involve much choreographed movement runs the risk of essentialism, meaning that there is an assumption that women will behave in a certain way because they are women. Feminist gender studies includes theories suggesting that women are socially conditioned to act in a prescribed manner. While Judith Butler maintains that the very concept of gender is constituted through repeated actions, at the other extreme some French feminists take a more essentialist view, promoting the idea of women celebrating the unique qualities of the female body. Paula Cooey describes the French feminist concept of *phallogocentrism* as a symbolic form of "male power." It "connotes the extent to which woman's body, her sexuality, her language, and her subjectivity . . . are defined, denied, or treated as a means of exchange in patriarchal culture."[56]

Judith Lynne Hanna offers a slightly different view of issues of gender, ritual, and the body. As an anthropologist who studies performance as a means of constructing gender, she notes that through dance the body is a powerful medium for communicating and *also altering perceptions of appropriate gender behavior.* "The body language of dance may carry a more immediate wallop than verbal communication in commenting on sexuality and in modeling gender" with its " motion-attracting attention, language-like qualities, replete multilayered meaning, [and] multisensory assault." At times, therefore, it is a powerful and dramatic text, because it speaks more loudly than words.[57]

Hanna describes dance as a physical means of changing "attitudes and opinions" through "sexuality": "dancing can lead to altered states of consciousness," she says, "and hence to altered social action." The examples she gives include Greek bacchanals and the "corrupting dance of Salome," as well as clerics who "speak of abuses of dance, which was an accepted liturgical art form." She then defines dance as a *"medium through which . . . producers interpret, legitimate, reproduce, and challenge gender and associated patterns of cooperation and conflict that order their social world."*[58]

It is possible to say that Sephardic women, caught in a patriarchal Jewish system, danced in prescribed ways in order to survive their social order. If they taught these dance patterns to their children, they then conveyed religiously acceptable and *prescribed behavior* through ritualized patterns. So *Sephardiyot* lit candles and baked Sabbath challah loaves using specific ritualized gestures. Yet in order to consider Hanna's statements on dance as a language that might lead to defiance of social and religious norms, dance must also be viewed as a means of effecting changes in prescribed behavior. So in private women's gatherings, the *Sephardiyot* belly danced. Although it had many variations, this dance style might be read as a movement of defiance and self-empowerment for women.

Dance is a preverbal activity that can challenge existing perceptions of reality and offer new interpretations of life. Hanna's research and conclusions regarding dance and gender suggest that women sought release and self-empowerment through dance performance, including movement that celebrated the unique aspects of a woman's body. Within a patriarchal setting, such use of dance may be an unconscious choice for dealing with oppressive circumstances. While women may have played out preestablished gender roles in accepted movement behavior, dance among women provided a socially acceptable means of defining their circumstances, at least temporarily.

Using established movement conventions for the creation of new patterns of social behavior is still a matter of ritual performance. According to Bell, this process of "ritualization" enables a person to gain "an instinctive knowledge of schemes [or movement conventions] that can be used to order his or her experience." Ritual conventions are authoritative, and transmit acceptable patterns of social behavior. The ritual patterns thereby establish a set of standards for movement in a society.

However, in practice, ritual might also be viewed as "part of a historical process in which past patterns are reproduced but also *reinterpreted* or *transformed*." Likewise, Driver considers ritualization an essential part of ritual. He defines it as "the making of new forms through which expressive behavior can flow," where ritual "connotes . . . already known, richly symbolic pattern[s] of behavior."[59]

Bell's statement begins to explain what Van der Leeuw meant by being able to "attain to all manner of things by 'dancing.'" When new or different movements are used in ritual performance and dance, perceptions of authority may change for an individual. Self-expression and a sense of personal power may arise, for through the practice of ritual movement, a person may, through the "everyday production" of meaningful motion, "acquiesce yet protest, reproduce yet seek to transform their predicament."[60]

Ritual patterns are "magical," in that they provide a means of creating self-expression that alters one's perception of reality. Changing conventional ritual patterns of movement can provide individuals with the power to reform authority and convention, offering them a means for personal expression. Yet Driver notes that because ritual is powerful, it can be used abusively. As an example he mentions Hitler's propaganda minister Joseph Goebbels, who used ritual extensively.[61] Such rituals, however, lack a true quality of ritualization, encouraging personal expression or exploration. Without the possibility of ritualization, such events might even be considered simply propaganda rather than ritual.

Dance is a form of conventional activity that can especially allow for ritual self-expression and ritualization of standard forms of movement. Dance was apparently open to Sephardic women as an outlet for expression in the Mediterranean and North Africa, with outstanding examples including belly dance and the *zar* cult. Both relate directly to Sephardic women's dance in terms of shared culture and social conditions. Significantly, women's dance traditions in this part of the world were often for women only. In some sense this segregation was liberating, as it gave women an opportunity to dance as they pleased. According to Buonaventura, outside the male gaze women enjoyed the skill and power of other dancers, and were "quick to . . . encourage a good dancer with the *zhagareet*, and by clapping time to the music." She also notes that by dancing, these women "in many respects" were defying Islam's "laws concerning the conduct of women in society."[62] Likewise, some of the Hadith sayings of Mohammed were interpreted to mean that dance is simply unacceptable behavior.

Nevertheless, *raks al-sharqi*, or belly dance, was a common form of dance among the women. This is perhaps the epitome of the French feminists' concern with celebration of the female. Historical evidence ties this form of movement, with its focus on stomach rolls that mimic birthing contractions, to the Goddess worship of pre-patriarchal society in the Middle East and Mediterranean. The abdominal movement supposedly honors the creator of new life, whether that is the great mother or another deity. Some dance historians tie the dance form to flamenco, and the type of dance used by the Sephardic women as people of the Mediterranean.[63]

Overt ritual use of belly dance may have ended with the advent of patriarchal religions in the Mediterranean world, but the dance itself continued, primarily performed by women for women. Buonaventura notes this phenomenon in her study of belly dance, observing that nineteenth-century paintings portraying "oriental dance" in North Africa clearly indicate that women showed more interest in performances than men. "Middle Eastern women sometimes remark that they are the ones who really appreciate the dance," she comments, "and it is true that men and women enjoy it for different reasons."[64] She illustrates her point by referring to a painting by Gaston Saint-Pierre titled *Women's Wedding Party in Algeria*. "The women," she points out, "are entertaining each other in the courtyard of the house, and their delight and involvement in the performance are evident." In contrast to paintings that include men, these women "watch with the kind of appreciative concentration which anyone who has been present at such an occasion would instantly recognize." The painting depicts women dancing for one another, as part of a celebration for a wedding event. Buonaventura contrasts this painting with others by Jean-Léon Gérôme and Eugène Delacroix that show women dancing to entertain men. In both instances, there is less involvement and interest displayed by the male observers than by the women in Saint-Pierre's depiction of the wedding party.[65]

In the following chapter on Sephardic women's wedding dances, a similar cycle of women's wedding celebration becomes an important focus. Here it appears that women's dance traditions were partly a means of release within a male-dominated society. In *Priestess, Mother, Sacred Sister*, Sered also mentions the *zar* cult, citing it as an example of women dancing for fulfillment. Women of the *zar* were deprived by society, she writes, and they danced to relieve tension caused by their social conditions. She applies this idea broadly, claiming that "by periodically participating in exciting religious rituals, women blow off enough steam to enable them to continue functioning in an overall cultural context that denies them the freedom to control their own lives."[66]

Given the patriarchal establishment of Judaism in medieval Spain, dance by Jewish women at that time was perhaps a means of expressing feminine power, or it might have been a way of celebrating femininity. Ritual, being prescribed behavior, and ritualization, being the creation of new symbolic behavior, suggest that both possibilities existed. Because Jewish women were deprived of religious leadership, it is especially intriguing to think of them as seeking power and release in their dance gatherings. But to say that the "voicing" of their power was a Jewish text—a form of Torah teaching—is another step in the process of understanding Sephardic women's dance and recovering Jewish women's history.

2 Movement Matters

> Yes, of course, it meant something. Everything meant something. My mother was correct in looking for the story in the gestures. In Shatapda's view, stuff and action were thoroughly intertwined; my mother's concern with gesture showed a remarkable Mesopotamian sensibility, but multiplicity and ensemble must be kept in mind-soul-body. She said it as though it were hyphenated, and she drew in the air at the same time. Separation was to be avoided. Separation could lead to fall.
>
> —Cass Dalglish, *Nin*

When I teach a class called "The Movement of Meaning," my students learn about how we perform religious values. In the novel *Nin*, author Cass Dalglish outlines the background of a similar idea in her colorful tale that involves two women, Enheduanna and Shatapda, the first writers. When the main character in the book, Nin, has a conversation with these ancient Mesopotamian women writers, she discovers that they have an expansive concept of language. They tell her that each character they wrote in cuneiform can also be interpreted as a gesture or action, not separate from the meaning of the word but part of its multiple meanings.

Dalglish's story suggests that words are more than just written text, and by extension, that Torah is more than the letters and words on a scroll. Text is also about actions and motions. In Jewish terms, you might say that the words of Torah are not just words, but indicate gestures and actions that give life to Torah concepts. The body in the text, indicated by words, is then as important as the words themselves.

According to Enheduanna and Shatapda, it is this wholeness of meaning that gives words their power. How is this so? That is the main question of this chapter, which discusses an embodied reevaluation of Torah and shows why words and motions are always a linked reality. Looking at some answers to this question may also help to explain why women's dance and movement in Judaism might be considered at the heart of Torah tradition, as a symbolic means of teaching the importance of embodied belief.

Dance, Torah, and Gender

Since women, words, and ritual gestures were connected in the ancient Near Eastern world, it should not be surprising to find women's dance rituals in the written Torah text. Overt examples include Miriam leading the congregation in dance, women leading ritual dance outside the Temple, and the whirling Shulamite woman of *Shir HaShirim*.

> Then Miriam the prophetess, Aaron's sister, took a timbrel in her hand, and all the women went out after her. And Miriam chanted for them:
>
> > Sing to the Lord, for He has triumphed gloriously;
> > Horse and driver He has hurled into the sea. (Exodus 15:20–21, JPS translation)
>
> the women of all the towns of Israel come out singing and dancing to greet King Saul with timbrels, shouting, and sistrums. The women sang as they danced, and they chanted:
>
> > Saul has slain his thousands;
> > David, his tens of thousands! (1 Samuel 18:6–7, JPS translation)
>
> Turn back, turn back,
> O maid of Peace (Shulam)!
> Turn back, turn back,
> That we may gaze upon you.
> "Why will you gaze at the Shulammite
> In the whirling dance?" (Song of Songs 7:1)

There are passages in Jeremiah that also imply women's role as ritual dance leaders. One mentions mourning, ordering women to "keen":

> Summon the wailing women to come,
> send for the women skilled in keening
> to come quickly and raise a lament
> for us, . . .
> Listen, you women, to the words of the Lord,
> that your ears may catch what he says.
> Teach your daughters the lament,
> let them teach one another this dirge. (Jeremiah 9:16–17, 19)

This passage is connected by implication to the well-known verse about Rachel weeping for her children. Jeremiah's prophecy contrasts a mourning dance ritual at the time of Judah's exile to Babylon with the joyful return to Israel that will come. It will be a time for the entire country to dance and rejoice. The prophet uses the images of women, almost always the timbrel players, to represent the nation as a whole. Such imagery perhaps reflects the Miriam passage of Exodus 15, but it also indicates the importance of women-led dance and music celebrations. Another example states:

> I will build you firmly again,
> O Maiden Israel!
> Again you shall take up your timbrels
> And go forth to the rhythm of the dancers. (Jeremiah 31:4)

Rather than read these passages as interesting trivia, one might read them as texts recording the importance of ritual and gesture in biblical Jewish life. The stories were written down, but they were also transmitted orally. Sephardic women could have identified with these stories, because they also lived in the Mediterranean world and led dances for celebrations, weddings, and funerals. We have little in the way of written text recording Sephardic women's views, but we do have records of *Sephardiyot*'s dance and ritual. Sephardic women's dance might inform us about their understanding of Jewish practice, and "reclaim" them as part of Torah tradition.

To some extent, Judith Plaskow proposes just such a possibility in the now-classic *Standing Again at Sinai*. She argues that women may be acknowledged through a "render[ing] visible" of women's place in Jewish history and culture. She promotes the recovery of women's history in "the presence, experience, and deeds of women erased in traditional sources" in order to "tell the stories of women's encounters with God and capture the texture of their religious experience." While Plaskow acknowledges the Torah in a strict sense as the "five books of Moses and traditional Jewish learning," she claims that a change to a more inclusive historiography would allow "women's words, teachings, and actions hitherto unseen" to also be part of Torah tradition.[1]

Unlike their Mesopotamian ancestors, Jewish women, especially Sephardic women, often could not read or write. They probably did not have access to traditional means of recording and interpreting Jewish history and belief. To follow Plaskow, examining their "presence" in their communities and their "actions" and "experience" as another form of discourse might shed light on their lives as Jewish women. She makes a convincing argument for pursuing such an interpretation.

In Plaskow's analysis of Jewish history, writing women back into the record is possible though an extension of her ideas concerning Torah interpretation (*midrash*), Jewish law (*halakhah*), and ritual as part of living Torah history. What she says is similar to Enheduanna and Shatapda's concept of text and story in *Nin*. While the text of Torah is set, the story of Torah is not. In rabbinic understanding, the text also grows in meaning over time, so it is important to know interpretations of Torah through history. How the story conveys meaning and how it is told also matters in rabbinic Oral Torah tradition. Part of the story is the action that results from its telling. Another part involves the actions and life experiences that cause the story to emerge and be retold. In this view, the story begins and is completed through embodied reality.

Oral Torah and Feminist Views on Jewish Tradition

A rabbinic *midrash* tells us that the Torah was written with black fire on white fire. Plaskow uses this description as the basis for her argument about how women might reenter the history of Torah tradition. "According to many ancient Jewish sources," she says, "the Torah preexisted the creation of the world. It was the first of God's works." She adds that "for the Kabbalists, this preexistent or primordial Torah is God's wisdom and essence . . . Our Torah of ink and parchment is only the 'outer garments,' a limited interpretation of what lies hidden."[2]

Just as a true definition of God is elusive, a true description of Torah is impossible. True Torah is elusive; it cannot be completely grasped in one interpretation. Because the earthly version is only a shadow of the actual heavenly Torah, continual interpretation and explanation of the revelatory experience of Torah is possible. The Torah text is violated when the concrete meaning of Torah is separated from its interpretation and lived reality. That includes women's lived reality, and Plaskow stresses the importance of using extratextual materials to gather historical information.

Since the publication of *Standing Again at Sinai*, some Jewish feminist critics, including Miriam Peskowitz, have objected to Plaskow's use of the rabbinic framework of *midrash* to re-present history, claiming that it yet again relies on a structure created by men.[3] However, Plaskow's method of recovering Jewish women's history does have its merits, as does her continuing work to incorporate physical, embodied reality into academic discourse.[4] The rabbinic concept of Oral Torah allows for an interpretation of Jewish history that is expansive, and inclusive of *per-*

formance of the tradition. Plaskow reminds us that this broader view of Torah is necessary for a more inclusive history:

> Torah is Jewish memory as it lives in and forms the present, and Israel is the people that remembers and transforms memory. If, from a feminist perspective, it is essential to recapture and recreate women's Torah, *the nature of Israel must be such that women's Torah can be remembered and lived.*[5]

Plaskow informs us that history is not based solely on presumed fact; it is based on interpretation of the past. As the Mesopotamian women writers of *Nin* remind us, even interpretation of written text is purposely selective. If you neglect the performance that the words represent, you drain them of their power. Applying this to the study of Jewish history, a broader view of Torah forces us to question our selective memories of Judaism, and what we have excluded. Expansion and reinterpretation of Jewish history that includes recognition of performance may make it possible for the lives of Jewish women to enter Jewish memory, as an enactment of Torah tradition.

But how can Jewish women's history be recovered? Plaskow thinks that "historiographical research is crucial to a new understanding of Torah because it both helps recover women's religious experiences and revitalizes the Torah we have."[6] Some noteworthy examples of recovering and retelling Jewish women's stories include Tikva Frymer-Kensky's *Reading the Women of the Bible* and Rabbi Tirzah Firestone's *The Receiving: Reclaiming Jewish Women's Wisdom.* However, they focus on well-known women, and not specifically on women's ritual leadership. Avraham Grossman's *Pious and Rebellious* is a seemingly thorough account of the lives of medieval Jewish women, considering their education, family duties, and religious practices. However, he defines their actions primarily in terms of patriarchal rabbinic standards for Jewish life, relating information in a factual manner, with only a small section on women's music and dance leadership. He has little in the way of a hermeneutic of suspicion about written records, and describes North African women's wedding dance leadership as unusual and in violation of rabbinic ruling.[7]

In contrast, Plaskow emphasizes that ritual is an important aspect of Jewish life, and a powerful way of interpreting Jewish memory. For her, "prayer and ritual, the liturgical reenactment and celebration of formative events . . . the cycles of the week and year have been the most potent reminders of central Jewish experience and values." Some examples she provides of memory preserved in ritual include "weekly renewal of creation with the inauguration of the Sabbath, the entry of the High Priest into the Holy of Holies on the Day of Atonement, the Exodus of Israel from Egypt every Passover." She points out that actions are involved in the retelling of history for these holidays, which "are remembered not just verbally but through the body and doubly imprinted on Jewish consciousness."[8]

Plaskow addresses women's ritual involvement in Judaism with this statement, stressing the significance of embodied practice. The history presented by Grossman seems to miss this point, as he is more concerned with medieval Jewish women's social and economic circumstances. But despite Plaskow's inclusion of the body, she seemingly continues to adhere to the necessity of written text, in this case the words of liturgy. Just as limiting Torah to a written text is problematic, by Plaskow's own assessment, limiting Jewish liturgy to oral rabbinic prayers is also restrictive. For as Peskowitz states, the patriarchal prayers might "bolster and protect these historical and cultural narratives of rabbinic and other forms of Judaism" that exclude women.[9] Yet Plaskow points out that even the patriarchal rabbis were aware that "Jewish consciousness" occurred through performance. The embodiment of prayer was equally as important as the written narrative. It is a modern interpretation that limits Judaism to written text, rather than the patriarchal rabbis.[10]

If Torah is lived memory, it may be rendered through actions of the body as well as written words. Stressing the action side of the equation, we might expand Torah tradition by including the ritual performances of Jewish women, even if they occurred outside the synagogue. With Jewish consciousness set in their bodies through ritual, the *Sephardiyot* might well have expressed their understanding of Torah through their dance.

Torah Text and the Biblical Roots of Word and Gesture

Torah text is verb-rich in story and in ethical guidance.[11] In this regard, its language can be seen as consistent with ancient Mesopotamian understandings of word-as-gesture. Within Jewish history, the power of Torah has been in ethical and ritual performance. In *The Magic of Ritual*, Tom Driver quotes Jacob Neusner on ritual performance in Judaism, emphasizing that the order of ritual is to make the Torah text a lived reality. For Neusner, rites take "second place behind the ritualization of the everyday and commonplace, that is to say, the sanctification of the ordinary." Furthermore, he thinks that it was the performance of ritual that was most important. Driver himself notes that "In Judaism,

. . . certain rituals contextualize the text and secure its place within the ordered word."[12]

In Judaism as in other religions, ritual can serve as a bridge between belief and action. The actions and gestures performed in ritual set beliefs in the body. The motions create parameters for the body's use of space, force, and time in an edifying context. In this way, the choreography of ritual sets the limits for one's behavior in the world, based on how one might embody values in a sacred context. While the beliefs may be primary, words are not the basis of belief. Rather, the body and movement are the basis for the words that orally relate beliefs. Words are metaphors for our experience in the world. In *Metaphors We Live By*, linguist George Lakoff and philosopher Mark Johnson claim that movement in fact generates organization of language, and they demonstrate how movement is at the basis of our metaphors and conceptual, cultural expression. Among their conclusions are these:

- Most of our fundamental concepts are organized in terms of one or more spatialization metaphors . . .
- Spatialization metaphors are rooted in physical and cultural experience.

In sum, according to Lakoff and Johnson, we experience reality through our bodies, in movement. What we say is really about what we do. Even philosophic and mathematical thought is grounded on this basic reality of life, as the language used for logical inquiry is most often metaphoric, based on typical human motions.[13] In *Philosophy in the Flesh*, Lakoff and Johnson explain in more detail how metaphors of motion serve as the basis of not only language, but thought as well. "The mind is inherently embodied," they write. "Thought is mostly unconscious. Abstract concepts are largely metaphorical."[14]

One of their examples concerns happiness, which is almost always expressed in a language of elevation. The metaphor they used to describe happiness is "up." In a "metaphorical mapping" of this phenomenon, they note that it is the "primary experience" involved in the expression "I'm feeling up today." This means that "feeling happy and energetic" is equated with "having an upright posture." Lifting the body up, then, is referred to in language as being "up" or happy. Metaphorical statements based on movement also reveal spatially "bounded" regions, mapping space. For happiness, the boundaries involve the vertical plain of up and down. So in contrast to happiness, one can be on the "edge" of a breakdown or "deep" in depression.[15]

Lakoff and Johnson warn that verbs used in metaphors "do not all name the same concept . . . Each has its own logic," and thus requires interpretation, and "each is the product of a form of forced movement mapped onto the abstract domain of events."[16] We perform first, then apply our actions to the situation, using appropriate words. Our actions, gestures, and motions are never limited to a particular meaning, but are like the "black fire" of Torah, where words create meaning in context.

For Lakoff and Johnson, religious and theological understandings are also metaphorical and embodied. Plaskow's use of the rabbis' metaphor for Torah is a prime example of what they mean. Torah is described as letters in black fire against a white fire background, meaning that just as human hands are not able to grasp fire, human minds are unable to fully understand Torah teaching. According to Lakoff and Johnson, the essential metaphors of religion are body-based. This is because religion is essentially physical, and the mind itself is embodied. Therefore, spirituality is essentially embodied, a "passionate" experience with "intense desire and pleasure, pain, delight, and remorse." Examples can be found in "the world's spiritual traditions," with "sex and art and music and dance and the taste of food . . . form[ing] . . . spiritual experience just as much as ritual practice, meditation, and prayer."[17] In this assessment of language and metaphor, symbolic activity is often used to express spiritual experience. So when the Torah text describes women dancing, it seems to acknowledge them as leaders of significant religious expression.

Activities such as dance and ritual express rejoicing, but a rejoicing that is beyond mere words. An experience of God as redeemer who restores an exiled nation can be rendered through verbal and written texts, but it requires the use of metaphor. For "an ineffable God requires metaphor not only to be imagined but to be approached, exhorted, evaded, confronted, struggled with, and loved." These metaphors then relate the "vividness, intensity, and meaningfulness of ordinary experience," which "becomes the basis of a passionate spirituality." Some of the noteworthy metaphors that Lakoff and Johnson name include "The Supreme Being. The Prime Mover. The Creator. The Almighty. The Father. The King of Kings. Shepherd. Potter. Lawgiver. Judge. Mother. Lover. Breath." They close their argument on the bodily basis of spiritual metaphors by reminding us that "it is a neural mechanism that recruits our abilities to perceive, to move, to feel, and to envision in the service not only of theoretical and philosophical thought, but of spiritual experience."[18]

In this estimation of the relationship between human experience and spiritual expression, Torah is perhaps best understood as a book of metaphoric stories, records, histories, and poetry. On one level, they record human experience. But the metaphorical level is also present. This is hardly shocking to Jewish tradition, for rabbis have long maintained that there were at least four basic levels of interpretation, one of them being symbolic. Modern scholar Marcus Borg elaborates on this point, explaining that the stories of the Bible relate to the realities of life from a spiritual point of view. The text points to reality rather than itself being literal reality. He explains this through the use of a Buddhist metaphor. Buddhists often speak of the teaching of the Buddha as "a finger pointing to the moon." This metaphor helps one guard against the mistake of thinking that being a Buddhist means believing in Buddhist teaching— that is, believing in the finger. Thus "one is to see . . . that to which the finger points. To apply the metaphor to the Bible, the Bible is like a finger pointing to the moon."[19]

Borg's use of gesture to explain metaphor nicely maintains a unity between words and motion. Both can function as a vehicle to teach the meanings of the text. Borg clarifies that entire stories may serve as metaphors. For example, the story of Israel's deliverance from Egypt is a metaphor explaining God as a liberator who desires social justice.[20] The metaphor, of course, peaks when Miriam leads the women in dance and song. Symbolic gestures of dance convey the metaphors of the text.

Frymer-Kensky follows a similar understanding of the biblical text when she writes that the stories about women in the Bible are best explained as what she calls metaphoric "discourses": "woman as victor," "woman as victim," "woman as virgin (bride-to-be)," and "woman as voice (of God)." By typing them in this way, she is able to compare various ideas of "women" in the Bible, and to contrast those ideas with contemporary views. Modern women can relate to the stories of their ancestors in the Torah, as it conveys its message through metaphors about living women.[21] Enheduanna and Shatapda would probably approve of such evaluations of Torah, for they account for the use of metaphor in ancient writing. Frymer-Kensky suggests that the dancing women of Torah are a metaphor for a type of behavior. As such, the image was perhaps significant to Sephardic women, who also provided dance leadership.

Nin author Cass Dalglish explains in an essay that even the formation of letters and word signs in the ancient world was considered metaphor. She writes: "The style of reading and writing that I find in both hypermedia and cuneiform" can be described in terms of "metaphors which have been central to imagery used by women writers since before the turn of the second millennium BCE." That writing was the work of "scribes who sometimes etched stone but who often simply pushed pictographic signs into soft clay with a wedge-shaped reed." These were signs with "multiple meanings" that were combined in various ways with numerous other signs carrying "multiple values." The result was "patterns of writing and reading" that went beyond a single meaning. Dalglish calls this technique of writing a "virtual dance that poets, mythmakers, and mystics have been dancing throughout history."[22]

Jewish tradition maintains that each letter of the Torah contains value and meaning, while also insisting on the possibility for the text to have multiple meanings. Rabbi Gershon Winkler writes that the mystical tradition of Judaism makes much use of the concept, and cites *Sefer Yetzirah*, the Book of Formation. The text explains how something is created from nothing, and relates how the letters of the Hebrew alphabet make this possible. Winkler quotes the book, translating a passage on this matter:

> The Infinite One . . . hollowed out existence with thirty-two pathways [the letters] of wondrous mystery wisdom and then sculpted the universe within three spheres: *sefer, s'por, sipur*—text, number, and story.

Winkler goes on to say that this differentiation is important, as there is a difference within Judaism between text, number, and story, with story containing "the power of the feminine, the power that takes in the raw and refines it, builds it, unfolds it to fruition." But he defines text as the *"fact* of life," and number as the *"process* of life." In all, it is "story" that "doesn't go by the book."[23]

Winkler also demonstrates that in the original Hebrew text, the letters of the words did not have vowel pointings. Much as with cuneiform, then, multiple interpretation and word meanings were not only possible but intended. Winkler quotes fourteenth-century rabbi Bachai ben Asher on this point, noting that the purpose for uncertain meaning was "so that a person could interpret as they wish . . . Without a vowel, however, a person can derive . . . a great number of exceedingly wondrous and precious ideas."[24]

Winkler is a renegade, formerly Orthodox rabbi known for his creative translation of Judaism. However, he has a deep knowledge of rabbinic traditions. His interpretation of *Sefer Yetzirah* reflects this knowledge, and is in keeping with noted Kabbalah scholar Elliot Wolfson's comments on medieval Spanish understandings of the Torah. According to Wolfson, the Kabbalah scholars of the Zohar saw the Torah texts as a reflection of human activity. The body of the text was not Hebrew letters; the Hebrew letters and words of Torah were a reflection of the body. In sum, the words of Torah do not become flesh. Torah is the body or "flesh" becoming word.[25]

As a product of Sephardic culture, the Zohar's understanding of Torah is significant to the study of Sephardic practices. But it is also consistent with rabbinic concepts of Oral Torah. According to scholar Daniel
Boyarin, "midrash—the Oral Torah—is a program of preserving the old
by making it new." Boyarin recognizes that what results is not simply a
matter of speech, and is "supremely authoritative for both attitudes and
behaviors." When a new interpretation is made, it "preserves contact and
context with tradition while it is liberating" for the present. Interpretation teaches us how to *perform* in the present world.[26]

When translating Oral Torah as story, Winkler recognizes the performance level of text and comments on "animation" of the text itself.[27]
Much like Boyarin, he finds that it is at this level that the Torah gains
power, for it allows individuals to enter the story, relating their own life
to the text. The story literally changes how people behave. This takes
active participation on the part of the reader.

According to Dalglish, this type of active participation is alien to
modern readers, who "have gradually become more and more accustomed
to a canon of published writing which we use as though it were . . . in-
visible." The result is that this produces "a single controlling metaphor,
that certainly does not stop us on the page and make us consider shape
and color and multiplicity of meaning." Reader participation in the story
is then reduced to a minimum.[28]

If Torah is metaphoric story, a "dance" of meaning and action, and
if we are to participate in that metaphoric story, we need to incorporate
our own history, stories, and spiritual expression. As Plaskow points out,
traditionally, one way of doing so is through ritual action. This is how
Jewish women's dance throughout history might be described as Torah.
It is not just that there are archetypes of Jewish women leading ritual
dance in the Torah text, but that the Torah text invites new understandings through continuing, active expression.

Written in medieval Spain, the Jewish mystical book of the Zohar
stresses the importance of both ritual and ethical actions. In this text,
active prayer is especially important as a means of redeeming the world.
Sections of the book indicate important gestures and actions to be performed for "elevation of the *Shekhinah*," the feminine presence of God.
The "mystic" did this by "lifting her out of the ashes of despair, cleans-
ing and purifying her once again, and dressing her in preparation for her
long postponed wedding with her groom."[29] The Zohar's explanation of
the Temple rituals and sacrifices in the Torah provided Zoharists with
reasons for doing so. Yet the Zohar stresses contemporary interpretation
of Torah and performance of prayers and Sabbath rituals as a more im-

portant means of assisting the *Shekhinah* with her reunification.[30] For spirituality involves the physical world and our relationship to God, with the results of our actions affecting the entire universe.[31]

The Zohar also provides specifics about how one is to gesture during prayer, making the connection between the body, movement, and spiritual meaning. These statements clearly join theological concepts to the body and gesture, with comments such as "When [one] arranges . . . [one's] prayer . . . in both action and speech, and ties the bond of unification [with the Holy] . . . [this] causes both the upper and lower worlds to be pleased." Thus, when actions and words are joined, happiness results. Furthermore, the Zohar insists that the "will to worship" is essentially embodied, and centered on the heart, "which is the support and foundation of the whole body." The result is that "good will then suffuses the entire body which will attract the radiance of the *Shekhinah* to dwell with them. [One] then becomes a portion of the Holy one . . . [by lifting up your heart]." To clarify the point, the Zohar even includes statements on the use of the hands in prayer. One is to "direct [one's] fingers toward the heavens . . . Just as Moses raised his hand [and] Aaron raised his hands." This will "bring blessing down from above."[32]

The Zohar is a rabbinic text, but an important one for examining the premodern culture in which the *Sephardiyot* lived. It was a world that still understood the relationship between words and gestures, and the deep value of ritual actions. Sephardic women understood that their actions had the power not only to affect the world in which they lived, but also to redeem the world. In a culture that valued movement this much, dance quite probably was a valuable activity.

The Hasidim, of course, realized the value of movement and dance described in the Zohar. While this may be overemphasized as *the* example of dance in Judaism, their theological reasoning is still informative about the significance of dance as part of Torah tradition. Their view of dance also demonstrates a Jewish understanding of thought as body-based. According to the Baal Shem Tov, the founder of the movement, dance was a form of prayer with deep historical roots. He "used to dance to attain religious enthusiasm . . . and communion with God," teaching his followers that "the dances of the Jew before his Creator are prayers." He supported this statement by quoting Psalm 35: "All my bones shall say: Lord, who is like unto Thee?" Furthermore, his great-grandson Nachman of Bratzlav "believed that to dance in prayer was a sacred command, and he composed a prayer which he recited before dancing."[33]

For the Hasidim, dance has historical roots in Judaism and serves as prayer. It also allows one to "unit[e] the Upper and Lower Worlds, Heaven and Earth" through gesture. Rabbi Zev Wolf of Zhitomir explained that this was possible because intention goes into each gesture of dance and "thought expresses itself through the body." But for Nachman of Bratzlav, motion allowed one to receive wisdom beyond thought, as the gestures of intentional dance are prayers. His example was "lifting the hands above the head," which indicates "going above [beyond] the intellect." This can be interpreted as meaning that "the gestures for dance have the same kind of symbolic meaning as those for prayer."[34]

But Is Torah a Dance?

According to the Hasidim, it is Jewish tradition to look at dance as a form of religious expression, and as a way to receive revelation. It is not necessarily a rabbinic argument, as the Hasidim were originally considered an unorthodox group. Yet Plaskow's argument for the inclusion of Jewish women in history makes brilliant use of rabbinic tradition concerning the relationship between words, actions, and meaning. She returns the body and gesture to the Torah story, and acknowledges ongoing revelation in Judaism. Her view is bolstered by modern scholarship as well as rabbinic interpretation. But for this study, the question still remains: While Torah can be metaphorically "danced" out, does dance produce Torah?

While the Hasidim might say "yes" to the question, the Jewish scholars of their day said "no." In the age of "rational" Judaism, ritual and movement were seen as less worthy practices within the tradition. It was an interpretation of Judaism that related to the then-current culture of Western Europe. However, it was a view that excluded Jewish mystical Kabbalah tradition, shunned traditional ritual movement, and devalued Sephardic culture.[35] By default, the rational interpretation also diminished the significance of Jewish women's practices. While there were women scholars in Judaism, for the most part Jewish women were leaders of home rituals, especially in the Sephardic community.

In the early twentieth century, Franz Rosenzweig wrote a counterview of Jewish tradition in *The Star of Redemption*. A rather dense book, it presents a view that Lakoff and Johnson might call "cognitive embodiment," as Rosenzweig (1) recognized that "revelation" or new interpretation comes through the body; (2) realized that there is a relationship between dance, ritual, and belief; and (3) understood Jewish theology as a lived reality that occurs in the body. What he says about dance in Judaism summarizes the tradition's understanding about movement, body, and text while also foreshadowing current scholarship on the significance of ritual movement and the body in Kabbalah:

For whenever man [sic] expresses himself wholly in gesture, there the space separating man from man falls away in a "wonderfully still" empathy. There the word may evaporate which had tumbled headlong into this divisive interval in order to fill it with its own body and thus to become a bridge between man and man by its own heroic self-sacrifice. Thus gesture perfects man for his full humanity. It must burst the space into which architecture had placed a multitude of others, and whose interstices music had filled in and bridged. This is accomplished on our festival of redemption by that prostration which is the ultimate gesture of all mankind; this prostration bursts every space and erases all time. The Talmud mentions this too among the miracles of the sanctuary in Jerusalem: the multitude assembles in the enclosed forecourt crowded so close together that there was not the least room left, but at the moment when those who were standing prostrated themselves on their faces, there was endlessly much room left over.

Dance is that form of art in which poetry thus emerges from between its covers, transposing itself from the ideal world of conception into the real world of exposition—dance and all that develops out of it, all such self-expositions as have no spectator or by rights should have none, as have only participants who, at most, may occasionally rest and relieve each other by turns. A people recognizes itself in festive processions and parades, in tournaments and pageants . . . Yet the dance of the individual remains the first thing . . .

Dance thus finds a place in the religious service itself only among us; the architectural power to create space and the musical power to fill space are first consummated in the gesture of the dance as it bursts space.[36]

Rosenzweig elevates dance in Judaism to a primary level, as movement is essential for human communication, creating and shaping relationships. Importantly, in saying that dance is a form of poetry, he also recognizes that a nonverbal, conceptual world can be embodied through dance. Those feelings, ideas, and thoughts, which are beyond words, can be spoken if they are first embodied. Dance allows for this experience because it is spatial and visual. It is also relational, involving the self in proximity to others. Concluding his point, Rosenzweig notes the Jewish people's unique relationship with dance, comparing the Christian processions of Corpus Christi with a Jewish *Simchat Torah* celebration. Remarking on the use of dance to rejoice in the giving of the Torah, he connects dance and movement with a Jewish understanding of Torah, with dance a unique Jewish conception of revelation and redemption.[37]

For Rosenzweig, movement comes first. Current ritual scholars agree with him, although they would not confine the importance of choreographed ritual movement to Judaism. However, they too find that there is a definite relationship between ritual gesture, dance, and performance of beliefs. Driver discusses the idea frequently in *The Magic of Ritual*. After quoting Ronald Grimes on the "epistomological primacy of the body," he states: "Religion's being danced out . . . with ideation playing a secondary role." He uses this term because he views religion as having an "intelligence . . . more similar to that of the arts than to conceptual theology." In his opinion, "this is a truth too little appreciated in theological seminaries, leading to an almost unbridgeable gap between . . . trained clergy with heads full of ideas and the practicing laity concentrated upon how religion is done."[38]

Driver recognizes the primacy of movement in symbol making and the embodiment of values. But he also realizes that it is in the choreographed movement of ritual that we form words that express beliefs. Conversely, "the closer dance is to ritual," the more the movement "articulates something never said before, brings it into being." What matters most is not so much the actual resulting dance, but the "act of shaping and forming the movement," which "is basic to any subsequent symbolic interpretation."[39]

Ritual theorist Ronald Grimes also connects ritual with dance and the expression of beliefs. In *Deeply into the Bone*, he outlines the human need for rituals and rites of passage, providing many examples of life-cycle rituals from various cultures. He concludes that ritual is "like inspired musical or choreographic knowledge," and not dependent on academic study or scriptural study. "Even in the so-called religions of the book, people learn what is in the book so that they can forget it, which is to say, embody it." He also concludes that "deep ritual knowledge" is something that "feels like the most natural thing in the world."[40] One would guess that, like Rosenzweig, Grimes would appreciate *Simchat Torah* as a danced ritual celebrating the Torah. But he also points out that significant rites can display values, even though they are not necessarily religious worship. So while Jewish women's dances for weddings, funerals, and birth celebrations were not religious worship of the synagogue, sanctioned by rabbinic law, they were still performed as an expression of beliefs.

Rosenzweig did not write about Jewish women's dances. However, he did maintain that each Jew "shares the Jewish people's covenant with God, made at Sinai and renewed through centuries of loyalty and practice." According to Eugene Borowitz, in Rosenzweig's view "the Jew's religious existence" was communal, but it was also based on "relationship," where "performance [of law] is not the test of Jewish legitimacy." However, ritual performance allowed for revelation within the body, and an ongoing reception of Torah.[41]

Rosenzweig says that movement in Judaism is different, because of Torah tradition. While Christianity may also have rituals that use symbolic dance movement, these rituals are not understood as revelation of Torah. Rosenzweig relies on traditional rabbinic vocabulary and thought to make his point, much as Plaskow does. He too values performance as a time and place that creates Jewish consciousness. What is more radical about Rosenzweig is that his "new thinking" breaks with philosophic tradition and embraces mystical thought and spiritual experience. While the thought was probably not a conscious one on his part, by reminding us that acting as a Jew is as significant as thinking as a Jew, he allows for Jewish women to be counted into Jewish history. While Rosenzweig's ideas about movement and dance in Judaism might provide a basis for addressing Sephardic women's performance, an important source of his thought also derives from their cultural setting—Kabbalah and the Zohar.

Like the Zohar, Rosenzweig tells us that movement matters. He does so by considering silence first, and then how silence becomes speech and word. He discusses what he calls a primordial "protocosmos," similar to the kabbalistic concept of the point of nothingness, stillness, and silence. This is the place of God or of *Ayin*, from which all creation, language, and motion stems. The kabbalistic idea derived from the Jewish belief that God created the world from nothingness, and the medieval Spanish Zohar reflects this belief, stating the concept in terms of revelation. Steven Fisdel explains that "The Zohar says that the Torah and the Divine Commandments are both hidden and revealed. It states that the Law and the Commandments are the manifestation of the Nothingness and Being."[42]

Completely in keeping with kabbalistic tradition, Rosenzweig also finds the origins of Torah as revelation existing in the emptiness of silence. Silence exists in the protocosmos and in art, "which is the language of the unspeakable, the language as long as there is no language, the language of the protocosmos." With "revelation" there is a "release of God, world, and man from their isolation and silence." And "this same transition can also be found in art."[43] What Rosenzweig means by this statement is similar to what happens when one quiets the mind for meditation. By silencing thought, one actually allows for new thoughts to arise from the unconscious. Enjoying a painting or music has a similar effect, as the verbal mind is allowed to rest; redemption comes as new revelations rise to the surface. The arts are one way of sharing revelation, with dance a supreme example of the transition from silence and revelation to the spoken word.

Rosenzweig makes this connection between silence, movement, and words through kabbalistic ideas. He does this for his account of "creation" early in *The Star of Redemption,* and again for the final section on "redemption" and liturgy. In his presentation of the feminine presence of God, the *Shekhinah,* and also in his passage on redemption, he tells us that revelation and language come about through movement and embodiment. He does so because he understands redemption as relational, so revelations of redemption must be shared. When we recognize the place of dance and ritual movement in Judaism, we can see that the symbolic expression in these activities is a means of sharing revelation.[44]

As the Hasidim remind us, dance is energizing and joyful. In that sense, it is redeeming to do or even see. Rosenzweig explains the process as "speech-thinking," and says that it is actually privileging speech, but not in a traditional philosophic sense. "Rather, overcoming the notion of hierarchy, speech-thinking consists of both speech and textuality." Here he is clearly in agreement with the rabbinic concept of Oral and written Torah. But for Rosenzweig, "complete redemption will be marked . . . not by the speech or silence of community but by the silence of God. 'God himself must speak the ultimate word *which may no longer be a word.*'" Art, which he calls poetry, may then be the superior way to receive redemption, because "poetry's content is the world as a Whole, and its little god, man the microcosm." In this holistic, embodied understanding, "poetry might be expected to supply man with the mood for finding his way to the ultimate redemptive silence."[45]

Rosenzweig seems to intuitively understand what Enheduanna and Shatapda said about words, but he adds that "word" is actually better understood as gesture. As we have seen, his theory of movement and communication is supported by language and ritual studies. On the more artistic side, dance critic Robin Collingwood also explains that dance and movement are the basis for language. Declaring that "speech is after all only a system of gestures," he then claims that "the dance is the mother of all languages," meaning "that each one of us, whenever he [sic] expresses himself, is doing so with his whole body, and is thus actually talking in the 'original' language of total bodily gesture." In conclusion, he writes, "The language of total bodily gesture is thus the motor side of our total imaginative experience."[46]

Rosenzweig understood the language of gesture from a theological perspective, although he perceived that through movement the meaning of words is enacted, and silently breaks the isolation between humans. Movement and gestures are thus a mode of redemption that goes beyond mere words:

> Poetry itself would first have to learn silence, for in the word it is still tied to the soul. It would have to free itself of the concept of configura-

tion . . . and would have to become gesture . . . For wherever man [*sic*] expresses himself wholly in gesture, there the space separating man from man falls away in a "wonderfully still" empathy.[47]

When Jewish women danced, their activity may have broken the separation they felt from the Torah tradition, for they were able to express what the tradition meant to them. Applying what Rosenzweig says, it is then possible to say that not only were the women dancing revelation, but they were participating in an immediate form of revelation. While Rosenzweig did not write of Jewish women's dance traditions, he did favor vision and embodied reception as a means of receiving revelation. For the body reveals all, as an image of the Creator's earthly "presence." "The epistemological consequence of such a move for both Rosenzweig and the Kabbalist is that truth becomes embodied . . . Finally, *knowledge* of the truth is gained in *seeing* the truth, which surpasses the experience of hearing the truth."[48]

Movement of the body might be viewed as even more essential to Rosenzweig's thinking than "speech" since it is immediate and visual. The body and movement are also theologically significant, as a reflection of God the Creator and as a place of learning truth. His ideas come partially from Sephardic culture, where women danced for celebrations, wedding, funerals, and holidays. The kabbalists were used to seeing women dance.

Rosenzweig and Modern Jewish Feminist Theory

For Rosenzweig, Torah as story and ongoing revelation is being danced out. Dance is the superior gesture, as it is highly symbolic and expresses the truth behind our words. The gestures of dance, and then everyday life, are also relational and may communicate compassion and understanding to others. Movement, the body, and relational theology are important to modern feminist scholarship as well as to Rosenzweig.

In this regard, Rosenzweig might be said to have paved the way for a modern Jewish feminist critique of Judaism and Jewish history. For him, Torah becomes living revelation, and because it is living, performance is operative. Thus Judaism as Torah tradition becomes defined through movement, not in the sense of "deed" or fulfillment of law (*halakhah*), but through living in relationship to God and one another. Metaphorically, this might be described as a dance. The relationship is symbolically expressed, then, through literal dance. In sum, it is no accident that women dance in the Torah, or that there are so many words for dance in the Torah and Talmud. It is an important means of symbolizing Jewish theology.

In Rosenzweig's presentation of Torah, history explains this non-verbal theology and underscores Plaskow's concept of the living of Torah tradition. It is a theology that can strengthen the position of Jewish feminist historiography and philosophy. Rosenzweig's dialogical position permits traditional categories of Jewish history while making room for expansion of history within the tradition. We can include Miriam as the dance leader, also understanding how it is important to her role as a prophet and an iconic figure of Jewish women's ritual leadership.

However, there is still a question of history. Rosenzweig recognized this in *The Star of Redemption*, where Torah and Sinai are operative as communal historical realities. But the written history of Judaism, including Torah, is considered interpretation rather than concrete reality. History for Rosenzweig is actually in the moment of personal experience rather than the concrete text. Consequently, there is permission to reinterpret history as personal revelation and experience: "we find truth not in ideas but only in the concrete living out of history."[49] Whether or not Jewish women's experience was recorded as significant, the significance of their activity does matter.

Like Rosenzweig, a number of Jewish feminists understand that history and experience structure an individual's theological perspective. According to Ellen Umansky, while the "specific theological concerns" of Jewish feminists may vary, "all seem to share an understanding of theology as rooted in personal experience," which is "shaped by specific cultural, historical, and economic [factors]."[50]

Saying that Jewish women's music and dance traditions are historically significant honors personal experience. But there were gendered differences of experience for Jewish men and women. Rosenzweig's thought allows for a different view of Jewish history that embraces embodied experience within the community. Since his theology also permits anthropomorphic images of a personal God, he leaves room for a conception of a Creator who moves and communicates through human bodies. For him, Judaism occurs in movement that is nonverbal, immediate in origin, and embodied.

In this view of Jewish history, Torah is still at the base of understanding what it meant to be a Jew, and how one was to live in the world as a Jew. This was true for Sephardic women's reality as Jewish women. Perhaps they could not read Torah text, and usually men set the boundaries of their existence. But they lived Torah tradition as they existed in a Jewish culture. Using Rosenzweig's understanding of history, one might say that while women's lives were shaped by the communal reality of the Torah tradition, their dance was a personal, artistic, poetic process and revelatory experience. It was like liturgical gesture, although outside the bounds of the synagogue. The *Sephardiyot* were performing their understanding of Jewishness through music and dance.

Whether or not Rosenzweig's existentialist version of Torah and Judaism is accurate, there is support for his position from rabbinic as well as kabbalistic tradition. *Midrash* as an art form is the basis for this support. But *midrash* is also about the cultural-religious spectrum within Jewish tradition. Given Rosenzweig's explanation of the process of art and revelation, along with an understanding of *midrash* as an art of interpretation, we can consider Sephardic women's dance an encoding of Torah, through a system of symbols utilizing movement. Torah interpretation might have been present in their ritual dance, rather than their dance being devoid of Judaism. Evidence for interpretation might be seen in the values displayed by their gathering as a group of Jewish women, dancing for specific occasions and specific reasons related to Judaism.

For Rosenzweig, Jewish tradition was very much about the art of living. *Halakhah* is less determinative, and primarily relational. Interpretive movement is what matters. History may then be defined through movement or performance, whether for legal, ritual, or artistic purposes. In this view, writing Jewish women back into Judaism is part of the process of history unfolding itself, and a means of receiving embodied revelation.

Conclusions

ORAL TORAH, LANGUAGE, AND DANCE

The dance of Jewish women might be viewed as Torah story, based on the composition of dance. Dance is highly symbolic movement encoding beliefs and values, expressed in a nonverbal and immediate fashion. From reading Rosenzweig, we might say that dance is the embodied version of Oral Torah. However, not all dancing is Torah. And not all movement need be rhythmic or choreographed to be significant. Lighting Shabbat candles and feeding children are other acts by women that might be regarded as symbolic of Torah ethics. But in ritual and the highly stylized and noncognitive activity of dance, one is more likely to stop deliberate thinking and to start embodying belief.

Embodied Torah is part of Jewish rabbinic and Jewish mystical tradition. Oral Torah is very much a process of embodying new unspoken and unconscious interpretations of Judaism. Rosenzweig and Jewish feminists remind us that the body and movement have been a part of the Oral tradition. Movement is the transition of the silent core of Judaism into words.

Movement is basic to life, and perhaps we too often forget this in historical interpretation. We have written documents from the past, and some pictures of human activity, but we of course have no videos or film. So we are prone to interpreting a static past. Rosenzweig's interpretation of ritual, then, seems especially appropriate for the study of the *Sephardiyot*'s dance, since Kabbalah was a product of medieval Jewish life in Spain, with imagery and concepts based on Sephardic culture. Spanish kabbalists explored meditation and movement techniques, appropriate gestures for prayer, and even and especially women's dance and song in the Torah. They looked at the world around them, and interpreted through words and movement. Examining the "Oral Torah" of the *Sephardiyot* is a more difficult matter, as we have only some paintings and some written descriptions of how they understood what they were doing. What people say they are doing and what they do are not necessarily the same.

Gesture creates metaphor, which can be read in multiple ways by the performer and observer. Considering all sources, it is possible and legitimate to interpret the metaphors, and how dance encoded women's understanding of Judaism. But it is only an interpretation. As Enheduanna and Shatapda inform us, the process is valuable, in that understanding symbolic gesture is a powerful means of reading written words holistically. Separating the two leads to a "fall," but many interpretations are possible.

Nevertheless, by discovering details about Jewish women's history, we may learn much about Jewish cultural history. Inclusive history that incorporates the symbol system of Jewish women's gesture, dance, and music might produce a bigger picture of the many types of Judaism that existed in medieval Spain, or throughout Sephardic Jewish history. Beyond the rabbinic world, there was a life and a culture practiced by those who lived as Jews in many ways within a society. For Talal Asad, understanding that world begins with "unpacking the comprehensive concept [of] 'religion'" into its role in society.[51] Questions about the function of Judaism in the arts, social culture, politics, and thinking among the Sephardim help us to better examine the tradition. This is significant. It requires looking at what might have been so common that it was regarded as trivial:

> I looked at Heduanna and Shatapda . . . Why were they still so unwilling to separate? Why couldn't one gesture be named as the most important?

"What survives is spectacle," explained Shatapda. "And that must often be practiced behind a curtain of triviality." "Triviality?" The gesture
I was seeking was trivial?
    "As you said, common. Hidden in everyday use." . . .
    "What matters is that we use it."[52]

Looking for specific signification of Jewish women's dance is a bit
like looking for the impossible. What matters is the broader meaning of
the dance—its overall metaphor and purpose. This is more a question of
why Jewish women danced than of what they specifically danced. Dance
in Judaism can be a rich study, exploring why Jews included music and
dance in their lives, and why it was permissible for them to adopt the
common cultural style of their host country. Jewish performance traditions can reveal the relevancy of Torah for Jews, including Jewish women.
The continuing reception and life of Torah may exist in performance,
with ritual movement a key factor.

A CONTEMPORARY EXAMPLE

While this concept may seem abstract, removed from a modern world
where people dance in clubs or onstage, the impact of ritual movement
is still felt. I experienced this at a Jewish Reform synagogue's Friday
evening Shabbat service. While I was expecting another cognitive, disembodied service, what I experienced was just the opposite. Led by two
women—a rabbi and a cantor—the service turned into a demonstration
of the power of movement.

It started with the traditional Reform routine of lighting candles
in a formal manner, with responsive reading. But then it changed. The
planned speaker for the day had canceled at the last minute, so the rabbi
had to think of what she could do to expand on the text of the week,
Noah. In the short amount of time she had to create a meaningful lesson
on the Torah portion, she decided to use movement. She assigned the
congregation gestures to accompany an overview of the story, complete
with stamping feet and clapping hands. Everyone from senior citizens
to small children suddenly smiled and began to participate with relish.
The rabbi walked up and down the central aisle as she told the story, cu-
ing people as to when they should add their motions. In the end, there
was an almost spontaneous singing of a camp song version of the story
of Noah and the ark. People stood and added the hand gestures they had
previously learned. After the services proper, more movement was added
to the event. There was a Bar Mitzvah that week, and the boy's family
decided to celebrate with dance. They formed a circle around him, danc-

ing and singing during the congregational after-services *oneg* refreshment time.

There is much to analyze about this service, and how gesture and dance were incorporated into the event. It may be significant that women were leaders that night, or that the Bar Mitzvah boy's family included Hasidim. But the point is that movement serves as an important means of religious expression even today, and we know it. In this instance, an understanding of the Torah story came through motion. People knew the vocabulary of the "dance" from other settings where movement was normally deemed acceptable. While we may attempt to suppress our symbolic motions, they always reveal themselves.

Judaism has a particularly rich history of dance and ritual gesture. It is a worthy endeavor to study why and in what way the Jewish community danced. Limiting the study to the synagogue or to Hasidic men's dance is blatantly sexist, especially when we know that women led dances for significant life passages outside the synagogue. The following chapters look in detail at Sephardic women's movement leadership for community celebrations, weddings, and funerals.

3 *Miriam's Dance*

Miriam is considered a prophetess, and she sang a
song of triumph with the Israelite women after the
crossing of the Red Sea (Exod. 15:20). A miraculous
well accompanied the Israelites in the wilderness
because of her merits. When she died, MIRIAM'S
WELL was transferred to the Sea of Galilee, where
its healing waters are still to be found. At the great
banquet, in the time of the Messiah, Miriam will
dance before the righteous.

Mystics believed that the water of Miriam's Well
helped refine the body, and those who drank from
it were thus able to understand the teachings of the
Kabbalah.

—Alan Unterman, *The Dictionary
of Jewish Lore and Legend*

Art and Symbol as Text

When I wrote my first biblical studies paper, I told the profes-
sor that I wanted to study Miriam. He attempted to persuade me to focus
instead on Deborah, because she was a general. While he did not have a
problem with the dancing Miriam as a topic, his concern was that there
was not enough critical evidence on the biblical character. At the time,
there was little historical research available on the dancing prophetess
and what she represented in the Torah text. The scientific study of religion did not seem to view a dancing woman as particularly important,
although rabbinic literature had ample mention of Miriam and dancing
women in the Talmud, *midrash,* and Zohar. There were also beautiful

depictions of Miriam and dancing women in medieval Spanish Passover manuscripts.

Legends in themselves can be a wonderful picture of a community's beliefs. In these stories of Jewish written text, the image is of a strong female Jewish leader who was a singer and dancer. The paintings might provide further insight into how the tradition was interpreted. According to dance scholar Judith Brin Ingber, through a reading of these pictures it is possible to discover a surprising amount of evidence about community history. If carefully interpreted, they might allow for a better understanding about the meaning of Miriam for the community, and how the tradition was embodied in the leadership of the *tanyaderas*, the women who served as dance and drum leaders of festive celebration.[1]

One purpose of looking at stories and paintings of Miriam is the recovery of history. The few available images provide essential clues. This is a worthy pursuit, as the movement depicted can relate a community's social and ethical values. However, a larger question looms: Why is the dancer Miriam so important? What symbolic value did she have in the original biblical text, and then later in Jewish communities? In sum, what was the Miriam tradition? Insight into Jewish women's dance rituals, especially in the Sephardic communities, can perhaps provide some answers, expanding Jewish history to be more inclusive of women.

Illuminated medieval Spanish Passover seder guides, *Haggadot*, offer beautiful and colorful views into the past. Four are known to be extant—the *Sarajevo Haggadah*, the *Golden Haggadah*, the *Hispano-Moresque Haggadah*, and the *Sister Haggadah*. All are from the fourteenth century (the *Hispano-Moresque Haggadah* may be slightly earlier), and all include a page or section on women dancing. In the *Golden Haggadah* and the *Sarajevo Haggadah*, there are large illustrations of Miriam and the women celebrating at the shores of the Red Sea. The biblical account of Miriam is quite memorable, and the paintings in these texts might simply depict this story. According to art historians, however, there is more present.

The depictions in these *Haggadot* are contemporized in terms of dress and stylization, as are the other pictures. So the manuscripts "allow us to discover aspects and scenes of medieval Jewish life through the biblical 'stories' they portray [in] the appearance and everyday dress of medieval Jews, through the biblical heroes at the time of the patriarchs." Thus it is possible to view Jewish understandings of life in these depictions, as "Jewish iconography was not bound by the conventions and strict codification of Christian iconography." Significantly, "the frequent occurrence of ritual images [in the manuscripts] provides us with a fairly complete picture and, hence, a more specific interpretation of the religious aspects of medieval Jewish life."[2] What we see, then, is at least as much about medieval Jewish life as it is about Jewish tradition.

Art historian Beth Haber considered the characterization of Miriam in the *Sarajevo Haggadah*, and what she perceives to be the dance style it portrays.[3] Detailed observations like Haber's require one to have knowledge of Jewish culture in medieval Spain and of dance history of the period. For instance, the women in the *Golden Haggadah* are holding hands, and there is a strong curve in their bodies. From what we know about the courtly activity of Jews and the influence of Middle Eastern and North African dance in southern Spain, it is possible that the women are doing a type of early Renaissance courtly dance. Ingber suggests that they are performing a Middle Eastern–influenced, hip-swinging line dance.

The images match what is known about Jewish women's dances in medieval Spain and about the drum-dance practice of Sephardic women. What is perhaps most striking is that the women are dancing with women. The reason may be the story of Passover, where the biblical account mentions that Miriam and other women danced in celebration of the escape from the Egyptians. Yet the depiction also matches much of what is known of Sephardic women's celebrations, especially those involving weddings.

Sephardic history provides strong evidence that women gathered and danced for such special events. The drum-dance leaders, the *tanyaderas*, were usually "a group of three women invited to sing and drum at all the ceremonies." These women were trained "not only in the musical repertoire, but in all the customs." Significantly, they were "actually the ones who conduct[ed] the ceremonies and supervise[d] the details." *Tanyaderas* "led the ceremonies and sang, amusing the women and making them dance."[4]

It seems probable that the *tanyaderas* conducted dance events for many celebratory occasions. Some are examined in the following chapters, but they are Sephardic rather than specifically Spanish. How the practices of the Sephardim in the Balkans and Morocco are connected to the practices of medieval Spain remains uncertain. However, it is reasonable to assume that within the culture of the Islamic and Mediterranean worlds, wedding event rituals were performed by Jewish women with a regional, Moorish, and Spanish flavor. The manner of dance is not outstanding, but the occasion for ritual dance leadership is impressive.

An examination of how the *Sephardiyot* danced might be a part of recovering their living history as Jews of the Torah tradition. Available details on courtly dance and *zambra* parties are informative about the type of dance done by women in Spain. Yet even while secular dance activity might reflect Jewish community values of the period, it would be difficult to qualify Sephardic women's dance as Jewish if only the manner of their dance is considered, or if only the rabbinic objections to their dance are noted. If, however, the *Sephardiyot* danced for times of Jewish religious celebration, then qualifying their behavior as living Torah becomes a valid possibility.

The paintings of the *Haggadot* might indicate the existence of a *tanyadera* tradition in medieval Spain, and that the artists were familiar with gatherings of women to celebrate religious events through dance and drumming. In contrast to social dance in the courts and *zambra* parties, such dances for ritual celebrations may have been spiritually significant. For the *Sephardiyot*, dance might have served as a symbolic means of expression, reflective of values relating to Jewish life.

In analyzing the pictures from the *Haggadot*, and considering hidden history through the "scrutinizing" of these visual texts, it may be possible to understand the significance of the women they depict. In her study on recovering women's history, *In Memory of Her*, Elisabeth Schüssler Fiorenza suggests this process for written texts, and it is possible for visual texts as well. Such study can provide important clues about Jewish women's music and dance leadership, and how Sephardic Jews might have understood what it meant for Miriam and the women to be dancing at the shores of the sea.

Medieval Spain, the home base of the Sephardic Jews, did have a significant amount of dance, so representations of this activity may have carried meaning that was eventually lost through the years of community dispersion throughout the Mediterranean. So reading the paintings involves digging through the life of medieval Spanish culture as it relates to the images. Feminist scholar Margaret Miles suggests that the symbolism of the images may be understood through a comparison of written and visual materials. Pictures such as those of the *Haggadot* might be "complementary or even redund[ant] to written texts" and have "similar and mutually reinforcing messages." Or there might be a "tension, in which text and image offer differing evidence that can be used to understand the community from which they come." There might also be an extreme difference between written texts and images, where there is a "contradiction." If so, it is possible that there were different understandings of an event, or that the text and images are complementary. Both must be considered if we are to gain a better understanding of the community.[5]

It is important, then, to compare different types of text in order to attain a richer understanding of a culture's system of encoding meaning through particular images. The result of such a comparison will be useful information that might provide insight into history. The four *Haggadah* paintings might offer insight into the mythology and meaning of women dancing in late medieval Jewish Spain, but written documentation from medieval Spain is still required for further understanding. Some of the texts cited in this chapter prove complementary with the images of the *Haggadah* paintings, especially the dance records, and somewhat in images provided in the kabalistic Zohar. However, historical records concerning women and worship in medieval Spain reveal a different picture of women's lives. There is a tension, if not a contradiction, between the visual and written images.

While medieval historical records provide a major source of information on how one might interpret pictures of Miriam, Jewish cultural traditions are also informative. Women's dance and drumming performance, for example, is evident in biblical texts, supportive archeological materials, and the continuing dance practices of Sephardic women. When this evidence is compared with the visual information in the *Haggadot*, the symbolic meaning of Miriam as a dance-drum leader appears to be important to Sephardic women's own dancing and drumming. I call it the Miriam tradition, as the image of Miriam dancing appears to carry deep symbolic meaning in medieval Spain, occurring in Jewish visual and written sources. Since written texts indicate that there was a continuous dance, drum, and song practice among Sephardic women, it seems legitimate to compare the older biblical material with the images of Miriam in the medieval *Haggadot*.

Records concerning women's synagogue leadership and participation are another eye-opening source of information. While the material may appear to stray from the subject of Jewish women's dance and music, it seems essential to consider it. Displacement of women's leadership in Jewish ritual is an issue, and the dance ensembles of the *Sephardiyot* perhaps developed as a result of women's status. As a result of exclusion, Sephardic women may have created their own significant rituals through music and dance.

Written records of Jewish women's history supply important data about women's participation in community. There is good reason to see their dance traditions as an important part of this participation, especially since physical movement patterns produce important clues that might be overlooked in written evidence. But when we are dealing with paintings of dance, the meaning of depicted gestures, postures, and implied actions must be read.

Visual Evidence of the Miriam Tradition

There are notable differences between the pictures of Miriam leading women in dance in the four existing medieval Spanish *Haggadot*. The difference in the dates of composition is one only of decades, a short amount of time compared to the longevity of Jewish women's drum-dance-song tradition in the Mediterranean world. Yet there are marked contrasts in the depictions that feature dancing and drumming women.[6] One reason for the differences between the images may be the change that occurred in Spanish life during the fourteenth century, around the time the *Haggadot* were created. Their stylistic features appear to reflect both Islamic and Christian influences. Islamic culture dominated the Iberian Peninsula well into the Christian *Reconquista,* which began in the eleventh century, and this basic historical point helps in reading these visual texts. Yet understanding how dance was depicted and why is equally important.

Joann Kealiinohomoku, a dance anthropologist, explains that the activity of dancing is always much more than the actual movement. She presents the idea of a "dance culture," meaning by this "an entire configuration, rather than just a performance," and including "implicit as well as explicit aspects of the dance and its reasons for being; the entire conception of the dance within the larger culture."[7] With respect to the Miriam paintings, this means that the dance scenes encode cultural symbols. More than a dance is displayed.

To understand the culture behind a "dance event," Kealiinohomoku calls for some very basic questions to be addressed. Required questions include "who, what, when, where, why, and how?" We can apply these questions widely, asking about the people involved, the setting, the time of year, any objects involved in the performance, and the reasons for the performance. According to Kealiinohomoku, "these criteria should include the negative as well as the positive measurements," as "the negative aspects [of a dance event] are often as instructive as the positive aspects."[8]

For the paintings of the women in the *Haggadot*, and in the following chapters, these questions might be formulated as: Who were these women? What music and songs did they use? When did they dance separately? Where did they dance: In the house? In the streets? Or outside?

Why did they dance? And, of course, how did they dance? The answers to such questions can then serve as a base layer for inquiry and analysis.

Since Kealiinohomoku also suggests looking at what is not present at a dance event, women's limited opportunities to participate in the synagogue and Jewish life are an important consideration. Questions for textual scrutiny might then include: When were women excluded from dancing? Where would women not have danced? Which women did not dance? What music and dance were unacceptable? And, in conjunction with these questions, what movement was unacceptable? When these questions are applied, the results allow for a very detailed view of the paintings.

THE *SARAJEVO HAGGADAH*

Although we know that the *Sarajevo Haggadah* dates from the latter half of the fourteenth century (1360–70), art critics do not agree about its place of origin. According to Thérèse Metzger, the painting is from Aragon, while Bezalel Narkiss claims that it is from Barcelona. Joseph Gutmann concludes that it must be from northern Spain because "the figures and drapery reveal the Italo-Gothic style so pervasive in fourteenth-century Catalonia." He is not specific about a city of origin.[9]

The motion of Miriam and the women in this painting involves a handholding line dance. Of the four women pictured, two have their arms lifted and bent at the elbow. They are looking at each other. The young woman closest to the tambourine-playing Miriam is at the near end of the line, and her free arm is bent. She and the young woman at the far end of the line are looking at Miriam. All are dancing against a background of blue squares, reminiscent of Islamic Spanish tile work, as there are fine white designs within the squares.

While this is not a picture from Andalusia, the women's movements display some features of what one would expect of women's group dance in southern Spain. The *how* of their movement appears to involve a pronounced hip swing. This could be considered a pose influenced by French Gothic stylistics, but the bend in the hips and the suggestion of motion are strong. Comparison with more French-influenced Jewish manuscripts reveals that the angle of the young women's stance is more extreme than the typical French Gothic pose.

What type of dance are they doing? French courtly dance may be a good guess, but there were regional differences in this style, especially in Spain. Visually, we have only a few paintings of dance from French, Spanish, and Italian courts in which to compare movement. Thérèse Metzger provides a comparison with a fifteenth-century picture of court dance from Italy, which differs in implied motion, body postures, handholding by the dancers, and characters. In the Italian painting, men are dancing with women.[10]

This might be a picture of a courtly social dance, but in Kealiino-homoku's view, "social dance, religious exercises, education dance, and concert dance" are all part of a total dance culture. Especially since the boundaries of ritual dance and movement in Jewish life are often blurred, the type of dancing that was done frequently defied clear categories. A courtly dance might have been done for a Passover celebration, because of the range of performance meanings that exist on the occasion for dance. It depends on whether the event inspires and uplifts or simply amuses. Performance scholar Richard Schechner terms the difference as one of *edifying* or *entertaining,* explaining that there is usually a mix of the two in religion and general culture.[11]

Textual information from Spain during the thirteenth and fourteenth centuries suggests that the *Sarajevo Haggadah* may depict a northern version of the *zambra*, the Near Eastern–influenced dance popularized in the Islamic courts of Andalusia. "Frequent allusions were made to the *zambra* [in the literature], alleged to be 'the most famous and artistic dance in the whole of the Peninsula,' but we are left to guess why. We are at least told that the dancers were 'holding hands' as is 'customary in this dance.' The *zambra* was often used in religious processions."[12]

French "court dancing" also had influence during the late Islamic period, but this element was an addition to the types of dance developed during Moorish rule, such as the *zambra*. Furthermore, at this time "dancing in the centre of the [Spanish] Peninsula flourished anew, consisting of native Castilian elements with oriental influence superimposed upon them." Given this description, the swaying hips of the *Sarajevo Haggadah* may suggest a southern Mediterranean, if not Arabic, influence on movement. Since the instrument played by Miriam is a hand drum, this may also suggest the so-called "oriental" influence.[13]

Most likely the *how* of the dance is a blending of courtly influence and Middle Eastern or Persian styling, just as in the music of the period. *Who* the women are is another factor to consider. The painting supposedly shows a mythic Miriam and some women who are depicted as escaped slaves in the Bible. The women are wearing fashionable clothes, and they are properly dressed, with Miriam shown as an older, married woman. Her head is covered in a white cloth, and she has a whitish-brown coat over her tunic. The dancing women all have long, flowing hair and are clothed in uncovered blue and red tunics, just as unmarried women of the day would have worn.

When and why they are dancing is an interesting aspect of this depiction, as it is in all the *Haggadot*. At one level the answer is because of the victory at the Red Sea. But the model for the dance is contemporary. The artist projects back in time, perhaps intending to portray the biblical version of Miriam and the women dancing. None of the paintings, however, include images of a seashore. The settings for depictions of Miriam in all of the *Haggadot* suggest that the artists portrayed contemporary scenes of Jewish women celebrating with drum and dance in medieval northern Spain.

When not and *where not* they are dancing become the more decisive questions. The women in this painting are not dancing at a wedding, at a funeral, or in a synagogue. The background of the *Sarajevo Haggadah* is blue, which suggests sky, but there are no trees or other natural objects to determine whether the setting is outside. Presumably, the place for the women's dance in this painting was a tiled court, even though the setting of the biblical account is outdoors. Some of the other *Haggadot* differ, indicating an outdoor environment through visual elements such as trees and landscapes. Why the women were dancing, however, is clear in context—it was in celebration of Passover. Thus it had an edifying, inspiring purpose.

THE *GOLDEN HAGGADAH*

Determined by most critics to be the work of two artists, the *Golden Haggadah* is from earlier in the fourteenth century than the *Sarajevo Haggadah*. The conventions employed in the settings and figures of this painting are French Gothic in manner, with some Italian features in the architecture included in the scenes of the biblical stories. This *Haggadah* takes its name from the background of the painting, which is golden foil with geometric figuring. In the scene with Miriam and the women, the geometric figures are also added to the instruments the women carry.

This version of the Passover story is somewhat similar to that in the *Sarajevo Haggadah*. Women are dancing in a similar manner, but there are noticeable differences. First, there are only two dancers proper, both in the upper right corner of the picture. They are looking at each other, and their back arms are raised, bent at the elbow. The forward arms are approximately at hip level. Here, too, the hips seem to be swayed past the French Gothic norm. Since the view of the dancers is from the side, the sway is more apparent than for the figures of Miriam and the other women, who play musical instruments in the foreground. The body position of the women musicians suggests a possible hip-shimmy movement.

All of the women, including Miriam, are depicted as young and unmarried. Their heads are uncovered, their hair is long and flowing, and their tunics are uncovered. For the most part they are musicians, with Miriam playing the box drum, the woman to the right of her playing a round drum, one woman behind her playing cymbals, another a percussive hand instrument, and one a lute. Metzger discusses the luxurious dress of the Jews in these paintings, saying that this was a typical, common depiction. Yet the elegance of their dress suggests that these were women of the courts.[14]

Where and why the women are dancing again remains a question. In the scenes of this *Haggadah*, inside settings are specified through architectural features. There are none for the Miriam frame, but also no marks of an outdoor setting, such as trees, grass, flowers, water, or rocks. Why the women are dancing is unclear, other than to illustrate the biblical story of Miriam leading a victory dance. Why this image is the one chosen for Miriam and the women dancing in celebration also remains uncertain, given the lack of visual clues to indicate the setting.

When one probes for answers to such questions, dance anthropologist Judith Lynne Hanna provides useful comments about dance and metaphor. In the painting itself and in the movement depicted, there seems to be a presentation of what Hanna calls a "common idiom" of medieval Spain. The idiom of dance provides metaphoric communication, which expresses what is beyond words and consciousness, much like a mythic story. In general, says Hanna, the purpose of dance in religion includes an "aesthetic" means of ordering the world. Here there is a blatant depiction of that artistic vision; we have a mythology of a dance, contemporized by medieval Spanish symbols. Using Hanna's terms, the meaning of a "common idiom" dance done for a religious occasion might vary. It could simply be for "worship or honor," or it might provide a way of "effecting change" in social reality. Hanna says that dance relates the symbol system through a cultural encoding in time and space. She therefore suggests looking at the structuring of dance within a community, as the activity "is a form of abstract language and it is an element of religion" that involves "symbolic thought and action."[15]

What is known about dance in southern Spain at this time suggests an idea of what dance symbolized. According to Anna Ivanova, it was a popular, if not required, activity for all well-bred young men and women, whether from Andalusia or Castile. It was a symbol of dignity and grace for young men and women, who danced a bit differently in the Castilian and northern Spanish regions. The occasions for dance apparently also differed in the north. Court sponsorship was still normal, but the courts were smaller, controlled by local lords. So the royal symbolism may not have been as distinct. Since the southern French region of Provence did have a sizable influence on the art and culture of northern Spain, French round dances à la the *caroles* were apparently popular. Connected more with the dance of the general population, the symbolism might be one of the importance of community.[16] This type of dance is perhaps what is pictured in the *Sister Haggadah*.

THE *SISTER HAGGADAH*

According to Bezalel Narkiss, the *Sister Haggadah* is so-called because of its similarity to the *Golden Haggadah*. After examining the various elements that make up the illuminations, he determined that this painting is from the same region of Catalonia, and the dating is approximately the same, but it was probably composed after the *Golden Haggadah*. Narkiss also finds that there is more of an Italian influence in the *Sister Haggadah*, with the dress and manner closer to Neapolitan, Italian styles.[17]

Elegant French Gothic styling is not present in the Miriam painting of the *Sister Haggadah*, but the dances of the women more closely resemble a French *carole* or *branle*, which Ivanova describes as a type of "round dance" that "always included singing, and in which the dancers were linked. It also contained a swaying movement, which accounts for the name '*branle*.'"[18] This is the type of formation and movement that the women in the *Sister Haggadah* appear to be performing. There are eight young women interlinking their arms, spaced in a pattern suggesting a circle. Off to the side, there is a Miriam figure playing a drum, and another woman with her, perhaps a singer.

The *how* is different here, but *who* dances remains in question. Could these be peasant women doing a folk dance, such as a version of the Catalonian *sardana*? The symbolic meaning of the dance then might differ from the courtly depiction found in the *Golden Haggadah*. According to Ivanova, "round, chain and processional dances were the three basic types of dance current in the Middle Ages, and were danced everywhere; in the homes of the nobility on ceremonial occasions and also in the open air by the people, at their rustic gatherings." Even if this is an outdoor folk dance setting, which might be indicated by the tree next to Miriam, the dance was probably similar to that done in the courts. Use of court-style dance for depiction of the biblical story of Miriam appears to be an accepted convention, although the only difference between the court dance and an open-air dance may have been a "coarser" and "rougher manner, heavier in quality because of the weight of the footwear."[19]

As to when and why these women are dancing, the *Haggadah* itself provides a script, repeating a phrase from Exodus 15:20: "And Miriam the prophetess took a timbrel [*toph*] in her hand, and *all the women went out* after her with timbrels and with dances" (my emphasis). The location and connection to the biblical account are made clear and direct with this inscription. Relating this original Passover celebration of Miriam and the women performing the dances of fourteenth-century Spanish Jewish women, again, was apparently not seen as unusual, given the depictions included in the *Haggadot*.

Answers to the questions of *who not, what not,* and *where not?* are the same for this half-page Miriam picture as for the *Sarajevo Haggadah* and *Golden Haggadah.* Who not is men. They are not involved even in the background or in the musical accompaniment. The focus of the biblical account is on the women. Men were also part of the story, and men are depicted throughout various scenes of the *Haggadot.* Traditional separation of men from women in the culture is perhaps evident. This is the *why not?* of the celebration pictures. In contrast to written texts of the period that lack mention of women, a question raised by the *Haggadot* depictions is *why only women?*

Some of these questions might be answered through an exploration of dance history in the Mediterranean world, the role of women dancing in Judaism, and their role in the synagogue. In *The Anthropology of Dance,* Anya Royce contends that a good study of dance involves "observation, description and analysis," as well as participation.[20] This is a difficult task of dance history, as it is possible to observe, describe, and analyze art and texts about dance practices, but not the actual performances. It is possible to participate in a *sardana* in modern Spain or a Sephardic dance celebration in Los Angeles, experiencing the dance tradition as it is now practiced. Yet observation and analysis will be skewed.

Dances change over time, even folk dances, and basing research on current information alone will often produce data that misrepresents historical reality. Reconstructing what a dance looked like and how it was performed is a possibility. Royce points this out in her chapter on anthropological methods for the history of dance, explaining how Gertrude Kurath determined the dance practices of ancient civilizations in Mexico. With no description, Kurath and Samuel Marti looked at all possible sources of evidence about dance in the culture, including post-Conquest descriptions written by Spaniards, along with "sculpture, painting, archaeological evidence for musical instruments, and comparison to present-day dances." Accounting for the "spacial and temporal qualities" of dance, they were able to infer what sort of movement was performed based on the poses of the figures.[21]

Royce notes that dance scholar Lillian Lawler did something similar in her study of dance in ancient Greece. Lawler had texts, artwork, "musical, archeological, epigraphical . . . linguistic, and anthropological" sources on which to base her analysis. She was able to produce a detailed account of the styles, function, and meaning of these dances.[22] With some texts, paintings, and a long-standing tradition, there is a possibility of interpreting the function and practice of the women in this *Haggadot,* as well as the others. It is an interpretation, with limited evidence. Yet any written textual materials would also provide limited evidence. As with all history, only an interpretation is possible.

Women of Sephardic heritage whom I interviewed agreed that music and dance is naturally a part of their culture. Generally, all acknowledged that the tradition is an important one, but they offered no specific reasons for why it is valued. The significance of the dance itself needs to be addressed, but is best explored through performance and observation of live dance. It is a matter of what Royce would call the "barefoot" difference. While watching women dance at a Mexican Zapotec wedding, Royce noticed that only lower-class or old women removed their shoes to perform a dance that was reportedly always done barefoot. While bare feet may have been the tradition, the idea was not really culturally acceptable. What Royce was told and what she observed were different.[23]

When studying dance of the past, or any women's activities with limited documentation, this type of observation is possible only through a keen examination of materials, and an effort to look for contradictions and consistencies among various types of text. Interpreting the function and meaning of dance and ritual in the gendered culture of medieval Spain requires keeping the "barefoot difference" in mind for an understanding of images, their mythology, and their meaning. Historical evidence about women dancing in Jewish tradition offers the best means of reading the symbolism of the paintings. But before examining that history, there is one other *Haggadah* to consider.

THE *HISPANO-MORESQUE HAGGADAH*

The picture of Miriam and the women dancing in the *Hispano-Moresque Haggadah* displays some significant differences from the other *Haggadot.* Stylistically, the paintings throughout this manuscript are different from those in the other *Haggadot.* Rather than fine Gothic characteristics, the details here are more primitive. For the Miriam painting, this is especially noticeable in the ill-defined features of the dancers. Narkiss labels this *Haggadah* "archaistic" and says that it may also depend on its Italian origin.[24]

What the women in this painting are dancing is a bit more obvious than in the depictions of dance in the other *Haggadot*. One of the two young, wreathed women dancing on either side of Miriam is holding percussive instruments in both hands. Her elbows are bent, with one arm raised and the other lowered. The other young woman's hands display curled fingers, as if her fingers were going to snap or turn. The dance depicted is decidedly more Moorish than in the other *Haggadah* paintings, judging from the hands and arms. The separateness of the women, plus the strong curve in the hand-percussionist dancer, also suggests Moorish influence.

Who the women are is again determined by their dress. Miriam is the drummer, and her head is covered, as was proper for a married Spanish woman. Her drum displays the *fleur-de-lis*, a mark of courtly Castile, where the *Hispano-Moresque Haggadah* is from. So the overall image might be of upper-class women playing in the court. The architectural columns framing the dancers in the painting suggest a court setting, as does the dress of the dancers.

In some sense, the written reports on dance in medieval Spain complement the images in the *Haggadot*, and answer the question of *who* these women are. The style of dance in painted and written text appears to match. However, there is also a tension between the text and the images. The written records report mainly on the courts. But if the women depicted in the *Haggadot* are simply entertaining the court, the question arises as to why their image is used to illustrate a biblical passage describing women (who were newly freed slaves). Several factors might be considered, including that Jews were predominant among the upper classes in Spain. All classes performed similar types of dances, so the *how* is not definitive. Rather, the issue appears to be one of iconographic traditions, as well as music and dance traditions among Jewish women. In this case, *who* is the operative question; that is, who was Miriam in symbol and reality for medieval Spanish Jews? Given the dance and drum tradition among the *Sephardiyot*, what did the symbolic image of Miriam mean for Jewish women in medieval Spain?

Miriam in History: Women and Worship in Judaism

Mentions of Miriam in written Jewish texts from medieval Spain provide clues to her symbolic value for the period. We know from written text that dance was a popular activity in medieval Spain, so the use of dance for religious celebrations by women might be interpreted as normative.

However, because of the strength of the images of Miriam in the *Haggadot,* the symbolic function of the figure of Miriam appears worthy of deeper exploration.

According to some Jewish scholars, the association between Miriam and Jewish women's drum and dance performance ensembles has a long history, stemming from biblical times. One simple interpretation of the *Haggadah* paintings might read Miriam as a symbol of the dance and drum practice. However, she is associated with much more than dance in biblical tradition, and her representation in the paintings might signify far more than the existence of dance among Sephardic women. She could be a Goddess replacement figure, or at the very least the image of a worship leader in ancient Israel.

In *Countertraditions in the Bible,* feminist scholar Ilana Pardes explores the meaning of the biblical Miriam. She examines Miriam's rank as "prophetess," the strands of biblical material that mention her, and her relationship to Goddess traditions in the Near East. Through her investigation, she finds a mythology of Miriam, partially continued by the rabbis in the legend of Miriam's well.

In contrast to Pardes, anthropologist Carol Meyers considers biblical stories about women leading victory dances, including the Exodus passage about Miriam. She examines archeological findings, and interprets the evidence through feminist ethnomusicological perspectives. She describes a drum-dance-song ensemble tradition as one with women serving as dance and music leaders in Israel, rather than representative of a Goddess tradition. Meyers uses evidence of terra-cotta figurines, found mainly in Cyprus, to make her point. Many of the figures appear to be women holding a round, flat object, such as a hand drum. While there is a noticeable lack of such figures in ancient Israel, she suggests that they are relevant, as they match textual information about women drummers and dancers in the Bible.

Meyers also examines biblical evidence, looking for details about women's performance ensembles. Citing passages that mention types of instruments and times of performance from Isaiah, Psalms, and history books, she states: "It is clear from artistic depictions of musicians recovered in archaeological excavations in the Near East that women as well as men played all the instruments." She adds that there was "a distinct musical tradition in which only women are the instrumentalists." These traditions are portrayed in the biblical text as "women playing drums" that "are associated with dances *(m'holot)* and also with song . . . Perhaps the best example is the so-called Song of Miriam."[25] Along with the Miriam passage from Exodus 15, Meyers cites passages in Judges

describing bands of women leading celebrations to greet victorious Israelite warriors. She concludes that biblical texts referring to women
drummers and dancers indicate that a women's performance tradition
existed in ancient Israel, and that their public performance constituted
a leadership role in the society.

Meyers stresses that there is an issue of "competency" involved with
a women's performance tradition. By this she means that the women had
a certain level of performance skill that required gathering for practice.
The performance leaders thus enjoyed some sense of "power" in their
lives, as "women participating in gender-specific groups are able to ex-
ercise control of themselves and their worlds." Furthermore, the women
performers were able to communicate with their audience through their
performance, giving them status in their society. Meyers notes that there
was an ongoing tradition of women's performance leadership in Israel,
including during the Second Temple period. Women were lament leaders, temple singers (Ezra 2:41; Nehemiah 7:44; 1 Chronicles 25:5), and
also "daughters of song" (Ecclesiastes 12:4).[26]

When this information is added to Pardes's claim that there are frag-
ments of a Miriam tradition present in the Bible, the total picture suggests that women's music and dance leadership existed within formative Judaism, and that it remained active through the ongoing music and
dance of Jewish women. However, Talmudic writings suggest that Jewish women's leadership eventually went underground; that is, women's
ritual leadership was marginalized, and was practiced primarily among
women, for women.

With respect to the biblical evidence, the Sephardic women's practice
of a drum-dance-song ensemble might be interpreted as a continuation
of Jewish women's displaced leadership. The *Haggadot* might depict a
drum and dance ensemble, as performed in Spain in the thirteenth and
fourteenth centuries, and indicate a continuing existence of women's
performance ensembles in medieval Spain. If so, the figure of Miriam
was important to a culture that valued dance. But the symbolic use of
Miriam might also indicate the worth of a women's dance and drum
ensemble in Judaism. While Jewish women did not provide dance and
music leadership for the medieval synagogue, their performance was apparently meaningful, and therefore is used in the *Haggadot*. The images
served as a model type for the "Song of Miriam."

Pardes offers information that supplements Meyers's work and provides
more insight into a mythology of Miriam in Judaism. Her literary analysis
of biblical stories featuring women focuses on "countertraditions"—those
stories that seem to break with the patriarchal structure of the biblical

text. With respect to Miriam, along with Zipporah, Yocheved, and other women of the Moses-Exodus account, she notes what appears to be a division of roles associated with the Egyptian Goddess Isis. Her point is highly worthy of consideration for understanding Miriam as a symbolic figure, and the drum-dance-song ensemble among Sephardic women.

Pardes's argument is based on the fact that Miriam was associated with water, just as the Egyptian Goddess Isis was. It was Isis who saved the dismembered pieces of Osiris from the Nile, whereas Miriam saved the baby Moses at the Nile River.[27] In the yearly celebration of the death and life of Osiris in Egypt, there was performance of dance and music. A description of this event was written by Plutarch, and involved passing through water before Osiris's resurrection. The participants danced "inside and outside the temple . . . The male priests in special dress, etc., represented Osiris and his companions, while the girls were Isis and hers [companions]."[28]

The story of Miriam in Exodus differs in the nature of celebration. Miriam the prophetess dances in celebration of the birth of the nation of Israel; the Goddess Isis dances for the rebirth of the god Osiris. Yet, like Isis, Miriam does have an elevated status, which adds symbolic weight and meaning to her activity as a dancer. The fact that she dances also raises the significance of women's dances in Israel, and in Jewish tradition. Thus, the drum-dance-song ensemble of the Bible and Sephardic culture *might* be labeled the Miriam tradition.

In addition to Meyers and Pardes, other scholars have written on the history of women's leadership in Jewish traditions, starting with the First Temple period in ancient Israel and continuing through European history. Altogether, their research suggests that women were performance leaders, in the fashion of the drum-dance-song ensemble. Women's performance groups remained active in Sephardic communities, and may have been part of a separate women's prayer group ritual. But as the synagogue replaced the Temple, the place for women's performance leadership became removed from sanctioned Jewish worship.

Biblical and Talmudic Accounts

According to Susan Grossman's analysis of the drum-dance-song ensemble portrayed in the book of Judges, "women sang and danced at festivals . . . However it is not clear whether the dances were part of the official cultic ceremony or just part of a general popular celebration of those who attended."[29] Examples include the daughters of Shiloh dancing for a festival (Judges 21:19), victory ceremonies that were "religious celebrations" at the time (I Samuel 18:6–7), Deborah's song, and Jepthah's daughter's dance (Judges 5:1–31, 11:34). In this description and elsewhere in her essay, Grossman suggests that the women song and dance leaders were either a part of the official cult or "just entertainment." Yet the extremes she presents seem counter to reality. Another interpretation might be that women led religious rituals that were meaningful to their community but were conducted outside the Temple or synagogue.

Of the Second Temple period, Grossman notes that "male and female singers are mentioned in Ezra and Nehemiah as part of the community returning from exile (Ezra 2:65; Neh. 7:67)." She concludes that "in both books, it is difficult to determine whether these women singers were part of the Temple retinue, as only male singers are mentioned when ceremonies or services are described." However, she notes that Heiman's three daughters are mentioned in Chronicles as trained for service in the Temple, and Psalm 68:26 describes "maidens playing timbrels among the musicians as part of the procession bringing the ark to its place, probably in Solomon's Temple."[30]

Meyers's research and studies by ethnomusicologist Alfred Sendrey strongly support the claim for music and dance leadership by women in the Bible. They conclude that in no way were these women denoted in the text merely as entertainment; they served a vital role in their performance of ritual in ancient Israel, as would be true for other neighboring cultures as well. In *Music in Ancient Israel*, Sendrey attributes the "entertainment" evaluation of the women singers to the medieval Talmudic commentator Rashi, and counters the claim by arguing that if the women were merely entertainers, they would not have prepared for a return to the Jerusalem Temple by practicing singing in Babylonian captivity. He considers it "indeed highly probable that the 'male singers and female singers' mentioned by Ezra and Nehemiah must have been in part non-levitical Temple singers" who still played a role in the life of Israel after the return from captivity in Babylon."

Sendrey concludes that scriptural passages in fact show that women were always part of the Temple staff of singers. He cites a passage from Amos, and another from Philo, regarding the Herodian Temple. Of Philo's comments he says, "the participation of women in the cult as dancers and also, possibly, as singers, is mentioned in several places in his writings." Finally, Sendrey notes that women were dance and song leaders at religious festivals that occurred outside the Temple. He describes these rituals as times of "entertainment," but not in a derogatory manner. Rather, he regards these events as "an indispensable requirement for certain ritual ceremonies." Dances done by women "brought [the events] to a climax by a popular entertainment, in which they were the main feature."[31]

Grossman's discussion of the Herodian Temple period mentions women's continuing participation in Temple practices for sacrifices and offerings, and also the water-drawing ceremony. Called *Simchat Beit ha-Sho'evah*, this ceremony occurred at the end of *Sukkot*, and involved a festival of dance and rejoicing. A celebration mentioned in the Mishnah, it raises the issue of whether men and women were separated for festive worship, as the text talks of men dancing in the women's court.[32]

In *The Hebrew Goddess*, Raphael Patai suggests that this water-drawing celebration was an occasion at which men and women danced together as a rite of fertility. The post-biblical Talmud reports that there was joyous dance and music for *Simchat Beit ha-Sho'evah* as part of the Temple harvest festival of *Sukkot*, with a water-pouring ritual, blazing torches, rabbis juggling, and men and women dancing together. Based on "descriptions contained in the Mishnah and in Talmudic sources," Patai concludes that these activities constituted an incorporation of old fertility rituals into Jewish Temple practices with ecstatic movement.[33]

Whether women participated or were separated in worship and celebration is at issue in these reports of *Simchat Beit ha-Sho'evah* festivities. Women's participation in the music and dancing might indicate their religious status during the time of the Mishnah. Women did lead ritual activities through dance, with the biblical and Talmudic texts strongly suggesting that there was a long history of such leadership in Judaism. When this historical information is compared with the images of the *Haggadot*, the representation of the tradition seems to clearly match written records. Yet research on the development of synagogue worship indicates that the value of the women's drum and dance ensemble changed, as dance and music by women became separated from official, sanctioned worship.

Miriam's Legacy and Women in Synagogue Worship

Although images from the *Haggadot* suggest that a Miriam tradition of women's dance and drumming retained a meaningful place in Jewish life, written evidence on the history of synagogue worship suggests that the importance of the tradition was devalued. While there is a tension between such records and the Miriam paintings, there is not a complete contradiction. Research shows that women were not totally separated from synagogue life, and in some cases from ritual leadership.

In *Women Leaders in the Ancient Synagogue,* Bernadette Brooten informs us that women not only participated in early synagogue life, but were also leaders of the synagogue. Looking at inscriptions on tombstones and archeological findings, Brooten found that women bore titles such as "Head of the Synagogue . . . leader . . . and . . . 'venerable'" and also "Mother of the Synagogue." She assumes that the titles had real meaning and were not honorary.[34] Adding to Brooten's findings, Hannah Safrai cites archeological evidence from the early synagogue period, and even "halakhic sources" about women, pointing out that women were not separated from men in worship during this early rabbinic period. However, she does report that there were restrictions on women. First, there are passages in the rabbinic Tosefta (Megillah 3:11–12) and Babylonian Talmud (Megillah 23a) indicating that women should not stand up and read the Torah. Even though this was not determined to be against *halakhah,* the Talmud explains that it would bring shame on the congregation. Safrai concludes that "women were permitted to be called up and recite the blessing during the Torah reading, but additional consideration served to distance them from this role in the synagogue."[35]

While women may have participated in synagogue ritual life to some degree, other evidence exists concerning their role as synagogue music leaders. After the destruction of the Temple, the use of music in Jewish worship was controversial, because of the rabbinic ban on the playing of musical instruments on the Sabbath. Singing was permitted, and some communities allowed the playing of rhythm instruments.[36] Dancing on the Sabbath was a sign of joy, and was used for worship to some degree, but rabbinic texts suggest that it was inappropriate save for weddings, when all were commanded to rejoice in the form of dance.[37] The rabbis of the Talmud even considered it important to suspend the study of Torah for processions, which can be considered a type of dance (Kethuboth 1:17a). The proof case involves Rabbi Judah ben Ila'i, who reportedly "interrupted the study of the Torah for the sake of a funeral procession and the leading of the bride [under the bridal canopy]."[38] Significantly, it was women who led the funeral processions.

Over time, changes in the use of music for Jewish worship affected the role of women as music leaders. An understanding of what was deemed proper behavior for women also changed. In the Near Eastern world, men and women rarely danced together. Women danced in separate groups, such as the dance and drum ensembles, although according to Meyers's research, women drummers may have performed in front of men, leading song and dance for festivities. The biblical text never indicates that it was considered improper to hear the voice of a Miriam (female song leader) singing praise, even for prayer.

In the Talmud, there was an attitude change: women's voices were determined to be "indecent" (*Kol b-ishah ervah*). A woman's voice was not to be heard during prayer, because it might distract a man, making him think lustful thoughts. Feminist scholar Emily Taitz translates this relevant passage (Sotah 48a), commenting that an actual ban on women's voices in worship was implemented in the Middle Ages, the period when the Miriam pictures were painted for the *Haggadot*. According to Taitz, rabbis of the period held an extremely negative view about hearing a woman's voice during prayer, determining that "if men sing and women respond . . . it is a breach of law, but if women sing and men respond, it is as if a fire was raging in a field of flax!"[39]

In effect, this interpretation eliminated all possibility of women's musical leadership within the synagogue. Because of these statements in the Talmud, "according to classical Jewish law, women are not permitted to serve as cantors nor as prayer leaders. Neither may they sing in a synagogue choir." Rivka Haut, however, suggests that women had their own prayer groups, and points to the Exodus passage about Miriam and the women dancing as the first example of a separate women's prayer group in Jewish tradition.[40]

Because of the *tanyaderas*, the Sephardic women's song and dance leaders, we know that Jewish women continued to lead music and dance for celebration and, as Haut describes it, as a form of women's prayer. Miriam and her "sisters" survived, but they survived outside the synagogue. Information varies on whether the continuing drum-dance-song groups performed only for women participants or for mixed company. Given the Talmudic restrictions on hearing a woman's voice, plus the custom of separate dance groups in the Near East and Mediterranean, the most likely answer is that women sometimes danced and played music in performance of Jewish ritual among women. While there were court entertainment performances for mixed company in medieval Spain, Jewish women still gathered separately for dance and music in the tradition of Miriam, with some evidence suggesting that they did so for ritual, prayer, and praise significant to their lives as Jews.

Jewish Women and Medieval Spain

The Jewish community in Spain lived under Islamic domination for centuries. A religion noted for extreme separation between men and women, Islam did influence some rabbinic decisions of the time, including those of the medieval Spanish Jewish scholar Moses Maimonides. His remarks on music and women's voices are similar to the comments in the Talmud in expressing strong opposition to men listening to female performers. Maimonides placed this prohibition at the end of his comments regarding the proper place of music in Jewish life. He wrote that "all music meant for amusement is absolutely forbidden." One should not listen to "a song with a secular text . . . a song that is accompanied by an instrument," to one that "includes obscene language," or to a "string instrument" or "passages played on such instruments while drinking wine." The "most severe transgression" was "listening to singing and playing of a woman."[41]

From the information available on *zambra* parties in medieval Andalusia, we know that both Islamic and Jewish communities had liberal interpretations of the prohibitions against music and women. Maimonides' restrictions seem to have been aimed at music for secular occasions, such as the *zambras*, where women played instruments and danced. Even so, Jewish women may not have been the singers and dancers at these parties of wine, music, and poetry.[42] Given Maimonides' comments and what we know about *zambras*, it is fairly safe to assume that medieval Jewish women were singing and dancing in front of men and, on occasion, with men. Rabbinic condemnation of mixed-couples dancing verifies this assumption.[43] But the objections to women dancing in front of and with men provide little information on what women were doing when they met together separately, and whether they used music and dance for their own ritual celebrations.

The Miriam paintings of the *Haggadot* offer a possible reading on this issue. The iconography of these paintings is curious given that men were prohibited from hearing a woman's voice during prayer. Yet if Jewish women maintained separate music or prayer groups, historical data from medieval Spain suggest that the Miriam imagery may derive from women's rituals that occurred outside the synagogue. Ethnographic studies show that while there was "rabbinic opposition to women singing in general," the "Sephardic women created their own time" for the "performance of their songs." Such times included "rituals related to the life cycle" and women's daily activities. It appears that the *Sephardiyot* "developed styles of communication and intimacy" through their own rituals that strengthened their sense of community.[44]

The imagery of the *Haggadot* might thus derive from women's gatherings for ritual, and the paintings may reflect women's separate ritual performance. Following Jewish custom and law, the women depicted in the *Haggadot* were perhaps celebrating a religiously significant event rather than performing a secular dance. What is sacred and holy and what is ordinary and mundane is never completely separate in a culture. Performance theory suggests that there is always a spectrum, or Schechner's "braid," of interaction between the edifying holy and the entertaining ordinary. In medieval Spain, women's dancing in front of and with men was at the entertainment end of the spectrum. The religious values of Jews in medieval Spain allowed for some members of Jewish society to accept the behavior. Yet since rabbis controlled the religious end of the spectrum for Jews, and they did not approve of women dancing in front of men, women's ritual performance apparently was removed from sanctioned rabbinic Jewish worship.[45]

The Miriam pictures might depict scenes from the courts of medieval Spain, with women dancing in the presence of men for entertainment. But they do depict a biblical scene. Despite the prohibition against men's hearing a woman's voice during prayer, the image of Miriam's ritual leadership retained enough meaning to be included in the visual rendition of the Passover story. So from another standpoint we might see the iconography of Miriam as a display of women's own ritual celebration. Miriam is a biblical figure in a story for Jewish celebration, where women led a prayer of praise. Artists for the *Haggadot* may have been painting what they knew of the Miriam tradition in their lifetime, with this tradition living through the dance and music of Jewish women of the period.

Jewish Women in Medieval Spain: Symbol and Reality

THE KABBALISTIC TEXTS

Questioning the meaning of Miriam and dancing women in Jewish history raises issues of symbolic and lived reality. How do we imagine our deepest values in visual form? What symbols do we create? And do our symbols, which are metaphoric, reveal more about our beliefs than we even know? These are important questions for today, as modern culture is as likely to produce visual texts as written ones.

Just as a modern film or an online image does not fully portray the reality of life, the illuminated paintings of the *Haggadot* are not complete representations of the lives of medieval Jews in Spain. Rather, they are an interpretation of biblical history, with parts of the Exodus story portrayed through chosen contemporary medieval images. The meaning of Miriam and the dancing women in the *Haggadot* remains in question, as does the impact that the images had for medieval Spanish Jews. On a simple level, they may merely portray courtly dance, or maybe they depict a women's prayer group, or both. On a symbolic level, though, there is probably far more being represented.

Understanding the symbolic value of the paintings requires another set of questions, such as: What did the Passover story mean to Jews in Spain during the thirteenth and fourteenth centuries? Why was the image of Miriam and the dancing women given a place in these illuminated manuscripts? What was the meaning of dancing women for the Jewish community? What did the image mean at this time? And what was the reality of the symbol for women?

One assumption has been that Jewish women were not ritual leaders of any significance. This is contradictory to what the tradition and some texts tell us. We know from textual information that the *Haggadot* present a picture of celebration that people would have recognized, or at least an image of women dancing within the strictures of a more conservative rabbinic ruling. They were separated from men for a special, if not sacred, purpose. But kabbalistic material from approximately the same time period offers clues about the metaphoric significance of the Miriam imagery.

From a passage in the Zohar (3167b) commenting on Miriam's victory dance, it appears that the *Haggadah* pictures were an idealistic but living image for medieval Jews. Impressively, the Zohar describes Miriam dancing in the royal courts of heaven. The Spanish mystics also directly influenced the culture of Castile and Catalonia during this time period, with Moses de Leon, the probable author of the Zohar, living in Catalonian Girona.

The Zohar is the primary text of mystical Spanish Kabbalah. Consisting of several volumes, it provides commentary on the first five books of the Hebrew Bible. This "Book of Splendor" contains passages on music and dance, and specifically on women's music and dance. Contrary to some rabbinic writings of the period, Spanish kabbalistic literature displays a highly favorable attitude toward music.

Abraham Abulafia was one Spanish kabbalist who had a lot to say about music. Abulafia, who taught a method of meditation based on focusing on the letters of the Hebrew alphabet, wrote that music and singing might produce the same meditative effect. For him, listening to music was thus a meditative technique that involved the body and the emotions.[46] Abulafia was not alone in his evaluation of the spiritual power of music. The Zohar portrays God and the angels in heaven singing, dancing, or listening intently to the music of humans. The commentary even states that when Israel sang after escaping Egypt, God silenced the angels to better hear the singing of the Israelites:

> On the night of the Exodus God orders the angels to stop singing be-
> cause Israel is singing on earth . . . At midnight when the Holy one,
> blessed be He, enters the Garden of Eden to delight with the righteous
> ones, the choir of angels, the trees of Eden, and heaven and earth sing
> his praises.

Almost paradoxically, the more pleasant sound is that of humans studying Torah. Since women did not normally study Torah, presumably their
music was less important.[47]

Statements on dance and Kabbalah must be made with caution, as the
kabbalistic literature displays mixed attitudes toward dance, especially
where women are concerned. Dance in general posed a problem for some
of the Spanish kabbalists, despite the favorable attitude toward music.
Later Jewish mystical literature from the Hasidic community of northern
Europe almost always portrays dance in a highly favorable manner, but
the thirteenth-century material seems concerned with movement as a
means of attaining a harmonious society. There is disdain of wild, ecstatic
dance, apparently because it might create disorder. Negative kabbalistic
attitudes toward dance are also found in an interpretation of Psalm 150,
with its mention a "*tof* (frame drum)," like that carried by Miriam.[48]

Despite the negative opinion of some women's dance attributed to
Spanish mystics, the Zohar contains the extremely positive image of
singing, dancing women given in commentary on Exodus 15:20. Shiloah's
discussion of this passage emphasizes the singing of women in the heavenly courts. The female performers constitute a third and upper "band"
of heavenly choirs, which includes Miriam. She leads the singing and
dancing of the women's choir. Additionally, Miriam's mother, Yocheved, sings with the women. They join her in singing "the Song of the
Sea three times a day." Miriam is mentioned in the song, which refers
to her taking up her drum. After she has the drum, the Zohar states that
"Yokheved sings alone."[49]

This is an amazing report for a medieval Jewish text because it shows
that women are enjoying a superior rank as singers. They are singing in
separate chambers from men, but they nevertheless have an important
role to play. Moreover, while in the biblical account Miriam is the leader
of song and dance and the composer of the Song of the Sea, her mother is
not even mentioned in Exodus 15:20. It is extremely curious why Yocheved takes over for Miriam in the Zohar's description of the women's
court. Possibly it is because the medieval commentator assumed that a
drumming woman also danced.

Rivka Haut gives her own version of this passage from the Zohar, stressing that women had separate prayer groups, and that the story is a reflection of the tradition:

> A scene of women praying together is found in the *Zohar* . . . An angel, privy to heaven's secrets, describes to R. Simeon ben Yohai a number of heavenly chambers for righteous women. In one of them, Jochebed, mother of the prophet Miriam, leads the women in paradise in praising God three times a day.[50]

In Haut's translation, "Jochebed" and the "thousands and tens of thousands" of other women with her give praise to "the Lord of the Universe," then "sing the Song of the Sea . . . and all the *tzadikim* in *Gan Eden* . . . listen to her sweet voice."[51] The distinction between praising and singing suggests the possibility of dance in connection with the singing. Biblical and Talmudic texts both use the word "rejoice" to indicate celebration conducted with dance and music.[52] Additionally, the name Yocheved means "glory of God," *kavod* meaning glory or majesty. In kabbalistic texts, the deity in this reference is interpreted to be the *Shekhinah,* the feminine presence of God.[53] The replacement of Miriam with Yocheved appears to be a visual shorthand. It is as if Miriam's drumming and dance brings in the *Shekhinah.*

There is apparently an idealized women's drum and dance group depicted in this passage. To what degree it was based on the reality of the life of Sephardic women is in question. For the Spanish kabbalists, what happened on the earthly plane affected the heavenly realm, and this world was an imperfect version of the celestial realm. So the Zohar passage on Miriam in the heavenly courts might be based on knowledge of women's song and dance practices in medieval Spain. The match with the Miriam pictures of the *Haggadot* is not exact, as the Zohar depicts an idealized reality. The most solid historical evidence indicates that women did not lead their own worship services in the courts. Yet a comparison and contrast between the images in the visual and written texts reveals striking similarities.

Haut suggests that the mention of singing and dancing women in the Zohar implies that the women's performance groups constituted a women's prayer tradition in Judaism. Supporting her claim, she provides a historical note relevant to the history of the *Sephardiyot.* She cites the commentary of Ibn Ezra on Exodus 38:8, where he explains the biblical verse by saying that a women's prayer group "would only come every day to the door of the Tent of Meeting, *to pray* and to hear about the *mitzvot.*"[54] That the Spanish Ibn Ezra would even think of the notion of a women's prayer group is remarkable. Yet the idea was possible for him as a biblical commentator of the twelfth century. His remark suggests that the Miriam paintings of the *Haggadot* might indeed portray a women's prayer group, due to his cultural vision as a skilled Spanish medieval poet and exegete.[55]

WOMEN'S REALITY

Images of women in the Zohar can be checked against the reality of women's lives through the *Geniza* manuscripts from twelfth-century Cairo and rabbinic writings. The Cairo manuscripts illustrate life in a synagogue during the Middle Ages, when the Mediterranean world was under Islamic rule. While women were not respected as leaders, the *Geniza* records reveal that they had some independence. The rabbinic writings indicate that there were attempts to limit that independence.

According to these documents, men and women were separated for worship, with women seated in their own gallery in the synagogue, but "men and women socialized both before and after prayer in the synagogue courtyard." Women were also educated to learn the prayers, their education depending on their social status. Women sometimes spoke from the women's gallery, and a woman could also take an oath. When she did so, it was "in the men's section, while holding the Torah scroll."[56]

Avraham Grossman's extensive study of Jewish women in the Middle Ages offers yet another perspective on the participation of women in synagogue life. First, he suggests that many Jewish women in Spain were educated, and thus capable of studying Torah. Then he offers evidence that they were capable of leading, and did lead, worship in separate women's groups. He quotes Maimonides' interpretation of Rabbi Eliezer ben Hyrcanus's statement in the Talmud on both of these points, demonstrating flexibility in actual practices in medieval Spain. According to Rabbi Eliezer, to teach women Torah is like teaching them *tiflut*— "licentiousness, lewdness, or immodesty."

Maimonides considered it permissible to educate women, but not in Oral Torah. He thought that "most women's minds are not focused toward studying," although this was not true of "all women." He also determined that it was permissible for women to lead prayers among themselves, although not in Hebrew. He referred to Mishnah Berakhot 7:2, where it says that women may "recite the invitation to Grace (*zimmun*) by themselves." In his view, this was not an option for women, but rather an obligation. However, they were not to "recite it with God's name."[57]

While women were separated from the men in the synagogues, the Cairo *Geniza* suggests that they were not entirely voiceless. Nor were they excluded from participation in synagogue life, even if they were menstruating. Two passages from the fifteenth-century *Shulhan Arukh* indicate that women participated in synagogue ritual in Sephardic communities. One states: "All those who are impure may read the Torah, recite the Shema, and pray," and "all those who are impure, even menstruants, are permitted to hold a Torah scroll and read it, provided that their hands are neither soiled nor dirty." From the earlier writings of Rabbi Asher ben Yehiel, Rabbi Jonah of Gerona, and "other Spanish sages," it appears that women did participate in synagogue prayer, but in the "vernacular." Rabbi Jonah even states in *Iggeret ha-Teshuvah* that women "should take care to pray evening, morning, and noon."[58] Still, in medieval Spain it may have been customary to exclude menstruants from services. A report from the school of Rashi (eleventh-century Provence) states that women did not attend service during this time, but that this was a "supererogation (*humrah be'alma*) and they are not obligated to act in this manner." Since the synagogue is "a place of purity," however, Rashi adds that the women "act properly, and may they be blessed."[59]

While the information from Cairo and the rulings of the rabbinic authorities indicate that women were participating in synagogue worship, other historical accounts differ on the medieval ritual life of Spain. Grossman reveals that some women received an education, but for the most part girls were poorly educated in Muslim Spain, and mainly learned from their mothers "spinning and various other forms of domestic work." By implication, this might mean that women could not participate fully in the recitation of Hebrew prayers in the synagogue. This was not always the case, though. Women did participate in worship services, but in separate locations; and in other countries during the same period, "men and women prayed together in the same hall."[60]

Research shows that women were less likely to participate in the worship life of the post-expulsion Sephardic community. Presenting an extreme example, Debbi Friedhaber describes a case of complete exclusion of Jewish women from worship in Kurdistan. The women were not allowed to participate in synagogue services, so while the men were inside the house of worship, the women created their own rituals through song and dance. They would first "do the necessary housework and then dress up in their Shabbat clothes and visit brides or mourners at home," then "young women would meet to dance, or sit on roofs and sing." They thus "passed on orally" their culture "from mother to daughter," though "few women knew how to read or write." The Kurdish *Sephardiyot* used dance, music, and speech as a means of sharing traditions of Jewish women. Despite being illiterate and completely displaced from

Jewish worship, they "passed on" Torah tradition, partially through their own dance and song prayer groups.[61]

Historical information from other Sephardic communities indicates that the Kurdish example was a drastic case. Women were not always excluded from the synagogue, but the place of their ritual function was at wedding celebrations and funeral rites. There was a unique blend of custom and faith combined in rituals for marriage and death, and Jewish women guided these life rituals through dance and music. So even though they were excluded from ritual leadership in the synagogue, presumably their leadership role did not disappear.

Displacement of women from Jewish worship may partially be due to women's association with dance, an event that became tangential to most Jewish synagogue worship over time. Yet dance never disappears in a culture. It provides a needed form of expression within a community, and always appears at some level.[62] Likewise, the dance- and music-oriented Miriam tradition of Jewish women apparently never disappeared among the *Sephardiyot*. Rather, it appears that the tradition was transferred to women's separate groups, perhaps for prayer, but undoubtedly for celebrations of life passages.

Conclusions

The various texts that inform us about women's roles in the culture and religion of medieval Jewish life in Spain do not offer clear and decisive information to help us decipher the Miriam pictures of the *Haggadot*. Historical and rabbinic materials imply that the restrictions on women's participation in worship were less severe than might be expected, even with the pronouncements against hearing a woman's voice during prayer, and with the influence of Islam on Jewish practice. Yet medieval Spanish women's reality is not entirely clear, as written records convey only certain aspects of their lives.

The *Haggadah* paintings offer some snapshots of women's existence in medieval Spain, which perhaps included separate women's music and dance groups—a type of continuing Miriam tradition. Along with kabbalistic writings and Sephardic cultural history, these paintings render much more than biblical illustrations for a Passover Seder. The imagery might reveal life circumstances for women of the period. In the *Hispano-Moresque Haggadah*, for example, as well as the *Sarajevo Haggadah*, there is a matron leading younger women in celebration. Additionally, the *Sister Haggadah* presents a singer with a matron's headdress singing alongside a Miriam figure. It is the matron who leads or teaches the song and dance. In the Zohar, Yocheved is portrayed as the matron who leads celebration, but who is also associated with the *Shekhinah.* The images of well-dressed women in the *Haggadot* matches the kabbalistic ideal of women dancing in the heavenly court. The historical evidence confirms that many of the Jewish women were living and dancing in the courts of medieval Spain. Yet the idealized imagery of the Zohar presents something different—an image of women with autonomy over their own worship rituals. This point becomes more relevant when we consider that the kabbalistic message was flourishing among the poorer classes, where women in general had less autonomy over their lives.[63]

The textual information of the Zohar and the visual imagery it provides imply that the kabbalists of Spain placed their own interpretation on the meaning of a women's drum and dance ensemble, signified through the figure of Miriam. Because there are visual texts of the women's ensemble available through the *Haggadot*, the kabbalistic interpretation appears to be based on the actual practices of Jewish women of the period. The kabbalists were not inventing a heavenly reality; they were looking at Spanish Jewish culture and rendering it in terms of their own understanding of life.

Again, this is a possible interpretation based on cultural influences in Spain during the thirteenth and fourteenth centuries, and the background of medieval Jewish culture in Islamic Spain. The *Haggadot* were painted by artists commissioned by wealthy families, but the artists' vision could have been influenced by kabbalistic ideas circulating in the culture. A comparison of visual and written texts suggests this possibility, even though the match is not exactly complementary.

Data on the literacy and education of Jewish women implies that women of the courts were capable of leading their own separate prayer group celebrations and participating in synagogue services. This may prove that a tension exists between written and visual materials. If women had been able to participate in synagogue services, their need for ritual might have been met in this activity. Yet while the *Sephardiyot* had other options, they still chose to perform *their* ritual as Jewish women, and perhaps their version of a prayer group.

Traditions of dance and music among Sephardic women may support the idea that the women's performance ensembles were prayer groups. The following chapter details some of the *Sephardiyot's* ritual practices for separate women's gatherings. *Tanyaderas* were the leaders of those rituals, and so they might have been considered teachers of prayer in the tradition of Miriam. They were not instructing women in traditional Jewish prayers, or even in Hebrew songs. Instead, they created times for rituals of dance and songs within the Jewish life cycle.

Music and dance may be considered Jewish prayer if it is defined through meaning rather than spoken word. Recall that Franz Rosenzweig regarded the silence of the body in motion as a part of prayer in Judaism, and the bridge to revelation. Jewish history and tradition conveys this metaphorically through the figure of Miriam. It is she who, according to the Zohar, "at the great banquet, in the time of the Messiah . . . *will dance* before the righteous" (my emphasis). Like Miriam, the *tanyaderas* led women in prayers of praise and celebration through the medium of dance. If their tradition is to be taken seriously, it must be in terms of the type of nontextual, movement-centered prayer encompassed in the extra-ordinary activity of dance.

4 *Miriam at the Wedding Celebration*

Y fuérame a bañar
a orillas del rio
ahí encontré, madre,
a mi lindo amigo
el me dio un abrazo
yo le di cinco.

I went to bathe
at the river's bank
there I met, mother,
my handsome friend,
he embraced me once,
I embraced him five times.

Por Dios, la nuestra novia,
cuerpo garrido,
qué es lo que os ponis
en escondido?
Si os ponéis albayarde
u oro molido?
Tan bien que le parecis
a vuestro marido.

Oh Lord, our bride,
beautiful body,
what is the cream that you
use secretly?
Is it white enamel
or gold dust?
You will look so well
in the eyes of your husband.

—"Y fuérame a bañar," translated by Eti Ben-Zaken,
from *The Bride Unfastens Her Braids, the Groom Faints*

Women's Torah Teaching: Life Ritual Celebration

In Judaism, women's dance traditions are often more than just entertainment. Biblical, Talmudic, historical, visual, and written records indicate that women's activity was important to the community. That is undoubtedly true with regard to weddings in the Sephardic community, where women were leaders of a large number of music and dance activities.[1]

What is a wedding dance? How and why do people dance at weddings? Current American culture might think in terms of a time after an official ceremony for excess drinking and bad music, with a few people moving around on the dance floor. For Jewish communities, the idea of a wedding dance is more established as an important social ritual. But the actual performance might range from a northern European and Hasidic-influenced line dance to a disc jockey playing rock music. In traditional Sephardic communities, the concept of a wedding dance was much broader, more specific, and elaborate.

The Sephardim had many unique wedding customs, reflective of their history in Spain and their life in the Mediterranean world. They fulfilled requirements for rejoicing at a Jewish wedding through distinctive songs and dances, which were usually led by women. The song above is part of the *Sephardiyot's* wedding repertoire, and was sometimes sung for the evening of the bride's ritual bath, the *mikveh*. As in many Sephardic wedding songs, the lyrics of "Y fuérame a bañar" reflect a mix of culture and specific Jewish ritual, with a notable sensual reference to the *mikveh* bath.

Jewish law prescribes the bride's *mikveh*, and as practiced for weddings in Sephardic communities, it was clearly a special event for women. Songs and associated dance traditions such as those presented in this chapter also indicate that it was a time when the *Sephardiyot* taught each other about living as Jewish women. Quoting Sephardic scholar Esther Benbassa-Dudonney on the nature and meaning of this ritual in Turkey, Paloma Díaz-Maz remarks that while the event could be raucous, it was also meaningful. She notes that "they ate baked goods and they drank *raki* while singing and dancing in the bathhouse." This activity might be dismissed as insignificant; however, "it can be said that it was a ceremony for the women, and of great importance."[2]

There are other women's dance ritual events in Sephardic wedding tradition, notably the henna ceremony. But in general, all aspects of the wedding experience involved forms of dance and ritual movement, with the ritual bath holding unique status as a women's event specific to Judaism. So ritual movement involved with the *mikveh* ceremony might demonstrate how the *Sephardiyot* used dance as a means of expressing lived Torah.

Dance often supplies visual clues to a culture's means of creating symbols. Without specific pictures of Jewish women's ritual bath gatherings, the most immediate source of information about what occurred is the songs sung at the event in the traditional Sephardic world. The lyrics are simple, and are more concerned with life ritual than with the conscious reflection of beliefs. Yet in their own right, the songs are an amazing source of information.[3] Along with knowledge of the tradition of dance as part of the women's wedding ritual, they might shed light on the circumstances surrounding the *mikveh* event and on the possible purpose and meaning of the dance and movement among the *Sephardiyot*.

In order to gain some understanding of the setting and religious background of the Sephardic wedding dance tradition, we must once again look to many sources for insight. An overview of Sephardic wedding customs and specific Moroccan and Eastern Mediterranean variations can provide some insight into the cultural background of these specific songs and dances. Considering the context of the performance, it is then possible to investigate the women's wedding songs and associated dance practices.

Ethnomusicologists report that many of the songs are quite sensuous and playful, as are the dance styles. However, the occasion was not always a joyful one for the bride. The larger context of Jewish weddings includes a patriarchal framework that was at times used to oppress women. Marriage circumstances and conditions sometimes proved to be less than ideal. In her study of elderly Turkish, Syrian, and Yemenite Jewish women currently living in Jerusalem, Susan Sered provides a number of descriptions of unhappy marriages. Some of the Sephardic women she interviewed were forced to leave their parents and marry at a very young age. Some were in arranged marriages, with husbands and in-laws who did not care about them. The women had the right to divorce, but they received no financial support beyond that agreed on at the marriage. One of the sadder wedding songs from Syria tells about a "bride" who is "crying and hiding to escape marriage."[4] Yet these are reports of women who lived in poverty under severe restrictions.

Songs of the Moroccan and Eastern Mediterranean *Sephardiyot* presented in this chapter certainly imply happier circumstances. Some Sephardic women did endure horrendous treatment because of marriage; however, this was not the case for all *Sephardiyot*. Historical evidence indicates that the wedding rituals themselves were comforting rather than punitive. Amnon Shiloah comments that while the brides in these arranged marriages were sometimes very young, one of the functions of the singing and dancing wedding rituals was to ease anxiety.[5]

While Sephardic wedding rituals were meant to be supportive, circumstances differed. Of Mediterranean Jewish decent herself, Sephardic singer Stefani Levi suggests that setting was a crucial factor. Women who lived in oppressed communities were more likely to be married quickly, and in less happy circumstances. She recalled that as a child she observed Jewish women from Syria who were forced to leave their home country to come to America for arranged marriages. She remembered that they appeared quite grim. However, she stresses that the songs for the women's separate gatherings were often bawdy and burlesque. Many of the lyrics show that when women were given the opportunity to create and shape ritual in seclusion from men, that is exactly what they did.[6]

Nevertheless, questions of women's circumstances arise when one is scrutinizing details of how women's Jewish religious values influenced their performance for weddings. Written texts on the laws and customs of Jewish weddings in these communities provide some understanding of the background of their practice and rabbinic prescription. This chapter explores such aspects of the Sephardic wedding, once again outlining how movement matters deeply to a community, and how Jewish women's dance leadership might have served as an embodied teaching of Torah tradition, perhaps even in defiance of patriarchal limitations.

Sephardic Wedding Dance: An Overview

More accurately described as a continuous dance event, a Sephardic wedding usually included a special party for the bride-to-be, a *mikveh*, and a henna party. How the women danced varied, depending on where they lived, but in general they danced like their Muslim neighbors. For instance, at a Moroccan wedding the dances of women included fast shaking of hips, and in the Turkish and Balkan areas the style of movement was reminiscent of Turkish belly dance patterns. During the weeklong wedding event, times for full, expressive dances were sandwiched in between separate rituals. For each ritual, there were often specific movement patterns, interlaced with special music and opportunities for free-form dance expression.

Whatever the style of movement that women performed for weddings, they almost always presented many dances. The wedding event in Sephardic communities included numerous pre-wedding ceremonies and rituals, with celebrations on the eve of the wedding day proper and post-wedding celebrations for up to a week. There were engagement and contractual ceremonies, the night of the *mikveh* celebration for the bride, a similar party for the groom, a display of the bride's trousseau, the blessings and ritual moment of the wedding, and a post-ceremony feast that included community singing and dancing. Moroccan Jewish weddings often occurred on a Wednesday night, with a pre-wedding gift-giving ceremony. The bride and groom's families and friends presented the bride with gifts, which included "sweets on a tray, flour, a garment to wear, [and] some kind of fabric or ribbon with which to adorn her head."[7]

The Moroccans also had a wealth of practices for the *noche banyo* (the night of the *mikveh*), a women's event honoring the bride. Also called *noche de novia* (the bride's night), the evening celebration included a henna ceremony, followed by a trip to the *mikveh*. Interestingly, from a description of the event in Tangiers, we know that rabbis were present at the beginning of the night, to escort the bride to a special chair. "The rabbi and two 'Edim' (religious witnesses) [came] in carrying candles and singing 'Piyutim' (religious songs)," then led "the bride to a throne set up with three chairs" for the henna ceremony. Women sang an "Arabic song" for the event, and ululated for joy. At the end of the night, when there were no men present, the women escorted the bride into the *mikveh* bath. Her mother greeted her as she left the water and gave her "a mirror . . . to view her face and entire body."[8]

This description of women's wedding practices provides a colorful slice of Sephardic life. At the same time, the details about the *mikveh* answer some basic question about the *who, where,* and *how* of these dance and music events. As reviewed in the last chapter, these particulars are important for evaluating the *why* of the proceedings: Why did *Sephardiyot* practice such elaborate customs or *minhag*? Why did these customs have religious significance? Why were specific songs and dances performed?

The answers might differ by community, as details do vary. However, there are also many commonalities. The Spanish Jews in Turkey followed a similar procedure of pre- and post-wedding festivities, with weddings often on Sunday rather than on Wednesday, but they also included many special songs. One notable song for an engagement party was "Que la novia era mia y non del rey"—"the bride belongs to the groom and not the king." This part of the wedding event was called *amostrar ashugar* (showing the trousseau). At this ceremony, sweets were served on a tray, and there were also songs for the display of the bride's "trousseau."[9]

On the night of the bride's *mikveh* in this community, the mother-in-law hosted a special party prior to the bathing ritual, called the *bogo de bano* (bag for the bath), at which gifts of toiletries were given to the bride. In contrast to the custom among Moroccan Jews, this event was "usually held in the early afternoon." The trip to the *mikveh* followed, and then the bride's mother hosted a women's party called a "*cafe de bano,*" where "special coffee and fancy cakes and pastries" were served.[10]

Paloma Díaz-Mas, a scholar of Sephardic descent, relates some of the same details in connection with the festivities for Jewish weddings in Morocco. The material she presents captures more of the unspoken, for she mentions when and how dance was included. In detailing the presentation of the bride's trousseau, for instance, she includes a description of a ceremony at which the bride's hair was unbraided while the women chanted "*ulalé*" (ululations). After sweets sent by the groom were served, women friends of the bride then "retired with the bride, unbraided her hair, tied it with the ribbon, and covered it with a *meherma*, or silk cloth." Afterward there was music and dance, followed by a march through the village that included a "*guisandera*, who played the *sonaxa* [tambourine]." Those in the procession went from the bride's house to the groom's house "with the candles lit, preceded by one member of the family who held a large candle," and "shouting *ulalé, ulalé.*"[11] This entire ritual was choreographed, from the unbraiding and decorating of the bride's hair to the procession to the groom's house. The procession occurred outside the home, with the celebrants led through the streets by the tambourine-playing *guisandera.* Notably, the chanting of *ulalé* for the procession reflects the women's chant during the unbraiding ritual.

Díaz-Mas also describes a procession that occurred after a wedding. This procession included men, and was "accompanied by music and song." In Eastern Mediterranean communities there was a great deal of music and dance for the seven days following a wedding, called "the week of the *huppa.*" Reportedly, "during that week the groom did not work and was to stay with his bride." There was continuous music and dance, with "mandolin and tambourine" providing "accompaniment to these pastimes. Old women sang ballads in Judeo-Spanish."[12]

For the Sephardic community, the wedding was a dance and music event. The wedding process involved performing formal ritual movement and more informal, less structured music and dance. Processions could serve as the bridge between these occasions. When there were specialized rituals, songs predominated, and when music was played, dance occurred. Processions were apparently transitional for music, chant, and movement, although they were not labeled a dance.

Research shows that women almost always led the music and dance at weddings. Ethnomusicologists Susana Weich-Shahak and Judith Cohen also note that women played the featured role during the wedding events.[13] For example, while Díaz-Mas's report of a procession to a Turkish bath (*hammam*) mentions male musicians, only women relatives went with the bride for the bath itself. "Her mother, sisters and aunts accompanied her, carrying the cleaning utensils sent over the previous night . . . by the groom." Significantly, she adds that "the bride wore luxurious clothing and a great deal of jewelry." A women's party followed, with food, drinking, and dancing.[14]

When the dance and ritual movement at these parties are fully examined, they provide insight into the role of women in the Sephardic community, and what the focused celebrations of the wedding meant to them. Unlike the scenes in the Passover *Haggadot* depicting an idealized biblical event, these accounts of women's dance and drumming for celebration describe actual women's practices. The *Haggadah* pictures do, however, suggest that medieval Jewish women maintained similar practices, and the *Sephardiyot* continued this tradition in the Diaspora.

The *Sephardiyot* definitely maintained the Spanish language through their songs, as they sang them in their Ladino dialect, primarily Spanish but with some added Hebrew. The melodies of their songs followed the patterns of Spanish *romanceros* and *cantigas*, with wedding music consisting primarily of the more simple *cantiga* songs. These songs were accompanied by dance, which was featured throughout the wedding festivities. Why was there so much dancing? What and how the *Sephardiyot* danced in mixed company can serve as a starting point for interpreting the meaning of their wedding dances.

Historical accounts are helpful in answering this question. Reports of women dancing as part of the post-wedding celebration describe details on the general nature of their dance style, and on what and how they danced. In an account from Samuel Aaron Romanelli, a Jewish writer from Mantua, Italy, who traveled to Morocco in 1787, we learn that he saw a young woman performing a free-form dance as part of a wedding celebration. With "her head tilted sideways," he wrote, she "holds an edge of a kerchief in each hand, one high above her head, the other pointing below her waist at her stomach, and then slowly, lithely, she reverses the position of her arms." He also mentions that she "was accompanied by young girls beating quietly on goblet drums." The style of dance Romanelli witnessed might be labeled *dans du ventri* or "belly dance," which is common to the region. Among the pre-wedding women's practices, he also mentions a wedding procession. It occurred at night, when women would "lead the bride to the home of her groom accompanied by [a] warbling woman and drums." The bride did not move at all when they dressed her, and was "like unto a monument of stone until she comes out from under her bridal canopy and has been placed upon her bedding."[15]

A report from the French painter Eugène Delacroix in 1832 echoes Romanelli's observations. Delacroix created a painting of the event he observed, and also recorded his visit to the wedding in a journal. He describes the dancing as "performed only by women, each woman rising in turn and dancing alone," and says that the event involved "participation of Muslim neighbors in the festivities of the Jews." Also, the musicians who played for the event were Jews.[16]

A few years later, in 1845, the French writer Alexandre Dumas visited Tangiers and wrote an entire chapter on his experience at a Jewish wedding there. His account is similar to Delacroix's, describing a dance troupe taking turns soloing, and "ten or twelve women" who "danced, one after another." He notes that the dancing was spontaneous, "with all the female relatives taking part as an active expression of their participation in the festivities." The dancers were paid with coins that were "placed . . . in the peaked headpiece" worn by one of them, while the bride "remain[ed] as immobile as a Japanese statue."[17]

The wedding reports of these travelers are valuable documentation of Jewish musical traditions, and can help us understand the changes that occurred in the practice. They provide details "not only of the wedding but of broader aspects of Jewish musical culture" that incorporated local styles.[18] This also applies to the dances described by the travelers, which were obviously influenced by the surrounding culture. Yet a clear study of how the Jewish community used local customs as a means of celebrating a Jewish wedding is valuable for understanding the *Sephardiyot*'s dance. An intriguing, if not crucial, question is why weddings with a "belly dance" would be part of Torah tradition for Sephardic Jews. These dances embodied traditions through a particular symbolism that might have particular religious significance in the context of a Jewish wedding, depending on the dance idioms of a given culture.

Sephardic women in the travelers' reports performed in a Moroccan style with a unique purpose. Dance scholar Judith Lynne Hanna explains that the language of dance carries a particular weight and meaning in a particular culture and is unique to a particular setting. She found, for instance, that when women danced in mixed company in Yugoslavia, they were, in part, displaying their potential as a mate. So "young nubile women are judged for their strength, endurance, and health in dance performance." Her remark suggests that one purpose for the seven-day Sephardic post-wedding dance celebrations in the Eastern Mediterranean was for young men and women to meet and find a potential mate. In contrast, for Islamic women of North African countries such as Morocco, dance as a means of courtship was usually not possible. Because of strict Islamic regulations, Muslim women dance for women only, even at weddings. According to Hanna, their "decorous female dancing" is confined to "the private female section of the house, with its enclosed space, drawn curtains, and closed doors."[19]

Hanna adds that within Muslim culture, there are occasions when women do dance in front of men, including at weddings.[20] As a point of comparison, the paradox of Islamic women's isolated and public wedding dance performance suggests how Jews might have interpreted culture within their respective settings. Considering the travelers' reports, Jewish women were perhaps less restricted than were Islamic women in Morocco. Hanna's research on wedding celebrations in the Eastern Mediterranean indicates that culture was apparently less limiting of women there as a whole, whether they were Jewish, Muslim, or Christian.[21]

The *Sephardiyot* did not necessarily have to celebrate in isolation. The custom, practice, and meaning of these women's dance rituals becomes all the more interesting and curious if they were not a product of repressed expression in the community. Apparently, some *Sephardiyot* could dance in public, at least for weddings. But if the women could publicly perform ritual wedding dances, a question then remains about the meaning and purpose of their separate women's gatherings.

Women's Wedding Practices

Events at which the *Sephardiyot* danced, the times when they danced with or without men, and the connection of their dance with Jewish practices becomes a point of significant contrast to their neighbors. The travelers' reports provide us with some of the differences, but other sources might illuminate the significance for Sephardic women of these dances, and of performing as a meaningful expression of their lives as Jewish women.

In addition to the accounts written by travelers, Sephardic women's "songs of the bride" (*cantigas di novia*) provide "a graphic picture of a variety of customs." Among them are "a song [sung] to the mother-in-law on her way to meet the bride, one for displaying the dowry, another for the bride's ritual bath," and "a song of leave taking." An example of how these songs were performed comes from Salonika, Greece. The event was led by *tanyaderas*. One of them started off by "jingling the miniature cymbals that surround[ed her frame] drum." All the women present then joined in with "wedding ballads," which included "familiar innuendoes" that would cause "much laughter and increase the happiness and joy."[22]

Moroccan wedding dance events were also led by *tanyaderas*, and included singing and dancing at the henna party. This was an event that involved painting the hands and feet of the bride-to-be with henna paste, a practice shared with Muslim women. This action was believed to bring good fortune to the bride and groom and to ward off evil. A Yemenite interpretation provides a good picture of the general process. "First, there was a procession. Then the bride sat, as henna paste was painted on her hands and feet." Next the bride was "seated in a place of honor where she remain[ed] motionless throughout the hours that pass[ed] until the henna ceremony itself," with "vocalists helping to make the time pass pleasantly by singing and accompanying the dancers." After hours of "music and dance," the remaining henna was quietly removed, "spirited away by the guests as a good luck omen."[23]

Depending on the local community, the bride's trip to the *mikveh* either followed or preceded this ceremony. For instance, Weich-Shahak presents a slightly different order of events from that given in the report from Tangiers. Among the North Moroccan Sephardim she interviewed, Monday was the night of the *mikveh*, before the henna party, and was called the *baño de la novia* (ritual bath of the bride). The ritual involved the "married women (except for widows) of the bride's family," who would take the bride to "the ritual bath," where "special honours [were] given to the groom's mother and the bride's own mother." This included "undress[ing] the bride, with the help of the other women, before the bath," and "dress[ing] her again afterward." The henna ceremony occurred the following night. Called *la noche de la novia* (the night of the bride), it was "celebrated at the house of the bride's family." The bride's hands were "painted with *alhena*" for the ceremony, and then, with "her eyes closed," she was "led by her parents to the groom's house." A "*hevrah*," consisting of "a choir," accompanied her, "adding to the festivity of the occasion."[24]

Dance anthropologist Joann Kealiinohomoku's base questions about such a ritual are important for interpreting the *mikveh* and henna parties as dance events. Reports vary concerning who was present for the two rituals. The who changes, and sometimes the when. The how is fairly consistent. Mothers and married women attended the *mikveh*, which was always presented as an isolated women's event, with music and dance. At both the *mikveh* and henna rituals, the why is at issue. Why the henna? And why the *mikveh*?

From Weich-Shahak's research, we know that Sephardic wedding music was performed primarily by women, that women were often the only ones present for specific rituals, and that when men were present, "they may [have] join[ed] in the singing, but generally follow[ed] the women's lead." She lists the instruments that were normally played for these rituals. All are percussive and associated with women's dances, including the "tambourine called *sonaja*," and also castanets, worn by the singers.[25]

Such details, along with descriptions of movement and dance for the women's private gatherings, are needed to determine the meaning of the dance events and why they were performed. Arcadio de Larrea Palacín offers an abundance of such details for *el dia del lavado,* the day of the *mikveh,* and the *noche de la novia* in his report of a Jewish community in the Moroccan city of Tetuan. According to Larrea Palacín, the bride's *mikveh* was preceded by a gathering of married women from the groom's family. They met at the home of the bride, dressing her in a prescribed manner, with an outfit that included a skirt, a shawl, a breastplate, a red silk girdle, and a black scarf for her head. As gifts to the bride from the groom, the articles of clothing were presented in a specific process.[26]

Larrea Palacín reports that the bride was already dressed when the groom's relatives arrived at her house. The women relatives then took the red silk girdle and covered the bride's face with it. They used two eggs that had been wrapped in a handkerchief to make a mark on the front of the bride, and a bit of egg was also put on the back of her neck. Then they chanted "Este y no mas"—"this (man) and no other." This chant was meant to ensure a good marriage. The women also wrapped a *retoño* (a type of handkerchief) around the bride's neck and chest five times, knotting it at each turn. This action ensured that she would have children.[27] Next, the women relatives sang, played instruments, and put the rest of the special clothing on the bride to prepare her for the ritual bath. The *guisandera* (tambourine player) removed a ribbon from the bride's hair. She took it to the groom's house, where she bargained for a delivery fee. Upon delivering the ribbon, she said, "Atado quedtis"—"You take the bundle."

Given the elaborate procedures involved in dressing the bride for what appears to have been a fertility rite, what followed for the *mikveh* ritual is especially intriguing. The bride was stripped completely of all her special new clothes for her ritual bath, and unlike the earlier bath that she had taken, called a *lavado chiquita,* which involved rose-scented water, this one involved pure, fresh running water, in conformance with Jewish legal requirements.[28] Larrea Palacín then describes the actual ceremony at the ritual bath:

> The groom's mother gives the bride, completely nude, to the *bañera,* or the woman charged with assisting her, who enters the bath with the bride, making sure that the water covers her completely, that her body does not touch the walls of the pool, and says the purification prayers . . . it is the mother of the groom who puts the chemise on the bride, and the other women in the groom's family dress her in the rest of her clothing, which is white, so that the life she is about to begin will be bright and happy.[29]

A women's party usually followed, with music and dance.

In this detail-rich account of ritual procedures for the pre-*mikveh* gathering, the colors of the clothing and the formulaic statement bestowing best wishes on the bride and groom show the mingling of Sephardic customs with a Jewish legal requirement. The motions of the pre-*mikveh* ritual are of special interest, as actions encoding meaning. An analysis of them might reveal the meaning of the post-*mikveh* dance celebration.

In this report, there is a specific use of space, direction, and motion on the part of the participants, involving a set of actions that involve going in and out of event settings and taking clothes on and off. The women relatives of the groom come into the bride's house, bringing her special clothing. The bride then goes out to the *mikveh*. But even before this, the direction reverses. Starting with the *guisandera*, the motion begins to be one of going out of feminine space. The ribbon is removed from the bride's hair, after which the *guisandera* takes it out of the house to the home of the groom. The bride goes out to the *mikveh* and comes out of the *mikveh*. A similar pattern can be seen in the putting on and taking off of clothing. Female relatives of the groom offer the bride a gift of clothes, putting a girdle and handkerchief on her.[30] After being enveloped in these special clothes, she takes them all off for the Jewish *mikveh*.

The in-and-out pattern of events might be viewed as an entering into the Jewishness of the night. It might also be viewed as an intertwining of Sephardic custom with Jewish practice. But the turning point seems to be the sending out of the tambourine player. Her power in this situation is a reversal. Up to this point, the groom provided everything. The groom's family has even sponsored the party. When the *guisandera* arrives at the groom's home with the ribbon for ransom, the movement changes in terms of control. It is the women who are now offering the bride to the groom.

There are no records of what the Sephardic women might have said about the meaning of this event. Since they were not taught to reflect on their ritual, it is likely that the answer would not be an abstract theological statement. Yet in accordance with Rosenzweig's theory on the relationship between symbolic action, words, and Jewish ritual, the movement of the ceremony relates the unspoken.[31] Based on descriptions of the ritual actions, the stripping off of the ritual clothing suggests that there is a sense of stripping away a particular status. After all, the wedding *mikveh* signifies an important change in life. In the lives of Sephardic women, marriage meant that the bride left her family to join her husband's household. At the time of the *mikveh*, she was in between roles as daughter and wife.

Noting a person's in-between status at a time of life transition is a more traditional anthropological observation. Considering women's dominance in the Sephardic wedding dance event as a whole, another reading might see this as one of the rare occasions for women to lead a Jewish ritual. So the description of the *mikveh* might represent being stripped of control, perhaps even male control. While the removal of clothes was required for taking the *mikveh*, the use of special garments and the dressing and undressing of the bride by women suggest that more was involved with the disrobing than necessity. It was a statement of faith for Jewish women to observe the legal obligation of the *mikveh*, but at the same time the *Sephardiyot* appear to have developed a sense of ritual ownership.

This is a twenty-first-century reading, based on an embodied feminist view of what was perhaps the perspective of the *Sephardiyot*. Some factors coloring this observation include the occurrence of a cultural "little bath" preceding the *mikveh* night. In contrast, the *mikveh* bath night was a Jewish event. Additionally, in the lyrics of *mikveh* songs, women are mentioned as supporters of the bride-to-be for the *mikveh*, assisting her in and out of the water. The presence of women is notably emphasized in many *mikveh* songs, indicating that women considered the Jewish wedding bath night their special event.

According to the lyrics of the *mikveh* song "Ay, que si te fueres a bañar, novia," when the bride entered the water she was accompanied by her mother and her soon-to-be mother-in-law. When she came back out, she was greeted by women from the groom's family offering support and protection, symbolized in the offering of a beautiful chiffon robe. In sum, the women's cultural addition to this very Jewish ritual of the *mikveh* perhaps taught the bride that she could draw power and comfort in her new life from the support of other women in her husband's family. She would now have a relationship with them, as well as with her new husband.

According to Esther Benbassa-Dudonney, *Sephardiyot* in the Balkan area followed a similar pattern. Her details on the post-*mikveh* music and dance event continue the story of the ritual. After the dressing of the bride (or at times the application of the henna), the removal of all ritual objects, and the emergence from the ritual bath, the rite was completed with a women's party. Benbassa-Dudonney stresses that the post-*mikveh* event was considered important, yet the ensuing party often included wild dancing.[32] While women in the Mediterranean world commonly have boisterous wedding dance parties, in a Jewish context the transition from the *mikveh* to the party is especially noteworthy. A controlled Jewish ritual turned into a rowdy women's dance event.

In the Near East and the Mediterranean, Muslim women's wedding parties were and are typically exclusive. Women are completely isolated from men for this part of the ritual; even the musicians are women. Kay Harvey Campbell, a musician and scholar who lived with Saudi women, described what she observed behind the closed doors of women's wedding parties in a strict Islamic culture. According to Campbell, one aspect of the parties involves social release through dance, helping to ease tension for women living within tight patriarchal strictures. Another function of the dance party, she says, is inducing an ecstatic state. Campbell described a Saudi women's wedding dance party as a "huge event, the bringing together of families, and it can go on for days," with even "a couple of hundred women in attendance." Since the women celebrate separately, they are "uninhibited, doing the latest dances they've learned on trips to Cairo . . . The high comes from dance and music."[33]

While Campbell's description does not report an extreme situation of ecstatic release such as that found in the women's *zar* cult of North Africa, her use of the terms "uninhibited" and "high" is striking. The women are not working themselves into an ecstatic trance, but they are dancing themselves into what might be described as a changed state, akin to that experienced from a mood-altering substance such as alcohol. Working with Middle Eastern dance choreographer Cassandra Shore, Campbell created a story to share her knowledge of these parties. Shore commented on what resulted, with insight from a dance perspective. She remarks on the social function of the wedding dance event, the women's dress, and their movement:

> Beyond the male gaze, these dances can be unbelievably rowdy . . . Without men present—and men are absolutely not allowed—women can do anything they want. It's freedom from any social pressure to be polite or conform. And the dresses! They're huge, unbelievably gorgeous and theatrical and colorful. You think of black! Wait until you see these hot green, pink and orange stripes. Totally wild.[34]

Obvious differences exist between the wedding parties of the Saudi women whom Campbell and Shore describe and the women of Sephardic cultures of previous centuries. The *Sephardiyot* were Jewish women, and were apparently less sequestered than the Saudi women. The *Sephardiyot* even drank alcohol. Although it is doubtful that Jewish women of the past were frequent travelers to Egypt, there are enough similarities to make some comparisons. Common to both the modern Saudi women and the *Sephardiyot* is the gala wedding-as-dance-event, lasting many days, as is the practice throughout the region. In both cases, the separate gatherings of women involve the use of clothing as a means of expression, the participation of women musicians, and wild dancing at the women-only parties.

The use of dance as a means of tension release appears to operate heavily for both events. Women were under patriarchal rule in the Sephardic world, where it was the men who controlled religion and associated rituals. Weddings were one of the few times women exerted control over ritual activities. A wedding also usually meant that a young woman was going to leave her mother to live under the rule of her husband and his family. There would understandably be a good deal of anxiety for the bride and her family. The ritual movements surrounding the *mikveh* and the post-*mikveh* dance offer a means of blessing the bride. Descriptions of the ritual relate activities done for well-wishing, fertility, and fidelity. Such activities might have reduced the stress of the bride's transition to her new life, especially since the women in the groom's family were involved in offering her support.

The blessings of the ritual are completely in keeping with Jewish practice, even when mingled with cultural customs. While the formula and type of blessings may match those of the general region, the use and timing of them might be viewed as fitting within a Jewish pattern. The cultural idiom serves the Jewish practice of offering blessings. For the Sephardic *mikveh*, women provided blessings through their words and actions. The power that women attained by blessing the bride, and the support offered the bride, might indeed have reduced tension and social stress. The release of tension perhaps factors into the wildness of the dance that followed, but it does not explain it completely.

Through the use of percussive instruments, the drinking of the liqueur known as *raki*, and the uninhibited dance movements, there was apparently a mood-altering function in the ritual process of the *Sephardiyot*. Sephardic women went wild with the dancing just as modern Saudi women do. There was music and some dance throughout the day of the *mikveh* ceremony, but it was only after the Jewish *mikveh* ritual that the women burst forth in unstructured dance.[35] This dance was probably patterned, but it was still free of the strictures of ritual exactness and rabbinic dictate.

Removed from the confines of their normal, subservient roles as Jewish wives, the women appear to have lost their inhibitions. In a way, we might expect such behavior for a rite of passage involving dance. The ecstatic and anti-structural quality is reminiscent of Victor Turner's description of rites of passage and a state of "liminality" as a mark of changing status. By liminality, he meant a threshold state, where one has an ambiguous relationship to one's community. For the *Sephardi-yot*'s *mikveh* ritual, the bride-to-be was liminal because she was not yet a wife, and yet she was no longer an unattached young woman.

The *Sephardiyot*'s bride's night dance occurred during a transitional stage between the *mikveh* and the wedding ceremony. While the *mikveh* involved a sacred performance and the dance party involved foolish fun, all of the actions were part of the rite of passage. The bride, the groom's family, and the bride's friends and family all had distinct roles to play. Those distinctions may have disappeared after the *mikveh*, but the bride was still the main feature of the event, complete with her special clothing. Rather than minimizing sex distinctions, the party celebrated women, with the risqué references in songs seeming to emphasize the differences between men and women.[36]

Feminist analysis of women's ritual behavior suggests that the *Sephardiyot*'s *mikveh* ceremony enacted more than an anti-structural, liminal rite of passage. In one sense, the women were already liminal in their patriarchal society. They really did not have status. As Jewish women, they occupied an ambiguous position within the society in which they lived, and ritually, there were fewer rites of passage available to them than for Jewish men. Because Jewish women lacked a religious rite of passage at puberty, such as a Bar Mitzvah, the wedding was their major rite of passage. The *Sephardiyot*'s dance party took place outdoors, outside of the synagogue, and outside of the male community, and was therefore also liminal.

For the *Sephardiyot*, who were always at the edge of Judaism, a rite of passage was more than a time of the bride's liminal status, between single and married life. In fact, the *mikveh* ritual might not even be considered a rite of passage. Susan Sered claims that women's religions and ritual are unconcerned with such rites, although she does allow for the possibility of ritual that helps women deal with their reality.[37] So a ritual for women might change their social status for the time being. Their lives have not changed because of the ritual, but the occurrence of the ritual helps them cope with the confines of their lives. Sered explains how the ecstatic dance of the *zar* cult fits this description. She emphasizes the separation of the participating woman from her husband and the wedding-like quality of the ritual, which "includes singing, drumming, dancing, and incense (techniques to invoke trance)." The participant is also "referred to as the bride of the *zar*, and the entire ceremony has ritual, symbolic, and linguistic parallels to weddings."[38]

In reviewing Sered's work, feminist scholar Lesley Northup has determined that women do have rites of passage, and what she concludes is pertinent to the Sephardic women's wedding dances. According to Northup, women's rites of passage tend to concentrate on the body. "Even among the religions Sered investigates, there is clear evidence of a fuller embracing of women's bodies than is found in patriarchal religions." Additionally, "none of them incorporate the outright condemnation of women's sexuality that characterizes, for example, developed Christianity."[39]

Northup mentions women's traditions that focus on the body and utilize ecstatic dance. She includes the Sande, Afro-Caribbean traditions with trance dances such as *vodoun*, and *zar* cults. As is typical of many ecstatic traditions, these women begin to dance through slow, specific ritual, then literally move into the free-form dance session. The behavior can become uncontrolled, and as with the *vodoun* or *zar*, there is a sense of possession. No report of the post-*mikveh* or henna dances claims that women were possessed by spirits, but the risqué lyrics and percussion-heavy music suggest that they performed free-flowing, spirit-lifting, joyous dance. As Shore indicates, in the wildness that sometimes occurs at these women's wedding dance gatherings, the bounds of structure might be pushed to the edges, or even reshaped.[40]

Despite the evidence that *Sephardiyot* performed an unstructured, mood-altering dance for the post-*mikveh* dance party, there is no indication that they were practicing a women's religion or dances of possession. Rather, they danced themselves into an exuberant state as part of the rites for a Jewish wedding. As a Jewish event, the wedding also involved certain rules of conduct, reflecting specific beliefs about what marriage meant. To understand the *Sephardiyot*'s wedding dance party behavior more fully, we must consider the broader Jewish context of the celebration.

Jewish Practices: Legal and Theological Issues Regarding Weddings

It is difficult to understand the symbolic meaning of the Sephardic women's dance traditions without an expanded view of their culture. At issue is how legal aspects of a Jewish wedding were interpreted for the *mikveh* ritual in the Mediterranean Jewish community. Kabbalistic use of bridal metaphors might also explain the meaning of some Sephardic wedding dance activities, especially since Kabbalah arose out of Sephardic culture.

Legally required ritual for Jewish weddings includes an established practice called a *ketubah*—the wedding contract. This contract was developed as a form of security for the bride, who in the ancient Near East had no legal rights or protection. It guaranteed that she would receive some money in the case of her husband's death or divorce, as it "set aside a certain amount of money as the wife's separate and sole property" that "would go directly to her as her inheritance or her alimony." The intention was for the wife to retain some "money and resources of her own."[41]

Among the other legal requirements for a Jewish wedding are the betrothal ceremony and the official wedding. The wedding proper, the *kiddushin* (meaning holiness), involves a "betrothal blessing," which "praises God, who permits proper marriages . . . and sanctifies the Jewish people by means of marriage." The blessing is recited "over a cup of wine."[42] The wedding ring is given to the bride, and then the marriage vows are recited. Traditionally, the groom reads the vows in Hebrew. Finally, the *ketubah* is read.

For the Sephardim, the betrothal ceremony involved rituals of music and dance and included the giving of gifts to the bride by the groom. Performance of the *kiddushin* adhered to legal requirements. However, the groom read the wedding vows in Aramaic or Ladino. The vows normally included "obligations of both the bride and the groom, and the dowry."[43] The entire process of the wedding in Sephardic communities gave women some status in a male-dominated world. Marriage did not grant them equal rights, but it did provide some compensation for them within the Jewish community, and a chance to participate in Jewish ritual.

Because of the *ketubah,* ideally a Jewish wedding offered the woman some form of redemption. In part, the *mikveh* dance party might have been a celebration of rights granted the bride through her marriage. It is not that this would have been untrue for northern European Ashkenazi women, who also received a *ketubah.* Nor does it mean that the *Sephardiyot* celebrated differently than did their Islamic women neighbors. Rather, dance was their cultural means of expressing themselves when a woman gained status in their patriarchal community.

Occasions for relief from patriarchal rule may have been truly rewarding for the *Sephardiyot.* The use of a Jewish purification ritual for women perhaps afforded such an opportunity. Additionally, the *ketubah* possibly changed the meaning of the rite of passage for the *Sephardiyot.* Rather than simply "letting loose" at the post-*mikveh* dance, it appears that the women were celebrating a liberating moment afforded them as women of the Torah tradition.

Any sense of redemption that might have been gained through the *mikveh* ritual can perhaps be attributed to a sense of community with the other women. Rather than being totally restricted by patriarchal rabbinic dictates, there is good evidence that in the context of their own community at the *mikveh,* the women often defied the limits of the imposed culture. As Kwok Pui-lan reminds us, we must not assume that women living under patriarchy were all servile, or in Slingerland's words, "inert repositories" upon which the culture imposed restrictions. As Hanna also informs us, dancing may have served as a means of altering their reality.[44] (See chap. 1.)

We know that there were forced marriages of girls, and that wives were sometimes treated cruelly by their in-laws. Becoming a bride was not always a happy occasion. Yet women's gatherings for the bridal celebrations were apparently meaningful to many *Sephardiyot*. In Jewish traditions, the metaphor of the bride and dance is well established in both the Bible and Talmud. The entire book of *Shir HaShirim*, the Song of Songs, describes wedding preparations, and includes a passage on the bride and her dance (7:1–9). In the Talmud, the house of Hillel and the house of Shammai even debate how one is to dance "before the bride."[45]

The bridal metaphor traveled from Spain as the Sephardic Kabbalah spread throughout the Mediterranean after the expulsion of the Jews from Spain in 1492. Starting in the sixteenth century, the Sephardic mystics of Safed implemented the practice of greeting the "Sabbath bride." It became a regular Friday evening ritual among these mystics to conduct a processional to meet the Sabbath bride, as one would do for a wedding. Their processional involved singing "Lekhah Dodi"—"come, friend, to greet the *Kallah* (bride)." The imagery in the song "goes back to Talmudic times, when the Sabbath was welcomed as a queen and bride." Jewish mystics also stress the "union of the male and female" with the imagery of the Sabbath bride. So "in hopes of Messianic redemption," the "Safed Kabbalists" would "go out into the fields, dressed in white, to welcome the Sabbath bride as the sun began to set on Friday evening."[46] The kabbalist texts *Iggeret ha-Kodesh* and the Zohar also envision that the mystic might be united with the female *Shekhinah* through sexual relations with his wife on the Sabbath. The Sabbath bride and marriage were a metaphor for this union.[47]

There are several possible points of connection between "Lekhah Dodi" and Sephardic women's wedding practices. In *The Hebrew Goddess*, Jewish scholar and noted Sephardic folklorist Raphael Patai considers the greeting of the Sabbath bride as a leftover of Goddess worship of the "Holy Matronit." This is "the Zoharic image of God the King proceeding with his innumerable hosts to receive his bride the Sabbath," *Shekhinah*. It is an image of the feminine aspect of God. Patai adds that when they pictured her entrance, "the spirits of the marching group would rise to near euphoria."[48] As the Goddess Holy Matronit, the *Shekhinah* was in exile, and returned on the Sabbath.

This image of the *Shekhinah* might echo a sense of Jewish "otherness," and this sense of difference might have been doubled for the *Sephardiyot* as women and as exiles from Spain. During an actual wedding ceremony, the sense of their otherness was altered, for the *Shekhinah* metaphorically entered the synagogue. Typically male territory, the space changed when the feminine entered. According to Philip Bohlman, the idea of this feminine "other" entering "masculine ritual space" caused a transition in the community, redeeming women so they are no longer outsiders.[49] Bohlman concludes that through the Sabbath entrance of the *Shekhinah* into the synagogue, the *Sephardiyot* entered into the masculine Jewish world. While traditionally women lit candles and presented the bread they baked for the home rituals of the Sabbath, only the men attended the synagogue. When the *Shekhinah* entered the synagogue, masculine and feminine space and time were united. She went in as a bride, as weddings are "preparation for union" of the masculine and feminine. "Significantly, the music of the Sabbath" then "celebrates and ritualizes the union in these spaces cohabited by the feminine sacred and the masculine sacred." Bohlman illustrates his point through a Sephardic wedding song, noting that Sephardic women's music was sung in a space outside the synagogue, and involved the world of "reproduction and the physical body."

The question remains of how Jewish bridal imagery influenced the *Sephardiyot*. Examination of the lyrics of these songs and the associated dance practices can enable us to make a good guess. What is certain is that Sephardic wedding dance celebrations were elaborate, and the affect of the processions and dances was strong enough to be employed by kabbalists.

The women could have merely been following social customs rather than practicing religious ritual. But the boundaries established by Jewish law framed the wedding dances within a Jewish context. While men established the parameters of a Jewish wedding, the *Sephardiyot* used their own space, time, and actions to express themselves as Jewish women. According to the modern elderly Sephardic women interviewed by Sered, what separated the Sephardim from Arabs was Jewish law, for "the Arabs do not have *mitzvot*." Sered concludes that "halakhah functions to highlight their cultural identity as Jews."[50]

The larger framework of the *Sephardiyot*'s culture was Jewish, and the women created their wedding ritual within the context of Jewish legal requirements for marriage. Through the *ketubah*, they gained some status in the male community. But this and other legal requirements did not deal directly with women's domain of home and village. Their music and dance was perhaps a response to Jewish law, and a means of sanctifying their lives in their realm of existence. Sephardic metaphors of the bride suggest that sexual union was another reason for wedding dances, as a celebration of fertility rites. Yet mystic literature indicates that Sephardic culture associated sexual union with redemption. A broad perspective of Sephardic society, then, suggests that the *Sephardiyot* performed wedding dances in celebration of their partial redemption as outsiders into the male Jewish world.

The following examination stresses details of Sephardic women's music and dance. This is a necessary process for developing a rich and embodied view of these practices, and for being able to effectively interpret them. The lyrics, along with the accompanying melodies and rhythms, might offer a more expansive understanding of the meaning of the *mikveh* ritual as performed by the *Sephardiyot*.

Wedding Music and Dance: Origins and Background

The song "Ay, que si te fueres a bañar, novia" is sung on the occasion of the bride's ritual bath, and describes the events of that night. The verses give the bride instructions about the *mikveh*. The first two lines inform her that she should not be alone for the event, and that she should go with her mother.

Ay, que si te fueres a bañar, novia	Oh, If you go to the bath, bride
Ay, que si te fueres a bañar, novia	Oh, if you go to the bath, bride
lleva a tu madre y non vayas sola,	go with your mother and not alone,
para quitarte la tu camisa,	to help remove your chemise,
para meterte en el agua fria.	to help you into the cold water.
Ay, que si te fueres a bañar, novia,	Oh, if you go to the bath, bride,
lleva a tu suegra y non vayas sola,	go with your mother-in-law and not alone,
para sacarte del ague clare,	to help you out of the clear
para ponerte la tu delgada.	water to put on your chemise.

While her mother helps her into the waters of the *mikveh*, the point appears to be that it is important for the bride to seek support. The second part of the song describes the process of leaving the *mikveh*, and informs the bride that her "mother-in-law" should also be present at the bath. Here again, the bride is encouraged to have women relatives assist her in completing the *mikveh*.[51]

There is a good chance that Sephardic music traditions come from medieval Spain. The melody of this song reflects Spanish origins.[52] Sephardic wedding rituals can also be traced back to medieval Spain, and share much in common with Muslim culture, but the Spanish origins of the music do not indicate a uniquely Sephardic practice. Rituals specific to Judaism, however, such as the bride's *mikveh*, do indicate a distinct, important meaning attached to the event.[53] Likewise, dance practices similar to a Spanish styling might indicate their origins.

Details of the song reveal some helpful information about their purpose. This *mikveh* song is a simple *cante* or *cantica*, but Sephardic women also sang other types of songs, including "the *romansa*" of sung "narrative" poetry.[54] "Ay, que si te fueres a bañar, novia" reflects a typical simple basic patterning in these songs, with almost identical verses, both starting with the same theme lines. It forms a parallel structure through the singing of the main phrase and development of the main phrase in the last two lines of each verse.[55] Songs such as this one, or *cantigas*, are often "quite playful in words and structure."[56] The same words are used repeatedly, weaving through the song in a colorful manner. Playful, creative use of words can also be found in many wedding songs, which are often full of innuendo.

Because of the heavily structured lyrics in "Ay, que si te fueres a bañar, novia," the pattern of the song renders a particular meaning through mood rather than a story. According to Anahory-Librowicz, the lyrics "reflect a state of mind, with specific references to the festivities which accompany the lengthy and complex Sephardic traditional wedding."[57] The tone of presentation, the speaker of the song, and the rhythm and meter of the music are other elements that develop meaning in the *Sephardiyot*'s wedding songs.

TONE

Tones associated with the women's wedding songs include erotic, poetic, exemplary, playful, and bawdy or obscene. Each tone colors the song in mood and implication. "Erotic lyricism" is displayed in one song when a bride tells her mother about her dream involving a vision of the "seashore." In at least one version, this imagery is matched with a refrain that expresses the young woman's prayer to "the Creator," who fulfills desires. The water could be "symbolic," providing imagery with an erotic quality, expressing the bride's sexual longings. "The bride's deepest feelings about different stages of her life are also expressed," and "on a deeper level, the lyrics and tone also reflect . . . faith in creation and the Creator." "Songs which refer to bathing reflect the double symbolic dimension of water: it is at once purifying and erotic."[58] This is exactly the type of imagery that is present in "Ay, que si te fueres a bañar, novia." Within the context of the song, the bride's possible fears are revealed through the word "alone." The speaker's desire is that the bride not go alone, and that she accept assistance for the ritual bath. Erotic imagery is present with the mention of the bride's nakedness as she steps in and out of the *mikveh* waters.

SPEAKER

In Sephardic wedding songs, the speaker often conveys a "poetic tone." In "Ay, que si te fueres a bañar, novia," the speaker is a woman offering the bride specific instructions. In other songs, the speaker is the bride or a friend of the bride. The songs that describe the bride have a feminine if not something of a feminist touch, with references to the moon and the beauty of a woman's body. The "bride" might be said to "shine like gold and enamel, like the dawning sun." She might also be called "gallant" or "elegant," with a "face like a moon" and a "svelte/lovely body." The bridal songs can also have a raunchy tone, which was sometimes a problem with rabbinic authorities: "Alvar points out the Council of Agde's edict (506) against erotic songs and dances during weddings."[59] Apparently the concern was that "licentious" behavior might result as a response to the lyrics. Men and women dancing together also frequently gave the rabbis problems, as is attested in numerous *responsa*. The wildness of the women at a *mikveh* party was probably not as much of an issue for the rabbis, since they were not present at the women's parties. Yet the nature of the women's dance event does suggest that they were deciding what constituted proper behavior for their gathering, and that their own sensuous interpretation was displayed in their dance.[60]

RHYTHM AND MELODY

In "Ay, que si te fueres a bañar, novia," the rhythm is almost unmetered, allowing for melodic additions and improvisations. In Weich-Shahak's recording, a Moroccan woman sings this song in an open lyrical style, with free use of vocal embellishment, and without any rhythmic accompaniment.[61] However, many Sephardic women's wedding songs do use rhythm instruments, especially to accompany dance. By implication, the accompanying dance and movement could differ, which is fitting given the tempos and rhythmic patterns that were common to a community. In other words, the how of the dance event and the dances may have differed even for the same song. Yet the why of the dance event appears to be consistent, and in keeping with Sephardic women's traditions.

RITUAL MOVEMENT AND DANCE

A *mikveh* wedding song such as "Ay, que si te fueres a bañar, novia" is usually not danced, as a steady rhythm is not present and the song is rather slow. Still, the ritual process leading to dance might be implied through the details of the music. As seen in the lyrics of this song, there is a set pattern of words that could be performed in a new manner. In an audio recording of the song, the singer offers variations by altering phrasing and melody. Performing without accompaniment, the singer extends notes and adds ornamentation freely. In the "doing" of a song for the set *mikveh* ritual, "creating" the performance involved change or ritualization "through alteration of set patterns." Such change allows for "expressive behavior" within a ritual of "already known, richly symbolic pattern of behavior."[62]

For this *mikveh* ritual song, the words, music, and described movement all suggest that ritualization was occurring, in terms of space for variations in musical performance. The quality of the singing and the slow rhythm allowed for this possibility. However, these same factors could make it difficult to alter ritual movement; the lyrics and melody dominate the song, and drumming is absent, so a strong rhythm for dancing is lacking. Nevertheless, women were performing the ritual required by patriarchal Judaism while creating their own variations. It is the improvisation within the tight structure of the ritual and the song that suggests the possible formation of new variations. The teaching or "Torah" of the event might be seen in the lyrics, which stress that the bride should not be alone; as she goes into the waters and comes out, she will receive support.

"Ay, que si te fueres a bañar, novia" combines Jewish ritual and women's performance. Because the post-*mikveh* celebration included free-form dancing, the process suggests that the women metaphorically created their own interpretation of a Jewish ritual, translating its meaning for their lives. Of course, this is only one possible reading, considering that the fewer words involved in ritual, the more room there is for expression through dance. The free-flowing post-*mikveh* dance might indicate that because of their changing status, the *Sephardiyot* were taking the opportunity to assert what little independence they had, expressing their "Jewishness."[63]

Within their own individual women's dance community, the *Sephardiyot* could still be Jews, through the ritual context of the *mikveh*. Such individual expression through set ritual is possible because Jewish culture provided patterns for enacting new behavior. "As participants in culture," the women "learn[ed] but also [taught], mostly by example." Their "individual learnings-by-doings were not left to pure invention and experiment but mostly followed ways [of Jewish tradition] marked out by cultural predecessors."[64]

Sephardic Women's Festive Wedding Dance

While the *Sephardiyot*'s behavior implies that the *mikveh* dance party was an important means of expressing their beliefs, the lack of sung verse for the occasion means that verbal clues to specific meanings of the event are missing. There is one known song specifically for dance in Sephardic repertoire, which might offer such insight. This is "Viva Orgueña." Because it involved performance of dance and words, it might provide a more complete view of the process of the women's wedding dance event.

Viva Orgueña lo afecha en su arenal
y asi lo afecha, viva Orgueña

Chorus· Y asi metira sus pied en el mar
y asi me enserñaran a bailar.

Viva Orgueña . . . a, lo sembra en su
lo sembra su arenal
y asi lo sembra, viva Orgueña
Chorus: Y asi metira sus pied en el mar
y asi me enseñaran a bailar.

Viva Orgueña, lo planta . . .
Chorus
Viva Orgueña, lo corta . . .
Chorus
Viva Orgueña, lo coge . . .
Chorus
Viva Orgueña, lo lleva . . .
Chorus
Viva Orgueña, lo seca . . .
Chorus
Viva Orgueña, lo mole . . .
Chorus
Viva Orgueña, lo amasa . . .
Chorus
Viva Orgueña, lo come . . .
Chorus

Viva Orduenya, she is sifting in her sandy
yard, she is sifting, viva Orduenya

she puts her feet in the sea

and I am learning the dance.

Viva Orduenya, she is

sowing in her sandy
yard, she is sowing, viva Orduenya
she puts her feet in the sea

and I am learning the dance.

Viva Orduenya, she is planting . . .

Viva Orduenya, she is cutting . . .

Viva Orduenya, she is harvesting . . .

Viva Orduenya, she is carrying . . .

Viva Orduenya, she is desiccating . . .

Viva Orduenya, she is grinding . . .

Viva Orduenya, she is kneading . . .

Viva Orduenya, she is eating . . . [65]

"Viva Ordueña" is a pantomimed dance, with "movements" that "follow the acts described in the text." So for the first verse, the dancers act out sifting flour, then "sowing," "planting," "cutting," "harvesting," "carrying," "desiccating," "grinding," "preparing bread," and "eating." For the chorus, the dancers move as if they are "stepping" into the sea to learn how "to dance." According to the musical score that Weich-Shahak provides, this dance is accompanied by castanets (*castañuelas*) and/or a tambourine (*sonanjya*) and drum (*darbuqqa*).[66]

A different account of the dance provides more details about the *bailes de la fiesta* that were done for the seven days following the wedding ceremony. Women performed "Viva Ordueña" in pairs, facing one another and acting out the song. For the chorus, the partners step forward toward each other, then step backward. Next, in pairs they take each other's arms and turn around twice. Those who are not dancing provide accompaniment by *palmades*, clapping their hands to the rhythm. Supposedly this is a very old post-wedding ritual; the song is almost exactly the same in different Sephardic communities, so its origins may derive from practices in medieval Spain. As for the dance's place within Jewish tradition, it might have been "a rite of fertility" (*que es considerado rito de fecundidad*).[67]

The basics of this dance event again involve women, water, and fertility. Despite the lyrics outlining how the song was performed, there are still questions about why this dance is part of a Jewish wedding celebration. Blessings for fertility are one answer, but the mention of women, water, and dance in the lyrics of the song presents the possibility of other layers of meaning, especially as part of a Jewish women's fiesta.

As for the details, the words and music in this song are in a tight union of meter and rhythm, with syllabic singing. The musical meter matches the verse exactly, and remains throughout the song. Even the lyrics do not vary greatly. Only one word changes per verse, and none for the chorus. According to musical transcriptions, even ornamentation is kept to a minimum. The melodic line will not vary much when the song is performed, and the accent is clearly on rhythm. So the complete structure of this song lends itself to dancing.

Nevertheless, it does feature words to some degree, but only because they are accompanied by movement. The descriptive step-by-step verse development—how bread is created, starting with sifting, then moving to planting, sowing, and so forth—is important for several reasons. A text about sowing seed for a post-wedding celebration is certainly suggestive of a ritual encouraging the newly wed couple to reproduce. Within a Jewish context, the words when pantomimed might carry other associations for women. In their daily life they were the ones who prepared food for the family. Sered points out in her study of Sephardic women that this preparation itself took on ritual significance. Even the manner in which she describes their process of preparing the food for daily life, the Sabbath, and holidays appears to echo the pantomimed words of "Viva Ordueña":

> For these women food preparation is sacred because it embodies, concretizes, dramatizes, and ritualizes the central elements of Judaism, as understood by the women themselves. The basic ritual building blocks of their religious world include sorting, cooking, serving, and cleaning—tasks that were simultaneously and inseparably essential to both physical survival and spiritual fulfillment. The women both domesticate relation and sacralize the profane.[68]

In Jewish ritual practice, the connection between women, bread, and the Sabbath has a long history, so the particular metaphor used in the song is striking. Women were the ones who prepared the challah, the Sabbath bread. After the destruction of the Temple, women enacted a ritual of breaking off a piece of bread dough before baking the loaf and throwing it into the oven flames as an offering. Called challah, the ritual was in imitation of the priestly bread sacrifice. As a woman offered the piece of dough, she recited a blessing.[69] It was one of the few post-Temple rituals established to be inclusive of women, if not specific to them.

Rabbi Lynn Gottlieb's comments on the association between women and the baking of challah are helpful and significant. Not only does she make the association with a history of Jewish women's ritual practices, but she also establishes a connection between the challah loaf and the word *machol*, used for women's dances:

> The word *challah* appears to be related to the word for women's dancing called *machol* and refers to round dancing and holding bread while dancing and praying. Women baked cakes to the Goddess on the new moon as a way of celebrating the renewal of the substance of life and to give expression to her Presence through the bread.[70]

The "Goddess" Gottlieb refers to is Asherah, for whom women used to bake cakes. In an interesting parallel with the song "Viva Ordueña," Asherah was the Goddess of the sea.

If the performance of "Viva Ordueña" was a fertility custom, Gottlieb's statement also makes it clear that such fertility customs have roots within, or at least strong connections with, the history of Jewish ritual. Worship of the Goddess was, of course, never part of sanctioned rabbinic Judaism. Yet the practices implemented under rabbinic Judaism had direct ties to the baking of cakes for Asherah that retained meaning for the religion.[71]

The words "sea" and "dance" are emphasized in the chorus rather than the word "bread." In performance, a wide range of movement accompanies these words, with women moving forward and back toward a partner, then turning or spinning around with that partner. There are possible metaphoric meanings attached to these motions, such as stepping into life, or sexual connotations might be implied. Certainly the gesture of stepping into and out of the sea has a host of meanings for people who live in the Mediterranean world. In fact, the sea was often mentioned in Sephardic women's healing ritual prayers, or *prekante*. Additionally, before performing the *prekante*, "the specialist and the stricken one usually went to the sea," as "the sea is deep and can endure everything."[72] The same is true of the circling motion in the dance. Such motion can be rich in symbolic value, with turning implying a change of life or the cycles of life. According to Lévy and Lévy Zumwalt, Sephardic women who performed ritual prayer regarded such actions as highly important and attributed deep symbolic meaning to these movements.[73] Presumably the same would be true for the actions of a ritual dance.

Rather than attaching specific meaning to the motions, we can see the motions and rhythm of the dance as a process that offers an idea of purpose for the use of the song. With all the rhythmic repetition of words, and the strong rhythmic accompaniment, there is a sense of community building present, especially with group motion. Additionally, since singing and dancing can tax the respiratory system enough to increase oxygen flow, participants turning or spinning in this condition may have experienced a euphoric high.

The meaning and reason for the turning movement might be found in the song's chorus: *Y asi metira sus pied en el mar / y asi me enseñaran a bailar*—"she puts her feet in the sea / and I teach the dance." To learn or teach the dance is the point of the song. This is when the participants turn, and action denotes a change. The dance is, after all, for the ending of a ritual of passage, which is a time of a change of status. The dance metaphorically acts out this change. It serves as a symbolic language expressing what cannot be stated fully in words.

At another level, and in consideration that these were Jewish women who were doing a type of dance of life, the meaning of the lyrics and movement of "Viva Ordueña" might take on a different symbolic dimension. Torah is a path one walks in order to know how to live in covenant as a Jew. From a theological and feminist perspective, one possible conclusion is that this was a dance of Torah for these Jewish women. Their language of expression was in symbolic performance. In "Viva Ordueña," important Jewish values and beliefs about life were encoded through music and movement. Creating bread and producing children were both mentioned, and are both edifying activities for Jewish women.

If this is a dance with religious meaning, reflecting highest Jewish values, then it will be "efficacious," causing "transformations."[74] The dance of "Viva Ordueña" caused just such positive transformations in the *Sephardiyot*'s realm of existence. Literally teaching women about how to create bread, the performance of "Viva Ordueña" metaphorically encouraged them to create children and continue life. This was "the dance" they learned by stepping into the sea of life.

Conclusions

Judith Lynne Hanna's perspectives on dance and religion are based on both her awareness of the circumstance for dance and her knowledge of cultural paradigm. In gathering information to determine how dance serves as a vehicle for symbolic movement, she quotes a statement by Victor Turner in *The Ritual Process*. He noted that it is vital to look at a symbol's meaning from an "exegetic," "operational," and "positional" perspective. In other words, in a thorough study, an observer finds what a symbol means for participants, and how the symbols act in human relationships. One also explores how symbolic movements "relate to other symbol systems" in a culture.[75]

Talking directly with participants in a dance about the symbolic meaning of only their movement means that an objective perspective is lacking. In the case of the wedding dances of the *Sephardiyot*, an additional problem related to this approach involves history. These dances are seldom done today. First- or secondhand reports make it difficult to determine anything about the use of space, effort, force of movement, and flow. Given the lack of opportunity for direct experience, the added resource of music and lyrics might be essential for a consideration of how dances were performed, and what possible symbolic value they had for participants. The rhythm, flow, and tone of the music might be especially helpful for discussing significance.

An idea of the atmosphere and tone of the *Sephardiyot*'s wedding dance rituals is possible as a result of the current revival of their practices, such as Middle Eastern dance henna parties. Cassandra Shore's presentation of the Saudi wedding party is a prime example of American women's interest in such dance and the related traditions. I have attended women's groups that used Sephardic dance practices and noted the participants' interest in accuracy and attention to detail. There I saw Jewish women express a desire and a need to continue such traditions. On this point, Rabbi Lynn Gottlieb notes that ceremonies such as these are "very important in Jewish tradition," for they help us "honor and observe the natural rhythms of our lives, such as birth, marriage, and death." Furthermore, they allow women to "recall formative movements in our history and carry forward the values and ideals associated with those events." She also notes that these traditions allow us to "create bonds of community" as they "bring us together through the years."[76]

Gottlieb provides an example of what she means, describing a Sephardic women's gathering that allowed her to learn about the "rich history of Jewish ceremonial life practiced by women separately from men." In Israel she found "Jewish women from Sephardic, European, North African, and Middle Eastern communities" celebrating their "rich heritage of song, dance, storytelling, proverbs, and life cycle rituals":

> One evening I went with some of the Moroccan women to an engagement party . . . When the bride-to-be entered the room, all the women threw candy at her and began emitting a piercing sound made from the throat. I was stunned.

She later describes the belly dancing that occurred at such gatherings, referring to traditional drumming patterns used for the movement. She claims that these gatherings were traditionally a means for women to transmit Jewish values, and she finds the practice so meaningful that she employs their traditional dance and drumming for modern Jewish women's rituals.[77]

In their acknowledgment that there was some sense of joy and power involved in the Jewish women's traditional gathering, Gottlieb's remarks are in striking contrast to the songs of sadness and despair noted in some of the *Sephardiyot*'s wedding ballads, a part of their repertoire sung when alone. The songs and dances presented in this chapter are for group gatherings, serving as almost a prayer or blessing for the bride, celebrating a rite of passage. The theology present in the music and dance is not direct, yet the ideas and values of living as Jewish women are apparent.

These women presented their values in a language that was meaningful to them. While music and singing were common to the life of Sephardic women, dance was not an ordinary event. They were not dancing all the time, even though their culture appreciated dance. As a whole, then, the special wedding dance event stands out even more as an occasion for celebration, and as a rare opportunity for the *Sephardiyot* to rejoice in their lives as Jewish women.

5 *The Rachel Tradition*

DANCING DEATH

The herbs in this field
have changed color,
and my heart; it
cries with grief.

The herbs in the field
have turned to yellow,
and my heart,
it cries with sighs.

—Susana Weich-Shahak,
  Judeo-Spanish Moroccan Songs

Jewish Women's Torah Teaching: Death and Lament

Historically, Jewish woman have been experts on grief. Their performance of dance for death was seen as a means of dealing with the profound sense of sadness that comes with loss. As a symbolic dance of death, their wailing was a means of purging the body and soul of grief. Modern American culture tends to avoid such dramatic physical expression of sorrow, yet there are still songs of grief. Like the verse above, the following two verses are examples of such deep, heartfelt mourning:

I long to live
to see you and hear you;
now that you're not here,
I prefer to die.

I asked the moon
high in the heavens
to grant me if only an hour
with my companion.[1]

Oh! What sorrow and what pain
I carry nailed to my heart
Since my mother died.
How alone I remain,
of my Father and my Mother
I've lost their warmth.[2]

These two examples are flamenco *cante siguiriyas* and *cante soleares*. The example that begins the chapter is a mourning song from the Sephardic Moroccan tradition.[3] All were originally written in Spanish, and all may have their origins in mourning rituals in medieval Spain. Jewish women were the main lament leaders in medieval Spain, where they were called *qinas, playeras, llaronas,* or more commonly *endechas.*

There is a fair amount of historical data available on Jewish women's performance as *endechas.* In this chapter we explore yet another aspect of Sephardic women's dance and music history, their "dance of death" as living Torah. Medieval Spanish records and continuing Sephardic history reveal that the work of the *endechas* was an established tradition among Jewish women, and that they led funeral lament rituals for Christians and Muslims as well as Jews.

Records of the *endechas'* performance are fascinating as documentation of a woman-led ritual involving specialized movement and rhythm. I am defining their lament practice as a dance for two primary reasons. First, biblical and rabbinic texts contain evidence of a history of Jewish women's lament leadership, with specialized movement associated with the mourning women's practice. Additionally, comparisons of archeological material from Mediterranean countries clearly depict women leaders of lament in dance formation and movement. That is, their movements were extraordinary and rhythmic, used for mourning and death rituals.

To explore the background of the *endechas,* it is necessary to look once again at visual evidence paired with written records. For additional insight, flamenco serves as a surprising source of cultural background, offering clues to embodied expressions of lament in a Spanish idiom. Flamenco dance forms such as the *soleares* and *siguiriyas* might help us understand the symbolism inherent in lament dance.

Dances for lament and death are certainly not a unique Jewish practice. It is even more curious that Jewish women became the primary performers of cultural lament rituals. One explanation for their having assumed this role is the strength of the lament tradition within Judaism. To be sure, Muslim women were also leading laments in medieval Spain, but the Jewish use of lament appears to have left a lasting legacy of movement. Exploring the full use of Jewish lament for deep, detailed, and embodied description could answer many questions about the impact of the *endechas'* dance. Therefore, it is important to include material on flamenco history.

Flamenco music is rich in lament, and *duende* (deep song)—the deep, wrenching feeling of the music and dance—is considered basic to the practice. Flamenco in its current form is undoubtedly a Gypsy creation, combining the music and dance of several cultures. Yet classic flamenco studies have linked the *duende* of flamenco to Jewish lament.[4] The movement history in the deepest dances of the tradition is by many accounts connected to the Jewish *endechas*. While this is a difficult means of gathering evidence, the flamenco material is at least helpful for learning about symbolic movements for mourning in a Spanish culture.

The issue of culture and religion arises again with the discussion of the death dance of the *endechas*. Funeral practices often combine religious and cultural customs. In what way did *endechas'* dance reflect their culture and their religion? *How* lamenting women danced might answer this question, but it is also important to consider *who* was involved. The fact that the *endechas* were often Jewish is important, as they were ritual leaders. Consequently, Kabbalah literature again provides insight into Jewish life in medieval Spain.

If the dance of Sephardic Jewish women is understood as a performance of Torah, this is especially true in the case of the *endechas*. They literally were continuing the biblical lament tradition through their actions. More significantly, their death dance appears to have encoded Jewish theological teachings about life, which held a unique appeal to many cultures in the Mediterranean world.

Information gathered about the *endechas* offers new possibilities for viewing historical knowledge on Jewish women rather than determining exact historical fact. I am offering an interpretation of history, based on the pairing of evidence from embodied ritual history with written textual material. There is much more research to be done to achieve a better understanding of the lament tradition of Jewish women. I hope that this study will provide a means of viewing data from an inclusive perspective, recognizing women's leadership in Judaism.

Death Dance Leadership among the Sephardiyot

The previous chapters show that throughout the Mediterranean world and in Sephardic culture, Jewish women played in drum-dance-song ensembles for celebrations as a continuation of what might be called a Miriam tradition.[5] We have pictorial evidence of this practice, some wedding songs, and knowledge of dances performed with drumming. Beyond women's tradition of celebrating through their practice of music and dance, there is strong evidence that Jewish women often led Spanish dances of death enacted for mourning and lament. This might be called the Rachel tradition, as "Rachel, weeping for her children" is an image representing mourning in Judaism.

As Susan Sered reminds us, women wail and dance in response to death all over the world.[6] Jewish sources suggest that the connection between women and mourning was historically a part of the fabric of Jewish culture in many communities. Several music scholars have reached the same conclusion, noting that Ashkenazi women sang laments about widowhood, abandonment, and bad husbands. In fact, Shiloah found that in general, "lamentations are a type of song exclusively sung by women." This may be because of "the symbolic connection between birth and death" that women experience as mothers, but it is clear that there were "experts" in wailing, "professionals who specialized in . . . grieving and knew how to feed the flame of sorrow and weeping."[7] This association between women, birth, and death is an important one, and within Judaism it is an ancient link as well. Women were professional midwives as well as mourners in the Jewish community of medieval Spain. While laments were sung in synagogue communities for several occasions, women's laments played a unique role in Jewish funeral customs.

Historical accounts of funeral practices during both the Islamic and the Christian period of rule supply many details about these specific laments. Having detailed life for Jews in the Islamic period, Eliyahu Ashtor serves as a primary source of historical data on medieval Spain. The information he provides on Jewish death rituals is general, yet his description of a Jewish funeral from the eleventh-century diary of a Jewish man (Abu Ya'kub) includes details about processions, mourners, and special practices, giving us a sense of how the *endechas* performed their role as mourning leaders. He mentions the customs of shattering vessels and kissing the corpse before the funeral, then goes on to outline the specifics of the funeral, especially the processions that went through the Jewish quarters.

First, there was a gathering at the house of the "deceased," where "Abu Ya'kub . . . waited with the other men in attendance before the house until the funeral cortege left for the cemetery." There he listened as "men . . . spoke in praise of the deceased." The funeral party then made its way to the Jewish cemetery, which was usually "located . . .

near the city gate that was close to the Jewish neighborhood." The trip to the cemetery involved a procession with "prayers and psalms" that "moved along the Jewish quarter's main thoroughfare . . . After leaving the city by way of the 'Jews' Gate,' the procession turned right until it reached the cemetery." Following the interment, the funeral party threw pebbles on the gravesite, and "the oldest son of the deceased . . . recited the mourner's prayer (*Kaddish*) in a voice choking with sobs." Those who were at the graveyard would then "arrange themselves in rows to comfort the mourners."[8]

These details of a medieval Jewish funeral can be compared with more specific references to the *endechas'* participation in funeral events and processions. They are mentioned in another account of a Jewish funeral in Christian Spain, and paintings of Jewish life in Spain during this period offer a glimpse of the choreographed behavior of the women mourning leaders. We know from written reports that in fourteenth-century Seville, "Jewish and Moslem women were engaged as professional wailers by Christians as well as their own co-religionists." Furthermore, "it was customary for the Spanish Jews to have women wailers at funerals," and Jewish *responsa* literature of the period from Saragossa (Aragon) mentions the "employment of professional wailers."[9] The paintings visualize some of this information about the *endechas* (*qinot* in Hebrew), with a specific illustration of their lamenting motions. *Qina* was a widespread practice, especially in medieval Spain, so there are many depictions of the process.

Metzger and Metzger describe a fourteenth-century illustration that shows "*qina* (lamentation), beside the deathbed on which the corpse lies." The process of specific mourning then continued "around the coffin placed on the ground. Members of the afflicted family walked with their heads lowered and covered, their hands hidden under their robes." Women lament experts would have led them. Research on the gestures employed by lamenting women reveals that the process began at the home of the deceased. In the illustration that Metzger and Metzger note, "two weeping women mourners are shown making the symbolical gestures signifying grief." Their movements include "embrac[ing] the deceased, the other raises her hands in a gesture of despair. Such mourners also clapped their hands to punctuate the lamentations they sang."[10] In another illustration, a woman gestures in grief through lifted arms bent at the elbow, her hands flat, her thumbs separated from her fingers. The wide position of her arms and the hand position suggest that she is preparing to clap her hands. Unfortunately, the other funeral illustrations do not include pictures of *qinot* heading processions, although we know that *endechas* were most likely in attendance when the body was interred. Reports of Sephardic practices and customs in Spain tell us that even though the mourning women did not always lead funeral processions, they were fully engaged in carrying out significant symbolic movement for the event.

In a short, focused description of wailing women in Sephardic tradition as a whole, Paloma Díaz-Mas brings these illustrations to life. The details she provides are revealing, including mention of the dramatic actions, motions, and sounds used for *planto* (public mourning). The mourning process involved "gathering around the body to show one's grief at the death by shouting, crying, and injuring oneself. During the ceremony, it was not unusual for people also to sing dirges." Significantly, she notes that "those in charge of performing the ceremony were always women"—either family members of the deceased or professional mourners. She also mentions that specific dramatic actions were used by the dirge-leading *endechas*. These were paid "professional criers" who performed their "gestures and scratches, wailing and keening" to "enhance the memory of the deceased."[11]

These are vivid images of the activity of women mourners among the Sephardim, but there are some differing accounts as well. Rabbi Herbert C. Dobrinsky, for example, claims that women were traditionally not part of the funeral processions of the Sephardim in Diaspora, and that they did not participate in, or at least speak during, the *hakafot*, the circling around the bier.[12] Within Spanish culture and Jewish tradition, however, there was an established tradition of provoked weeping.

Manuel Alvar presents a highly respected account of *endechas* and of the lament tradition among the Sephardim and its place within Sephardic Jewish life. An older, classic study, his small book offers many details about the practice of Jewish women leading funeral chants in Tetuan, Morocco, featuring valuable firsthand reports. Alvar's focus is the poetry of lament, also called *endecha*, but he supplies background information about the wailing *endechas* in Spanish history. He calls them "*planyideras* (wailing women)," and tells us that they recited verses of lament "in the house of the deceased" while they performed a highly involved dance (*danza*) of strong, exaggerated movement, perhaps including contractions. They "flung themselves into mournful dances, as if possessed," he writes, "with tearing of hair, scratching the face, and piercing death cries." He comments, "this is a custom which was perhaps important in Spain, and disappeared."[13] Alvar questions whether this practice is pagan or Jewish in origin, but concedes that *endechas* were popular in Spain. It did not disappear from Sephardic tradition, however, and Sephardic women continued to lead other mourners in lamenting, especially in the home of the deceased.[14]

In *The Dance of Death*, Florence Whyte discusses this Spanish drama, which is related to mourning practices in Spain. Her commentary reveals even more detail than does Alvar:

> *Endechas*, or lamentation, formed a part of the repertoire of the medieval *jugular* in Spain . . . *Endechas* were sung at funerals by mourning women called *plañideras*. A sculpted group on a monument in the old Cathedral in Salamanca shows the soul, represented as a child, accompanied by the *plañideras*, who are tearing their hair . . . Lazarillo de Tormes going up the narrow streets of Toledo encountered a humble funeral procession; the corpse was carried on a litter, behind it came women in mourning . . .
>
> Customs derived from Oriental habits of mourning prevailed until a surprisingly late date in the Iberian peninsula, as may be inferred from the custom of tearing the hair that we have just mentioned.[15]

The implication of this quote is that laments were widely used as part of Spanish death rituals, that they were performed as a kind of dance, and that they were influenced by biblical tradition and Jewish practices. The "Oriental habits" Whyte refers to are supposedly Jewish, based on the similarity between a Sephardic lament from the Menéndez Pidal manuscript and a Spanish lament verse in the *Coplas de la muerta.* Whyte records that "there is, in fact, such a composition" where "verbal coincidences abound," with "entire stanzas parallel" to "lines of the *Coplas.*" They are laments (*endechas*), which "were sung by four Jews of Tangiers." The *Coplas de la muerta* were supposedly composed by monks "of Montserrat," who "expressed their intention of supplanting objectionable songs and dances by substitutes." This was because there were "ecclesiastical objections to profane dances in holy places" for funerals.[16] Yet a question remains about why some of the dances for death were regarded as objectionable, and whether the objections included opposition to women lament leaders.

Dance done for religious events was popular in Spain, and there were even dances for death watches and funerals. A "death watch" dance might include singing, castanets, and the regional dance called a *jota*, as indicated by an 1870s account of a group keeping watch over a dying child. The church did not necessarily disapprove of such activity, given that the theology was correct—hopeful concerning the afterlife. Performing round dances, hand clapping, beating drums, and laughing to scare away demons were part of the activity.[17] The Christian view apparently emphasized dance as a means of assisting mourners. According to E. Louis Backman, many people believed that "the dead are comforted and rejoiced by the dance performed for them in the night watch, before their last journey," and "the demons are forced by the dance to leave the dead alone." But "when the body is buried there is another dance in its honour . . . which illustrates both bliss in the heavenly paradise and also the approaching bodily resurrection."[18]

Some death dancing customs may even have been acceptable to the church if they stressed Christian belief in a happy afterlife. Presumably, however, lament and expressions of grief were not acceptable. Death dances in churchyards were the subject of numerous bans, because of other associated activity and beliefs. Two are particularly striking: one statement involves the participation of women in death dances, and the other concerns dance and ritual in Spain. According to Backman's description of one such ban, women were forbidden to dance in front of churches and at graveyards:

> In the eighth century a number of episcopal instructions were issued to subordinates *(Commitorium)* in which *dancing and singing by women in the church porch were forbidden*, as well as the "devilish" songs which the public used to sing for the dead at night time to the accompaniment of loud laughter.

Backman adds:

> At the beginning of the tenth century the *Patriarch John III threatened with excommunication those women who visited graves in order to beat drums and dance* . . . Similarly, at the beginning of the same century Regina, Abbot of *Prum* . . . posed the confessional question, "Have you sung devilish songs for the dead?" and forbade the public to sing them at funerals, or to dance, since it was the pagans who, at the instigation of the Devil, had invented them.[19]

Folklore, demonology, and dance customs differed throughout Europe, so some of the church bans reflected practices in northern countries rather than in Spain. Yet, as Whyte's assessment shows, church officials were concerned about the type of dance and music performed for all death rituals. Backman's description of Spanish death dances from northern Spain (Lerida, 1318) details some of the reasons for bans against their performance. They included "indecent ring-dances to the singing of songs, with violence, dice games and other forbidden things by which the churches and churchyards are desecrated."[20]

The church's objection to certain types of dance behavior appears to have involved far more than concern for proper conduct, however. Among the other issues were the role of women in ritual, religious purity, and concern for theology. The bans did not criticize the process of grieving, but the association of death dances with pagan customs is telling with respect to Jewish wailing women. The *endechas* encouraged grieving and performed what might be construed as a pagan activity. Alvar considers their practice to be pagan. He notes that rabbinic literature contains opposition to the mourning women. But he also claims that lament was more acceptable for Judaism than for Christianity, which stressed a happy afterlife and resurrection.[21] Whether the *endechas* led grieving because of Jewish attitudes toward death or because of pagan custom, their popularity suggests that the boundaries between religion and popular culture overlapped in Jewish death ritual.

Laments, after all, are a part of Jewish tradition. A majority of the biblical psalms are laments, and forms of lament are common for specific days of the ritual year, such as *Tisha b'Av*, the day that commemorates the destruction of the Temple in Jerusalem. Certain melodies for *Yom Kippur* also touch on the sound of lament. Beyond a repetition of biblical poetry in liturgy, new laments also developed in Judaism, and specifically in medieval Spain. In Jewish liturgical music this involved the use of participatory prayer, including laments. The congregation would sing in response to the cantor.[22]

As part of the congregation, Jewish women knew the tradition, and they may have been responsible for maintaining laments performed outside the synagogue, not just for death but for mourning of all types. While most laments were sung for funerals, others expressed "feelings such as sadness and despair, bad luck, and misfortune." In addition, the genre included "*romances* of tragic content."[23] Lament was written into the rabbinic cycle of the Jewish ritual practice, and into the life of Sephardic Jews. The *Sephardiyot*'s particular role as lament experts may be connected directly with the liturgical practices of the congregation, as well as with Jewish culture. Since their death dance is similar to others in the region, the unique aspect of their practice appears to be the richness of Jewish laments, and also the associated theology, which encourages grieving at times of loss.

Spanish Jews actively participated in the production of funeral ritual in medieval Spain. At the very least, according to most sources, Jewish custom influenced the practices of death lament and related ritual movement. While some literature lacks any mention of Jewish women leading these events, their presence is clearly noted in more in-depth information about the dances of death, such as Whyte's and Alvar's studies.

Whether or not Spanish lament practices had their origins in Jewish ritual remains in question. Within the Spanish context, however, Jewish musical traditions were highly influential, adding to the lament genre practiced in Spain. Significantly, the main transmitters of the tradition to the general community were Jewish women. Their distinctive practice was rhythmic, involved dramatic movement, and stemmed from biblical traditions. Just as many of the Jewish holidays are connected with fertility rites, and therefore not fully in keeping with rabbinic theology, the Jewish *endechas* appear to have carried on a Torah tradition with origins in Near Eastern pagan practices. Through use in a Jewish context, the mode of performance was Jewish.

Jewish women's lament traditions appear to have had unique qualities, which might explain why they were popular in medieval Spain— they were an acceptable alternative to other death dances. When the church banned the wild dance practices associated with superstitions about death, the dance-oriented culture of Spain had few other outlets for the expression of grief. One possible alternative was to employ people who had the freedom to conduct such rituals, such as Jewish *endechas*. Another was to develop stylized, theologically acceptable dances of death, which is what happened at Montserrat, or eventually with the use of *saetas* for religious processions.[24]

When the Spanish needed to lament and wail in grief, the monks' dances of death offered structured movement, but no chance for dramatic expression of pain and loss. These dances were then apparently more entertainment, as they contained no lament to aid mourners. During the medieval period, Jewish women in Spain practiced a biblical tradition that could provide a meaningful ritual of grief. It appears that they filled a gap, and as they were outsiders to the synagogue and church, they were allowed to perform this task. Because of their role as leaders of social ritual, the theological dimension of their lament became important.

Judaism has always had its own interpretation of so-called pagan practices, and this applies to the *endechas*. There is a cycle of life and death obvious in their lamentation dance. In Jewish traditional values, nature is not personified as a god of death. Rather, the Jewish God is "Master of the Universe," in control of nature and humanity. This God also responds to human actions, including lament.[25] At least in the Jewish community, women's lament served as not only a means of catharsis, but a reflection of a biblical tradition that symbolized that God was beyond the cycle of death and life. An example of this theology exists in the lyrics of songs from the Moroccan Sephardic community. The lyrics contain a dialogue with the Angel of Death rather than the devil. This is a significant difference from the Christian dance of death plays, which feature a devil or Satan figure. He sends all characters to meet their fate, and no protests or pleas can change his mind. Within the lament of the *endechas*, however, the biblical monotheism remained intact, and a "Rachel" tradition continued.

The Rachel Tradition: Jewish Women's Lament Leadership

The *endechas* appear to have practiced a uniquely Jewish interpretation of lament. It was a Torah tradition, although it was sometimes labeled a pagan practice. Just as a women's drum-dance-song ensemble in Judaism might be considered a continuation of biblical tradition, and embodied in the image of Miriam, the lament practices of Sephardic women might be seen as associated with the Torah through the biblical matriarch Rachel. Rachel never wails in the Bible, as the beloved of Israel/Jacob. However, in the prophetic book of Jeremiah, she is portrayed as the archetypal wailing mother of the nation of Israel. "Mother Rachel" appears in Jeremiah's poetic vision of the restoration of Israel:

> A voice is heard in Ramah—
> wailing bitter weeping—
> Rachel, weeping for her children.
> She refuses to be comforted
> for her children, who are gone.

In this passage, a woman is mourning the loss of her children. Rather than a generic "mother," she is labeled "Rachel." Why choose Rachel as the iconic figure for lamenting women? In this passage she seems to be the epitome of mourning. There are other passages from the period of the prophets that clearly indicate that women were lament leaders in Israel. So the connection with Rachel appears to be one of metaphoric association. Rachel is actually a mother who dies in childbirth, but her children form the nation of Israel. She is the eternal mother of the Jews. The association also appears to satisfy a role that the Goddess occupied in ancient Near Eastern culture.

Rachel is like the lamenting Sumerian Goddess who displays compassion for those who are suffering, much like the compassion and grief that a mother would have for her children. She wails for them and with them in their time of loss. The purpose of the Goddess's lament is to appeal for divine intercession for those experiencing grief. Implicit within the Sumerian tradition of an extreme display of passionate mourning, there is also a sense of hope and renewal. So when Rachel laments, "her weeping, like that of the ancient Sumerian goddess-mothers, is unconditional." It "brings the plight of the people continually before God, and finally moves God, in this vision, to remember and restore the people of Israel."[26]

In the case of Jeremiah's Rachel, the loss involves the kingdom of Judah under Babylonian siege, and the accompanying death and starvation of a nation. It is human loss that prompts the eternal mother's weeping. The Sumerian Goddess, however, weeps for the death of a nature god. In the Bible, Rachel replaces the Goddess as a *human* mother whose lament affects the one God, who might transform death into a new life. "In the same way, the cultural arts of learning, song and lamentation, once associated with Sumerian Goddesses, are human arts in the Bible." Laments "are written *for* God, but are written by people."[27] Rachel thus differs from the Sumer Goddess Geshtinanna, and especially the Goddess Inanna. They both weep for the god Dumuzi, who dies and is resurrected. The cycle of seasons is suggested by this story, with Dumuzi's resurrection a metaphor for the rebirth of the earth in spring. The Goddesses assist the cycle of nature through the singing of laments, which directly influence the life and death of agricultural seasons.[28]

Humans enacted this behavior of the lamenting Goddesses in an attempt to influence nature. They expected that a divine source would negotiate between the natural and the human worlds. As described by the Sumer texts, the movements of these laments were similar to those depicted in biblical texts, and also described in the accounts of the *plañideras* wailing their *endechas*. A description of their behavior mentions the Goddesses clawing their eyes and noses, the insides of their thighs, and their breasts, emitting "frenzied" cries and tearing their "hair like rushes," while uttering a bitter lament. This behavior was "almost certainly a reflection of mourning behavior on the human scene."[29]

There are differences between some of the movements and actions in this description and the reports of the Mediterranean Jewish wailing women. What is described in the Sumer text also appears less choreographed than the processions, arm thrusts, contractions, stamping feet, and clapping hands of the *endechas,* and is focused on self-mutilation. Yet the essential reason for the performance remains almost unchanged. The *endechas* led grieving to effect change: "It was a purposeful act, specifically intended to serve as an intercession."[30]

There is a fine distinction, however, between a theology based on humans' relationship to nature as god and their relationship to a God of both humans and nature. The passage in Jeremiah about Rachel as the archetypal wailing mother reveals that the connection between nature, women, and the cycle of life and death continued to exist within biblical tradition even though the status of the Goddess changed. Rabbinic Judaism altered the theological focus of the religion, and thereby displaced the importance of women's practices.[31] Jewish women continued to practice lament in the early rabbinic period, and at least through the medieval period, as evidence of this practice is found in Talmudic writings. However, rather than performing a pagan practice, like the other women of the Mediterranean, the Jewish *endechas* were different. It appears that they were popular mourning leaders in Spain because of the Rachel tradition. The basis for their lament dance was a biblical, matriarchal tradition of Judaic monotheism.

THE MACHOL OF DEATH

Near Eastern history and the background of biblical lament can help us understand the meaning of movement in Jewish women's "Rachel" lament. Jewish women performed their lament dance in the same way their pagan neighbors did, but in accordance with their own Jewish understandings of God. Specific biblical and rabbinic texts reflect an agricultural cycle of life and death that was interpreted within the framework of Jewish belief and practice. This interpretation indicates the presence of the Rachel tradition.[32] Passages from the Prophets and the New Testament that offer images of the Rachel tradition include Isaiah 30:29, Jeremiah 48:36, and Matthew 9:23, all of which deal with mourning. A related passage, 2 Chronicles 35:25, describes mourning at the funeral of King Josiah: "and to this day the minstrels, both men and women, commemorate Josiah in their lamentations. Such laments have become traditional in Israel, and they are found in the written collection."

In these biblical passages, there is a connection between the wailing women, the flute, and the choreography of the funeral lament. A passage from the Mishnah on a "proper" Jewish burial for a wife provides more detail on how and why wailing, the flute, and women are connected, as well as rabbinic attitude concerning the lament tradition:

> Rabbi Yehuda says: Even a pauper in Israel shall not employ less than two 'flutes (*halilin*) and a wailing woman' (*Ketuvot* IV.4). This however, was a time-honored custom, but it was not regarded as a religious duty that would overrule the commandment of Sabbath rest.

Then Rabbi Yehuda explains:

> 'One waits for nightfall close to the Sabbath-boundary when the affairs of a bride or a dead man have to be arranged' (*Shabbat* 23:4).

Those affairs included arranging for a flute to be brought to the event so that the process would not violate Jewish law by forcing a musician to carry an instrument on Shabbat.

The Mishnah text implies that there were no strict rules governing the carrying of a musical instrument. They were performing what the rabbis labeled "a time-honored custom," yet they were not allowed to interrupt a celebration with their mourning. According to the Tosefta, "it was not admissible to upset the joy of a holiday by carrying 'flutes' (*halilin*) to a 'house of mourning,'" though it was permissible to do so if one was going "to a place of festivity or banquet."[33] In this passage, the peculiarities of the use of musical instruments in Jewish ritual for the life cycle are contrasted with the rules regulating the Sabbath. Presumably, women's lament was also regulated by Jewish law—not a law banning the hearing of a woman's voice, but one determining the proper time for mourning and rejoicing.

Flutes were used for the holiday of *Simchat Beit ha-Sho'evah*—the water-drawing ceremony time at the end of *Sukkot*—as well as for funerals. This was partially a matter of "local customs," as was the use of flutes at funerals.[34] But if use of the flute for the funeral and the danced lament of Jewish women was merely a performance of local custom, Talmudic passages mentioning dance and women might be construed as a concession to pagan fertility superstitions. A biblical passage on women lament leaders offers a different interpretation. Besides the Rachel passage and the account of wailing women at Josiah's funeral, another verse in Jeremiah (9:10–21) explicitly orders the *qinot* to conduct laments for the people of Jerusalem:

> Summon the wailing women to come,
> send for the women skilled in
> keening
> to come quickly and raise a lament
> for us,
> that our eyes may run with tears
> and our eyelids be wet with weeping.
> Hark, hark, lamentation is heard in
> Zion . . .
>
> *Listen, you women, to the words of the Lord,*
>
> that your ears may catch what he says.
> *Teach your daughters the lament,*
> *let them teach one another this dirge.* (My emphasis)

According to this passage from Jeremiah, lament involves listening to "the words of the Lord," which commands women to teach *qinot* to their daughters. The lament tradition is not only proper, but also part of proper Torah behavior. The section immediately preceding this biblical proclamation further implies the correctness of the practice and the need for it in Torah tradition and biblical Judaism. The previous verses lay blame on pagan practices for the death and destruction occurring in the city, so Jeremiah would not have commanded the *qinot* to wail and keen if they were enacting pagan, Canaanite rituals of lament. Furthermore, the rabbis of the Talmud refer to this passage when they discuss the proper conduct for *qinot*.[35]

Talmudic and Sephardic records present verbal descriptions of the movements that were enacted for the process of "keening," including the clapping of hands the beating of limbs, and the playing of hand drums (*erus* and also *rebi'it*), both referring to clapping. The behavior was apparently typical of funeral dances and also habitual practices during secular dances. "Even when funeral dances have been abolished, these former attributes of the dance survived."[36]

Other action words that are associated with death rituals in the Bible and other Jewish writings include *misped*, meaning "beating the breast"; *bakah*, or crying for mourning; and *sabab*, "to go around," used for a funeral procession. The word *sabab*, "to go around," possibly reflects the Sephardim practice of circling around a funeral bier.[37] The Mishnah, Mo'ed Ketan, also indicates that such behavior was regulated, with "R. Ishmael" saying, "they that . . . are near to the bier may clap their hands," and also "on the first days of the months and at Dedication and at Purim they may sing lamentations . . . and clap their hands [for the dance]." However, no wailing, lamenting, or hand clapping was allowed "after the corpse has been buried." At the funeral, there was an intermediate stage that involved "walking seven times around the bier during which seven short prayers are recited or chanted." All prayers ended with "and continually may he walk in the land of life, and may his soul rest in the bond of life."[38]

As written texts on the *endechas* and their lament rituals in Spain reveal, the funeral processions were led by women, contorting their bodies and crying, and probably also beating their limbs and clapping their hands. While there is a gap in information about Mediterranean lament practice between the Talmudic period and medieval Spain, the patterns of behavior seem to have remained fairly consistent. Following Torah traditions, lament apparently continued to be a role for women, complete with choreographed movement.

In comparison with other Mediterranean funeral traditions, Jewish women's lament appears significantly different in intention. Ancient Egyptian art depicts motions similar to the ones described for wailing women in the Bible, and in later Sephardic tradition. Those actions appear to include clapping, stamping of feet, drumming, and even castanet playing. Yet the biblical and rabbinic Jewish beliefs and practices concerning death, life, and fertility differed considerably from those in Egypt, and also from those of Christianity. The biblical *qinot* danced for a different tradition than their neighbors did, holding a different understanding about death. Their actions were far more dramatic and tortured than anything we find in Egyptian relief sculptures or in Greek and Roman labyrinth death dance paintings.

Significantly, the Sephardic mourners wailed. This represents a contrast to Christianity of the time, which officially promoted the gentle singing of hymns and songs celebrating entrance into a heavenly afterlife. Jewish theology recognizes death as painful. In a later stage of the Sephardic funeral, a circling motion is made around the grave. This suggests a hope in life continuing after death, but the Sephardic Jewish tradition recognizes that a life has ended. Wailing first predominates, as the pain of death and separation is fully acknowledged.[39]

Spanish tradition and Sephardic Judaism appear to have shared beliefs about how best to express loss through death. From this perspective, the Jewish women might be seen as popular lament leaders, as their lament embodied Torah teaching that was seemingly meaningful not just to Jews, but to the wider community. It was how the *endechas'* words and motions went together that seems to have had an impact. Their practice was apparently so vital and relevant to the culture of medieval Spain that remnants of it can be found today in flamenco.

Lament and Flamenco

Flamenco music and dance are generally recognized as a product of the pain and suffering of the underclass of Spain, especially the Gypsies. But the earliest history of flamenco includes legacies left by the great cultures of the medieval period, which included Muslims and Jews. Jewish laments were apparently at the root of the oldest known flamenco songs.

The earliest history of flamenco can be traced through the song (*cante*), and although it is always controversial to claim clear knowledge of flamenco development, the earliest forms were the *cañas, polos,* and *saetas.* All of these songs express pain, loss, and lament, and are full of the deep emotion expressed as *duende.* Out of these "deep songs," the *cante soleares* evolved. Called the mother *cante* of flamenco, the *soleares* most likely derives from the mournful *cante siguiriyas*, which stems from Jewish music of medieval Spain. Notably, the deep songs of flamenco appear to contain remnants of the *endecha* tradition.

Women continued to lead funeral laments in post-expulsion Spain, and the practice apparently influenced flamenco. *Endechas* "had been banned in Malaga" in southern Spain "for their exaggerated hysterics, but in Seville they remained active throughout the eighteenth century." This is "a likely link to the emergent forms of flamenco," with the deep song *siguiriyas* possibly having "roots in the singing style of these professional female mourners."[40]

Jewish women were important leaders of the funeral processions in Spain, but according to post-expulsion historians, this would not have been possible past the fifteenth century, as Jews were officially expelled from the country in 1492. For flamenco historians, however, and more recently for Sephardic scholars, the picture is murky; they believe that some Jews may have remained in Spain, influencing music and dance development. An older flamenco theory considers that some Jewish outcasts went underground, hiding in the hill country of Andalusia with Gypsies, and thus directly influenced the formation of Gypsy flamenco. Another theory suggests that Sephardic musical traditions were influential in the formation of several *cantes*, including the *soleares* and *siguiriyas*.[41]

"JEWISH" FLAMENCO HISTORY

Less is known about the dance history of flamenco. Some of the movement patterns of the *soleares* and *siguiriyas* certainly appear to have been influenced by or copied from the *endechas*, and therefore might provide insight into the symbolic meaning of their death dance. Additionally, the religious rather than ethnic origins of flamenco are recognized by several scholars, especially for the *cante jondo*—the deep song with its heartfelt quality of *duende*. Typical flamenco dance movements used to convey *duende* include expressive arms, pained body, and saddened face, which perhaps reflects flamenco's history as a product of persecution during the Spanish Inquisition in the fifteenth century. The claim is that even though they were not supposed to be in Spain, Jews and Muslims did live in the back hills with the Gypsies, as all were persecuted at the time. They were then "joined by many Christian fugitives and dissenters, who added a fourth distinct culture."[42] Significantly, there is also a claim that "Spanish Jews who migrated to Flanders were allowed to sing their religious chants unmolested." Their "songs were referred to as 'flamenco' by their kin who remained in Spain, who were forbidden them by the inquisition." Flamenco music associated with these or other religious songs may be *toñas, cañas* and *polos, roas,* and *campa-nilleros. Toñas* are related to the *saetas,* a lament song considered to be Jewish in origin.[43]

While the history of flamenco is not clear, its "deep song" can be seen as a type of psychodrama of grief. It involves the "out" group, which may have included Jews. "There were many Jewish neighborhoods and settlements in the southwest corner of Spain," so "some Jewish contribution to the popular music of Andalusia in general and perhaps to flamenco in particular cannot be ruled out." One very dark song, the *peteneras,* might provide some evidence, as it does talk of a "Jewess."[44]

Mitchell attributes the hypotheses of post-expulsion Jewish influence on flamenco to a "German Jew writing under the name Medina Azara." Azara believed that the deep song of flamenco derived from "synagogal practices." Mitchell also notes that in a 1986 publication, "Manuel Barrios conjectures that the recurrent references in flamenco lyrics to exile, nostalgia, and the need for secrecy may reflect a [post-expulsion] Hebraic influence." Barrios also finds that "the strange superstition gitanos have regarding the *peteneras*" and the curse of death when performed "is a remembrance of its 'Hebraic singularity.'"[45]

The *endechas* might represent a link between Jewish dance practices and flamenco, because their death dance was accompanied by cries of mourning and loss. Their songs of deep grief are much like those used for the *soleares* and *siguiriyas.* The *peteneras* is also a *cante* whose lyrics unite death, dance, and Jews. A Jewish woman is named in a popular verse for *peteneras,* which suggests its pre-expulsion origins. This mention of a Jewish woman is striking, in that the *cante* is about death and is associated with death. Two traditional verses even evoke images of the *endechas* through mention of a funeral procession, a "Jewess," and a "synagogue":

> La Petenera has died
> and they are taking her to be buried;
> all of the followers of the process
> will not fit into the mausoleum . . .
>
> * * *
>
> Where are you going, beautiful Jewess,
> after hours and so fixed up?
> I going looking for Rebecco,
> who is in a synagogue[46]

Given the theories of social oppression and flamenco, claims of Jewish influence on *duende,* and the danceable *peteneras* associated with

Jewish women and funerals, the *endechas'* use of wailing, feet stamping, and hand clapping may have been the origin of flamenco movement.[47] In *La otra historia del flamenco* (An Alternative History of Flamenco), José Romero Jiménez dwells specifically on the Jewish and Arabic contribution to flamenco, including the influence of music and dance from medieval Spain. He sees the *peteneras* as proof of a Jewish contribution to flamenco. Through his extensive research on flamenco music, he finds that the current version of the *peteneras* stems from the "Judeo-Andalusia" song "A la una," and that it is in a true, original *maqam* (mode). Significantly, he notates this version of the *peteneras* in a *siguiriyas* rhythm, "en el modo arabigo andaluz" (in the Arabic-Andalusian mode).[48]

Jiménez's work is detailed, considering the rhythms and musical structures of flamenco *cante*. Dance development is primarily outside his study. However, the connections he makes between Jewish music and flamenco, plus historical accounts of death, lament, and dance in Spain, imply that the fundamental movements of the *endechas* influenced flamenco dancing. Given the available records, Jiménez concludes that the basic dance of the Jews and Moors set the foundation for flamenco, and the Gypsies then added to this structure. And while some Andalusian folk dance contributed to flamenco, the *siguiriyas* and *soleares* are truly unique forms.[49]

In sum, despite the uncertainty of Jewish connections to flamenco history, there is a strong indication that the *danza* movement of the *endechas* influenced flamenco music and dance. As with the mention of a Jewish woman in the *peteneras* lyrics, the connection is tenuous, but it is present. The subject matter and lyrics are about death and possibly a funeral procession, with a curious mention of a Jewish woman. Since mourning leadership was a social role often filled by Jewish women, the *peteneras* might be a reference to *endechas*, whose *danza* was full of *duende* in tone and ritual action.

Duende and Dance

Peteneras, soleares, and *siguiriyas* have no set dance patterns; nor were these flamenco songs always danced. Yet they exhibit typical structures of movement that match the tone of the three *cantes*. Typical movements for these dances are reminiscent of the reports of the actions of the *endechas*, suggesting a particular idiom of nonverbal expression of grief. It may be that the idiom was "Spanish" in origin, yet the pattern was associated with the *endechas*. That these patterns still exist does not lessen their connection with Jewish influence on flamenco; rather, it reveals that Jewish traditions left strong and lasting influences in Spain. Set rhythms for each *cante* establish the direction and dynamics of the dance.

The *siguiriyas* rhythm follows a pattern familiar to many dirges, with a phrase of two sustained notes followed by counts of three, like two wails and sobbing. *Soleares* have a similar rhythmic structure, although the accentuation, which is the opposite of that for the *siguiriyas*, changes the tone of the dance. Appropriately, the mood is less dark, one of moving through grief rather than being in mourning. The *peteneras* may also be classified as a *cante jondo* (deep song), yet it too has a dark tone, with the rhythm pattern today similar to that of the *siguiriyas*.

When a dance is performed to one of these *cantes*, it follows the tone and mood of the rhythm, accentuation, and lyrics, which often convey certain beliefs about the nature of life, the meaning of death, and edifying behavior in the face of loss. It is common to see stamping feet and clapping hands in all three dances, as for any flamenco dance. Yet because these are darker songs that deal with grief, there is a particular weight of movement in their performance.

The mood of the *siguiriyas* is often one of pain and loss, if not death. Body stance and gestures in the dance match the dark mood of the music and lyrics, with arms typically thrusting up strongly and sharply. Slower sections of the dance might include a lowered head, although this varies with the choreography. The *soleares* also expresses an introspective mood, with movements expressing grief or loss, but this dance customarily ends with a faster, uplifting movement. The mood for *soleares* is one of loneliness and loss, but not tragedy. Often the *cante* ends on a hopeful, proud note. The *peteneras*, in contrast, is rarely performed. It is so strongly connected with death that the Gypsies often still believe that anyone who performs this flamenco style will die or suffer bad luck. When it is performed, the typical interpretation includes some dancing, but it is subdued. Expressive arm movement is the main feature.

In sum, all of these dances deal with the process of loss. Some of the gestures, actions, and dance movements parallel those seen in descriptions of the *endechas*. In particular, the use of hand clapping and feet stamping in sorrow appears to be directly related to the funeral practices. The mournful gestures of the *peteneras* certainly recall the medieval and Sephardic descriptions of *endechas*. Such gestures were not unique to Jewish women, but the *endechas* had a unique practice, given the theology of their tradition. The development of the *soleares* out of the *siguiriyas* and the *peteneras*'s background both indicate that the movement of the *endechas* was fitting with Jewish theology, as well as Spanish custom. Mourning was to occur through dramatic grieving expressed through the body. Then life was to go on, and the bodily expression of grief must change.

For insight into Jewish understandings of grieving through the body, this passage from the Talmud is worth rereading:

> The women may sing dirges but they may not clap their hands. R. Ishmael says: "They that are near to the bier may clap their hands," and also "On the first days of the months and at Dedication and at Purim they may sing lamentations . . . and clap their hands [for the dance] but during none of them may they wail . . . After the corpse has been buried they may not sing lamentations or clap their hands."

It is in this passage from the Mishnah that the movement of lament first receives attention. Details of when the behavior was permissible convey an understanding of life and death. The expression of extreme grief was to stop when the body was interred. While mourning dance was appropriate for death, there must also be a pause for celebration.

Kabbalah and the Endechas

Jewish women were commanded to rest on *Rosh Chodesh,* as a holiday for women. This meant that there was no lament dance on this first day of a Jewish month, the time of the new moon. *Rosh Chodesh* was the one time in the official Jewish rabbinic calendar when women were allowed to have a role. It was not a leadership role, but one that recognized women, giving them a day off for this minor celebration. Yet traditional *Rosh Chodesh* practices involved a minimal amount of dance, even among the *Sephardiyot.*

Despite evidence that Sephardic women led wedding dance ritual and funeral processions, there is less clear evidence that they danced for the time of birth, the other significant life cycle event when they were music leaders. This was true even for the birth of the new moon. *Sephardiyot* could have sung, drummed, and possibly danced for this day, but little in the way of concrete data is available. Given the dance-oriented culture of the Mediterranean world, this is surprising.[50]

While flamenco might offer an idea of what the *endechas'* movement embodied, the Zohar may offer textual insight into their Jewish teaching. Not surprisingly, the Spanish kabbalists addressed the tradition of lament in their writings. The kabbalists implemented a midnight prayer service that involved reciting biblical psalms for a service of *Tikkun Rachel.* The service was related to interpretation of the passage from Jeremiah referring to Rachel weeping for her children, with the *Tikkun* (redemption) of the service in the recovery of the divine feminine *Shekhinah* from exile. This was accomplished through joy, as according to Jewish mystical tradition, the biblical Rachel attained redemption through tears and joy. So her practice of lament should be imitated. Rachel weeps for her children, who are in exile, but she is also "the true love of Jacob, and she won him . . . with joy." The midnight service of *Tikkun Rachel* then recalls Rachel's joy' "even when reciting the mournful *Tikkun Rachel*." Although it is mournful, it is also said out of joy, even as "we cry for the exile of the *Shechinah*."

> When the Besht got into the carriage he said to Rabbi Nahum, "Young man, if you are able to tell me the difference between *Tikkun Leah* and *Tikkun Rachel*, I will let you come with me." Without hesitation, Rabbi Nahum answered, saying, "What Leah accomplished with tears, Rachel was able to do with joy." Immediately the Besht let him into the carriage.[51]

The mystics believed that the *Shekhinah* was in exile. They mourned her absence, but at the same time their mourning led to their elation. They were thereby allowed to enter a process of redemption, where they might be reunited with the *Shekhinah*. There is "lament over the exile of the *Shechinah* and the destruction of the Temple in *Tikkun Rachel*," yet "through this mourning itself we also begin the process of joining with the *Shechinah*, and tying ourselves to Her in love."[52]

Tikkun Rachel is said for the midnight prayer service of *Tikkun Hatzot*. The midnight vigil service of the Jewish mystical tradition begins with mourning for the loss of the Temple and the exile of the *Shekhinah*, and ends with singing of praise and for redemption. It stems from practices of the Spanish kabbalists, and is "praised again and again in the *Zohar*." Rabbi Elijah deVidas, a "disciple" of "Rabbi Moshe Cordovero," said of the importance of the service of *Tikkun Rachel*:

> I have discussed this at length because it seems to me that this practice is a basic pillar for all the services of God. And it is not an accident that the Midnight Service is emphasized so much throughout the *Zohar*, innumerable times, more so than all the other *mitzvot*.

Quoting from the Zohar, deVidas describes anyone who takes part in this service as "a son of the Holy One, blessed be He . . . and there is none who stand in the way when appeal is made on his behalf to the King's palace" (*Totzaot Hayim* 20).[53]

Of course, men would have been the participants in this service. Women in medieval Spain had their own version of a *Tikkun Rachel*, drawn from biblical tradition. The *endechas* in the Sephardic community continued a women's lament or "Rachel" tradition, which pursued redemption through performance. This is one possible interpretation of their dance of death, based on reports of their activities. It is doubtful that the women were fully conscious of the symbolism and history of their practice. However, that does not mean their performance was meaningless to them.

The kabbalists would have been familiar with these women's practice. Women's leadership of mourning rituals and lament appears to have been a cultural form that was familiar to men. Insight into what mourning dance meant to the Jewish community of medieval Spain might also be seen in the kabbalistic writings. The text describing words and performance of the midnight service might be viewed as a male manifestation of a biblical lament tradition. The kabbalistic texts perhaps express some of the perceived meaning of the symbolism of mourning women, like the biblical Rachel.

Just as the image of Miriam in the Zohar's image of the heavenly courts appears to reflect the dance and music of the Jewish women in medieval Spain, so the mourning dance of the *endechas* seems to serve as a model for the Spanish kabbalists. The reasons given for services of *Tikkun Rachel* suggest that the dance of the *endechas* embodied a Jewish theology espoused in the culture of medieval Spain—one laments to gain hope for the living. It is a paradox, but the kabbalistic understanding of the *Shekhinah* is that the thought is the result of an understanding of the divine feminine as present and absent.

The *endechas*, their dances of death, and the *Sephardiyot's* dances for life passages again indicate that there was an active tradition in Judaism of recognizing the rhythms of life. Since the *endechas* were part of the culture from which the Zohar arose, these Sephardic women could have danced their kabbalah (reception), presented to the community in movement and music rather than written texts. As Caroline Walker Bynum states, "women's symbols and myths tend to build from social and biological experiences." They are clearly embodied. "Men's symbols and myths tend to invert" experience.[54] That inversion can and is often disembodied and static, written text.

Consider *Rosh Chodesh*. For Sephardic women, this was a time to slow down, light candles, eat special foods, and perhaps drum with accompanying dance and song. The emphasis on rest allowed for reflection. In contrast and comparison, biological death and loss involved performing the "Rachel" tradition. The Jewish *endechas* embodied the experience in dramatic movement and cries of grief. Where men had to do this by concentrating on words, letters, and syllables in kabbalistic meditation, the women did so through movement, pausing to consider life and death.

Conclusions

When Susan Sered interviewed Sephardic women, she found that they lit candles for *Rosh Chodesh* as a way to "signal divine attention and to elicit divine assistance." At the same time, the candles served as a means of connecting the living and the dead.[55] On *Rosh Chodesh* eve, the women visited cemeteries and lit candles for the souls of the dead, whether they were Jewish saints or family members. By doing so, they displayed a sense of history, and of their own personal identification with Jewish tradition.[56]

Today, Jewish women have created numerous ways to celebrate *Rosh Chodesh* through many different types of rituals. It is a way for them to connect to a Jewish tradition that specifically recognizes women. From *Miriam's Well* to *Celebrating the New Moon*, the richness, variety, and creativity of modern *Rosh Chodesh* rituals is an amazing blend of Jewish myth, modern *midrash*, song, and often dance. The newly created practices often circumvent or reappropriate patriarchal, rabbinic material. The practice of building new *Rosh Chodesh* traditions is a powerful move, and a construction of new Torah teaching by women.

Jewish women have long had their own traditions, as the history of the *endechas* shows us. Their practice of ritual movement is a matter of history, as are the newly created *Rosh Chodesh* ceremonies. They are embodied practices that go beyond mere social custom to encompass religious traditions in Judaism. Women's rituals have been a way for them to assert some sense of power within patriarchal structures. But their rituals also expressed their beliefs.

Judaism includes a wealth of traditions and practices. The lament dance of the *Sephardiyot* is only one of them. Although not necessarily sanctioned by rabbinic Judaism, the history of this practice stems from biblical times, and is epitomized by the figure of the weeping mother Rachel. I have reviewed this material in order to gain some understanding of the meaning of the lament dances for the *Sephardiyot*. Biblical and historical details indicate that, from one perspective, the dance of the *endechas* was a Jewish theology in motion.

Rabbinic texts reveal that there were particular uses of dance and movement for funerals. The rabbis neither approved nor disapproved of the stamping feet and clapping hands of the *qinot*. They did have some concern about regulating the behavior, perhaps to distinguish keening practices from those of neighboring cultures. Again, the main issue seems to have been a proper understanding of when one should mourn and rejoice in Judaism. Theologically, the practice was apparently important to the Spanish kabbalists, and their texts on *Tikkun Rachel* reflect a possible interpretation of *why* the *endechas* were important to medieval Spain. The *endechas'* movement reveals much about symbolic discourse of medieval Spain.

While *how* a dance is done is often not the most important means of interpreting a dance event, the reports of the *endechas'* formal dance and the movements of the flamenco *siguiriyas* and *soleares* make a dramatic impression. These are gripping, powerful dances. They were meant to lead mourners in and out of grieving, loss, and depression. As they were used by the Jewish *endechas*, a manner of teaching Jewish understandings of life was apparently encoded in their ritual motion. In this sense, their dance was Torah, incorporating women's customs for, and as a part of, Jewish tradition.

Conclusion

In the now many years that I have been teaching religious studies, I have found that students often face the same difficulties with the fieldwork I assign. Many assume that because they are not experts in religious study, their observations at an event are invalid—despite the fact that I provide them with guidelines for noting the basic physical components of an event, in terms of motion, space, and sensual perception. While many are able to describe the use of space, artwork, gestures, behavior, ritual objects, smells, foods, and even clothing worn by participants, just as many are unable to do so.

These students want to leap into a philosophical discussion, and simply do not have time for the physical details of the lived religion. This was the response of a few students who attended a very energetic, lively Tot Shabbat synagogue service. Although there were children running to and from the *bima*, occasional cries from the pews, and many gestured songs involving dinosaurs and challah bread, several of my college students could barely write a paragraph about the event. One even told me that he thought it was a cute service meant to entertain children, but did not see how it had anything to do with the deep values of Judaism. He was a bit surprised when I offered that such a service might suggest that this Jewish congregation valued family education, and that the service might be one active means of doing so. It was exactly what we had read about in the assigned textbook, but somehow the live experience did not seem to make sense to him at first.

Throughout this study on Sephardic women's dance traditions, I have tried to convey that what is done in religious practice is every bit as important as the theoretical aspects of a particular tradition, and very often makes practical sense out of seemingly abstract religious principles. When the embodied, lived reality of a religion is dismissed, much of its history and wisdom is lost. In the case of the *Miriam Tradition*, religious scholars seemingly forgot Sephardic women's community leadership. Ethnomusicologists and dance anthropologists have recorded and studied the history, but there is a notable absence of study of the practice as an active engagement of Torah tradition, even and especially in a gendered Judaism.

Describing their dance as Torah was one means for Sephardic women to tell their story as *embodied* text, understanding Torah as teaching. In a very real and physical sense, I have also dealt with *halakhah*—Jewish law—how Jewish women "walked" the Torah path of living a Jewish life. Overall, I am concerned with the performance of Judaism, in order to ground my work in the physical reality of the religion. Therefore my definition of *halakhah* in this study is broad and reconstructive, with consideration for rabbinic views. I find this a necessary step, for as Rachel Adler pointed out in *Engendering Judaism*, a feminist view of Judaism must also take traditional understandings into account. Rather than totally bypassing *halakhah*, then, which was a part of Jewish women's lives, I broadened its scope by first looking at the restrictive results of *halakhah*, and then looking for women's alternative activities. Additionally, the rabbinic understanding of Torah text and *halakhah* was highly embodied to begin with. I simply could not dismiss tradition as only a patriarchal imposition on women's lives.

Judith Plaskow and Rachel Adler have attempted to construct a Jewish feminist history grounded in some sense of rabbinic tradition. I therefore found Plaskow's use of the rabbinic categories of Torah, covenant, and Israel appealing for examining what I call the Miriam tradition. As she presents it, Torah is the structural, organizing principle of Judaism, able to encompass a broad range of Jewish history beyond written texts. Overall, Plaskow's work displays a keen sense of the importance of tradition and embodied practices. She does not completely dismiss the rabbis, yet she wants to include women in Jewish history, even if that history has yet to be discovered.

Without Plaskow, I might not even have considered the importance of the Miriam tradition. Yet to finally flesh out the implications of presenting an embodied version of Jewish women's history, it is worth considering Adler's presentation of rabbinic understandings of *mitzvot* (commandments) and *halakhah*. Adler presents them as categories that the rabbis understood as eternal, with lasting truths for developing ethics. Ethics involve action, or performance, so Adler's evaluation of rabbinic ethics is important for examining Jewish women's performance practices.

Adler states that while the rabbis emphasize *halakhah* and history as vertically connected with heaven, the horizontal, relational aspect of living these timeless truths is also important for Judaism. She thinks that including women in Jewish history requires consideration of ethical conduct—the living out of Torah truth. Women will not be treated justly in the future if women's performance in Jewish history remains hidden or denigrated. Adler suggests that a "bridge" must be built between the rabbinic recording of the past and an ethical Jewish future inclusive of women. If we want to construct such a bridge, we need to reach back into rabbinic history, renewing Torah for the future. We must also "extend Torah as we extend ourselves by reaching ahead."[1]

I saw Franz Rosenzweig's picture of Jewish ethics and history as a bridge between rabbinic accounts of Jewish history and new accounts that recognize the performance of Jewish women as part of Torah tradition. Rosenzweig was committed to this tradition, yet out of deep concern for the importance of ethics and relationship in Judaism, he struck a balance between acknowledging eternal values of Torah and ongoing revelation. Adler seems to echo the views expressed by Rosenzweig in *The Star of Redemption,* stating that while "the vertical dimension [of revelation] remains, it is the horizontal, human plane that requires revelation."[2] However, Rosenzweig's strong sense of performance distinguishes his work. He includes movement as a means of attaining new revelation.

The silence of women from the past needs to emerge so that we can close the gap between the past and the present and understand *how* Jewish women built bridges between their lives and their identity as Jews. There are now many highly detailed accounts of Jewish women's history, and knowing these stories is vastly important, instilling a sense of worth and belonging in the tradition for many Jewish women. In part, this is why I have made an effort to investigate the Miriam tradition. However, my focus on ritual leadership acknowledges that women also taught Torah values through nonverbal symbolic movement that embodied belief.

Religion and Culture in Judaism

There was fluidity in the relationship between Sephardic Judaism and culture. In the case of the *Sephardiyot,* their *minhag*—their cultural practices for weddings and funerals—was not simply local custom. Their culture said that ritual dance was an important activity for these life-changing events, and it became a part of Jewish practice rather than serving as superficial entertainment. These dances also relate a story about women's traditions within a gendered Judaism. Although Jewish women were restricted by patriarchy, they found a way to take leadership and even subvert or alter restrictions. Their *mikveh* party traditions are an example, as the participants created lyrics and dances that expressed their own interpretation of the Jewish ritual.

Much like Judaism in general, then, Sephardic women adapted to their circumstances. Judaism changed in dress and culture as it traveled from one country to another in the Diaspora. More accurately, the people of Judaism adapted their lifestyle in accordance with the culture in which they lived, even as Torah tradition remained. Likewise, Jewish women's dances may have changed over the years, but women still led wedding dances and funeral laments, just as women did in the Torah. It was a part of Jewish life and practice.

Written texts can inform us about the practices of Jews. Since the rabbis addressed *halakhah* in their *responsa*, their opinions might be viewed as the "really real" of Jewish life. Yet this view does not consider that *interpretation* of *halakhah* was based on cultural circumstance. Additionally, historical documents demonstrate that the "really real" was only one, narrow reality. If ethics, or enacted theology, is a vital component of Judaism, then consideration of more than a written text is essential, even for rabbinic accounts of history.

The examples I provide of music and dance among Sephardic women establish a positive means of dealing with the sometimes negative rabbinic accounts of history. In some cases, the story of the Miriam tradition might demonstrate how Jewish communities defied restrictive rabbinic rulings, perhaps determining their own "walk" with Torah tradition. Rabbinic complaints about popular dances provide some evidence that this did occur. Yet the rabbis never argued against dance itself.

The embodied text of the *Sephardiyot* was dance and music. Arguably, this might be considered a lesser text for Judaism, as a religion built on words. To restrict the understanding of Torah, however, is to reiterate a narrow view that there is one, unified Judaism. If women were denied access to the reading and study of written Torah, it was because patriarchy restricted the concept of Torah, to the exclusion of women. Women's dance practices were partially a countertradition. Their story might also be considered evidence of a Jewish women's prayer group practice, and such evidence has already altered Orthodox Judaism. There are now Orthodox women's prayer groups led by women in both the United States and Israel, and most likely in Europe as well.

My other concern for this study was the implication for people today, as history is always worthy of study for evaluating the present, often helping us dispel illusions and assumptions about reality. I characterize this age as one that generally does not acknowledge the importance of movement. In a past postmodern, computer-age society, keyboard stroking and walking to the coffee shop may be people's only forms of significant movement during a day. As a yoga teacher and dancer, however, I have also noticed an increase in popular interest in ritual and ritual-like activities such as yoga and tae kwon do. Symbolic, metaphoric movement is a part of these practices, with a ritual-like quality that may be structured and repetitive. As is true of good ritual, there is also an ever-evolving quality to these practices. It is quite the opposite of data processing and crunching numbers.

We desperately need ritual, especially during life passages, when words alone cannot express the deep realities discovered at these times. In an age fraught with depression, there is also a discernible need for these rituals to be embodied, and to move one toward joy. I was reminded of this fact at the death of my father. While there were no women to lead us in lamenting, a procession to the gravesite and the accompanying gunfire salute by the American Legion proved extremely helpful in dealing with grief.

Perhaps this need for ritual processing also explains the seemingly inordinate amount of money that young couples spend on complicated weddings. Yet while it is probably no longer economically possible to conduct weeklong wedding celebrations, it is possible to perform meaningful rituals that dispel the negative, build energy, and celebrate life. The lament, wedding, and celebratory leadership of the *Sephardiyot* provides a good example of how this might be done. The history of the Miriam tradition can open our vision to possibilities of inclusive means of creating joy throughout an entire community. This too is part of Torah tradition—to make one's bones rejoice again (Psalm 51).

NOTES

Preface: Why Movement Matters

1. "Red Sea" is the infamous mistranslation of *Yam Suf*, which correctly translated means "reed sea."

2. Langer, Lüddeckens, Radde, and Snoek, "Transfer of Ritual," 2.

Chapter 1: Women and Sacred Power

1. Gruber, "Ten Dance-Derived Expressions," 57–58. Although Gruber does not do so, some interpret the term to mean that the writhing was evocative of "a woman in labor." I refer to this interpretation in Sautter, "Searching for Biblical Roots of Belly Dance," suggesting that the writhing and spinning could be a description of belly dance, as it is a common form of dance among women in the Eastern Mediterranean.

2. Sendrey, *Music in Ancient Israel*, 445–46.

3. Abrahams, *Jewish Life in the Middles Ages*, 380–81; Friedhaber, "Bibliographic Sources in Research," 32.

4. See Grossman and Haut, *Daughters of the King*, especially the essays by Susan Grossman, Sara Reguer, and Emily Taitz.

5. Biale, *Women and Jewish Law*, 12.

6. Ibid., 21.

7. Ibid.

8. See Taitz, "Women's Voices, Women's Prayers," 61.

9. Shiloah, *Jewish Musical Traditions*, 120.

10. Shiloah comments on the use of secular poetry in the synagogue, noting rabbinic objections, especially in medieval Spain. He cites the severe criticism of R. Judah al-Harizi, a thirteenth-century Hebrew poet from Spain, who complained about a cantor. Ibid., 68–71.

11. Ibid., 211. Shiloah discusses in detail the prohibitions against playing musical instruments in mourning for the Temple, and how this ban was interpreted in the various Jewish communities: "this prohibition is never violated in the framework of synagogue ritual . . . It is less strictly observed . . . in events taking place in homes or even in synagogues on weekdays or at the close of the Sabbath" (75).

12. Adams, *Congregational Dancing*, 93, 101.

13. See Shiloah, *Jewish Musical Traditions*, 174–78. The Sephardic traditions will be detailed in the following chapters. While Maimonides' son disapproved

of women whom he viewed as dancing in imitation of "Gentiles," it is equally important to recognize his activity with Sufis, including the use of movement for meditation. He wrote about these techniques in *The Pomegranate.*

14. See Roth, *Jews in the Renaissance,* 276–81. Roth describes Guglielmo Pesaro, a courtly Jewish dance master who recorded his teachings in writing. Shiloah also offers descriptions of mixed-couples dancing in *Jewish Musical Traditions,* 211–12.

15. On dancing for *Rosh Chodesh,* see Novick, "History of Rosh Chodesh." Details on the use of dance at wedding and funerals will be elaborated in the following chapters.

16. Shiloah, *Jewish Musical Traditions,* 211–13.

17. See Baer, *A History of the Jews.* Paloma Díaz-Mas's more recent book *Sephardim* cites Baer as the best source for details of life among Jews in medieval Spain, and offers a limited list of new resources (33). Beinart, *The Sephardi Legacy,* offers essays with specific information about the economic status and role of Jews in medieval Spain. Grossman, *Pious and Rebellious,* offers a more in-depth view of the lives of both Ashkenazi and Sephardic women in the medieval period.

18. Scheindlin, *Wine, Women, and Death,* 20.

19. However, Eliyahu Ashtor reports that the women were not Jewish; *Jews of Moslem Spain,* 3:163.

20. All dance might be considered as being in the performative mode, as dance involves action. See Richard Schechner, "From Ritual to Theater and Back: The Efficacy-Entertainment Braid," in *Performance Theory,* 106–52.

21. Ivanova, *Dance in Spain,* 28. Ivanova provides the dates of 215 B.C.E–409 C.E. for the Roman period in Spain. She does not note exact dates of records, but mentions the Roman writers Martial and Juvenal.

22. Buonaventura, *Serpent of the Nile,* 43.

23. E. Louis Backman provides an extensive overview of attitudes toward dance in Christianity in *Religious Dances.* For Islamic attitudes toward dance and culture, see al-Faruqi, "Dance as an Expression of Islamic Culture"; al-Faruqi, "Dances of the Muslim People."

24. Brooks, *Dances of the Processions of Seville in Spain's Golden Age;* Roth, *Jews in the Renaissance,* 274, although he attributes the styling to its popularity in Palermo, where the dance procession was performed.

25. Lapson, "Dance," 462.

26. I am alluding to a phrase used in the Talmud that indicates rabbinic judgment on how Jews were to conduct themselves in their host country.

27. Ingber has done extensive research on dance in Judaism. She personally told me how she studied the dance history of the Sephardim. See the bibliography for a list of her works.

28. See Lapson, "Dance," 456, 461.

29. See Shiloah, "Ritual and Music of the Synagogue," 120–27, especially 121 on "*The Sephardi and Portuguese Style*"; Abrahams, *Jewish Life in the Middles Ages,* 254.

30. Lévy and Lévy Zumwalt, *Ritual Medical Lore of Sephardic Women,* 17–24.

31. Flood, *Introduction to Hinduism.* See Gupta, *Yoga of Classical Indian Dance.*

32. See Satlow, *Creating Judaism*.

33. Sered, *Priestess, Mother, Sacred Sister*, 121.

34. Asad, *Genealogies of Religion*, 53–54. Asad argues that "different kinds of practices and discourse are intrinsic to the field in which religious representations . . . acquire their identity and truthfulness" (53).

35. Paul Tillich, "Existentialist Aspects of Modern Art," in *Christianity and the Existentialists*, ed. Carl Michelson (New York: Scribner's Sons, 1956), p. 132, as quoted in Adams, "Theological Expressions."

36. Grosz, *Volatile Bodies*, 17–18.

37. Slingerland, *What Science Offers*, 82.

38. Kwok Pui-lan, "Unbinding Our Feet: Saving Brown Women and Feminist Religious Discourse," in Donaldson and Kwok, *Postcolonialism, Feminism, and Religious Discourse*, 62–81.

39. Slingerland, *What Science Offers*, 80.

40. See also *Journal of the American Academy of Religion* 76, no. 2 (2008).

41. Howard Eilberg-Schwartz traces the labeling of older rituals as primitive or "savage" in his introduction to *The Savage in Judaism*. The reasoning of the early religious anthropologists seems to be that because primitives danced, and because Western religions are not primitive, therefore dance is outside their existence. Typical accounts of sacred dance history are no better, sometimes stating that the Protestant Reformation's attack on ritual separated dance from religion. Cf. Margaret Taylor Doane, "A History of Symbolic Movement in Worship," in Adams and Apostolos-Cappadona, *Dance as Religious Studies*, 15–31.

42. Helpful general information on how this process occurred in Judaism are found in Lapson, "Dance," and in *Encyclopaedia Judaica* (Jerusalem: Macmillan, 1971), 5:1262–71.

43. Bell, *Ritual Theory, Ritual Practice*, 98; my emphasis.

44. Van der Leeuw, *Religion in Essence and Manifestation*, 374.

45. See also Apostolos-Cappadona and Adams, *Dance as Religious Studies*, 39.

46. Quoted in Spencer, *Society and the Dance*, 35.

47. Ibid.

48. Some Jewish women were literate in the Ashkenazic communities, and also wrote prayers called *Tkhines*. See Weissler, "*Tkhines* and Women's Prayer."

49. Hoffman, *Beyond the Text*, 133–36, 137–39.

50. My definitions of ritual and ritual within Judaism are based on those provided by Driver in *Magic of Ritual*; Bell in *Ritual Theory, Ritual Practice*; Hoffman in *Beyond the Text*; and Grimes in *Beginnings in Ritual Studies*. In general, there is agreement among these authors that ritual and ritualization are at basic movement-oriented. Driver goes so far as to say that ritual is like a slow dance, whereas Grimes suggests that a study of dance analysis might well serve ritual studies.

While ritual movement is certainly *like* a dance, there is a distinction between ritual motion, dance ritual, and dance. For instance, a Friday night Kabbalat Shabbat service includes bowing, which might be considered choreographed ritual movement. A joyful line dance done as part of the service might be a ritual dance. Dance done in a fellowship hall after services may be an edifying social dance that relates to values discussed in services.

51. On Hasidic dance, see Jill Gellerman's essays in Ingber, *Dancing into Marriage*.

52. See Bahat and Bahat, "Jewish Yemenite Songs from the Diwan."

53. Geertz, *Interpretation of Cultures*, 113; my emphasis. Geertz borrows the term "cultural performance" from M. Singer, "The Cultural Pattern of Indian Civilization," *Far Eastern Quarterly* 15 (1955): 23–26.

54. Not all songs were accompanied by dance. Yet when there is music, there is often an event that includes dancing. See Joann Kealiinohomoku on the dance event in "Dance Culture."

55. Northup, *Ritualizing Women*, 90.

56. Butler, *Gender Trouble*, 33; Cooey, *Religious Imagination*, 22–23.

57. Hanna, *Dance, Sex, and Gender*, 22–23.

58. Ibid.; my emphasis. Hanna cites Sherry Ortner and Harriet Whitehead, *Sexual Meanings: The Cultural Construction of Gender and Sexuality* (New York: Cambridge University Press, 1981). Regarding issues of political power, it should be noted that governments have banned dance and music as a means of suppressing rebellion and independence. For instance, in *Irish Dance and Spirituality* (Austin, Tex.: Sharing Press, 1987), I documented how, when they were occupying Ireland, the British banned the playing of Irish music and, in conjunction, dance. More recently, the Taliban prohibited music and dance in Afghanistan as a means of controlling the population. After their defeat in one city, a memorable 2002 news video presented Afghani men loudly playing traditional regional music on a radio and gleefully dancing in a local style.

59. Bell, *Ritual*, 82–83, my emphasis; Driver, *Magic of Ritual*, 30.

60. Bell, *Ritual*, 83, quoting Jean Comaroff in *Body of Power, Spirit of Resistance: The Culture and History of the South African People* (Chicago: University of Chicago Press, 1985).

61. Driver, *Magic of Ritual*, 8.

62. Buonaventura, *Serpent of the Nile*, 86, 16.

63. See Buonaventura, *Serpent of the Nile*; Jamila Salimpour, *Bellydancing, from Cave to Cult to Cabaret* (n.p.: Salimpour, 1979). Ivanova discusses ancient evidence for these patterns of movement in Spain and the Western Mediterranean in *Dance in Spain.*

64. Buonaventura, *Serpent of the Nile*, 86.

65. Ibid.

66. Sered, *Priestess, Mother, Sacred Sister*, 62.

Chapter 2: Movement Matters

1. Plaskow, *Standing Again at Sinai*, 28–29.

2. Ibid., 34.

3. Peskowitz cites Gayatri Chakravorty Spivak when she criticizes Plaskow. However, Plaskow's addition of the body in the text is a break from a rationalist, male framework that prevents women's activity from being recorded as significant history. See Donaldson and Kwok, *Postcolonialism, Feminism, and Religious Discourse*, for essays on these issues.

4. Plaskow continued to address the issue in a paper that she presented at the 2007 American Academy of Religion conference. Titled "Embodiment, Elimination, and the Role of Toilets in Struggles for Social Justice," it explored the lack of sufficient toilet facilities for women and the associated issues of power and

equality. In the paper she looked at theory concerning women's bodies as inferior to men's. Elizabeth Grosz discusses the belief that women "seep" fluid in *Volatile Bodies*, 187–210. Plaskow contrasts this image to a perceived paragon of a rational, male executive who denies his bodily functions.

5. Plaskow, *Standing Again at Sinai*, 76; emphasis in the original.

6. Ibid., 36.

7. Grossman, *Pious and Rebellious*, 197.

8. Plaskow, *Standing Again at Sinai*, 57.

9. Miriam Peskowitz, "Engendering Jewish Religious History," in Peskowitz and Levitt, *Judaism since Gender*, 28, 33.

10. Plaskow, *Standing Again at Sinai*, 57.

11. See Alter, *Art of Biblical Narrative*.

12. Driver, *Magic of Ritual*, 140–41, 142.

13. Lakoff and Johnson, *Metaphors We Live By*, 13, 17–18.

14. Lakoff and Johnson, *Philosophy in the Flesh*, 3.

15. Ibid., 50, 180.

16. Ibid., 186.

17. Ibid., 567.

18. Ibid., 567–68.

19. Borg, *Reading the Bible Again*, 34.

20. Ibid., 102–6.

21. Frymer-Kensky, *Reading the Women of the Bible*, Introduction, esp. xvii.

22. Dalglish, "Skipping, Jumping, Twisting and Untwisting."

23. Winkler, *Magic of the Ordinary*, 25–27; emphasis in the original.

24. Ibid., 24.

25. Wolfson, "Body in the Text," 492, 493ff.

26. Boyarin, *Intertextuality*, 37.

27. Winkler, *Magic of the Ordinary*, 27–29.

28. Cass Dalglish, from a paper presented at the Red River Conference on World Literature in 2004.

29. Ariel, *Mystic Quest*, 103.

30. See Tishby, *Wisdom of the Zohar*, vol. 3, sec. I on the Temple, sec. II on prayer, Zohar 2:135a–b; Matt, *The Essential Kabbalah*, 80.

31. For more on embodiment in the Zohar, see Wolfson, "The Body in the Text." Wolfson finds that rather than humans embodying the ideas of the text, the letters and words of Torah represent human bodies. While he does not deal specifically with directives for action in the Zohar, his overall view supports the idea that Torah does not separate body, action, and idea.

32. Tishby, *Wisdom of the Zohar*, 1035, Zohar III, 170b–121a; ibid., 9540; ibid., 1052, Zohar II, 56b–57a—commentary on God's right hand, Ex. 15.6.

33. Buxbaum, *Jewish Spiritual Practices*, 487, quoting "Dance," in *Encyclopedia Judaica*, 5:1267.

34. Ibid., 490.

35. See Biale, *Gershom Scholem*; Satlow, *Creating Judaism*.

36. Rosenzweig, *Star of Redemption*, 372.

37. Ibid.

38. Driver, *Magic of Ritual*, 84.

39. Ibid., 91–92.

40. Grimes, *Deeply into the Bone*, 144.
41. Borowitz, *Choices*, 137.
42. Greenberg, *Better Than Wine*, 44–45; Fisdel, *Practice of Kaballah*, 90.
43. Greenberg, *Better Than Wine*, 76.
44. Ibid., 76–77, 39–40, 136–37.
45. Ibid., 101–2, 124; my emphasis.
46. Collingwood, *Principles of Art*, 372.
47. Greenberg, *Better Than Wine*, 124.
48. Ibid., 114; emphasis in the original.
49. Borowitz, *Choices*, 135.
50. Umansky, quoted in ibid., 314–15.
51. Asad, *Genealogies of Religion*, 54.
52. Dalglish, *Nin*, 252.

Chapter 3: Miriam's Dance

1. For a list of Ingber's works, including her latest work on Jewish dance history, see the bibliography.
2. Metzger and Metzger, *Jewish Life*, 9.
3. Beth Haber, "Women in Biblical Art," in Adelman, *Miriam's Well*, 16. Haber provides commentary on various depictions of Miriam (15–18). I agree with her that the style of painting in this particular depiction of Miriam is "International Gothic" (16). However, I find her labeling of the dance as "courtly" a judgment that does not consider dance history or Sephardic culture. Her remarks on the "grid of convention" come from literary scholar Robert Alter, who wrote: "A coherent reading of any art work . . . requires some detailed awareness of the grid of conventions upon which, and against which, the individual work operates." Alter, *Art of Biblical Narrative*, 47.
4. Shiloah, *Jewish Musical Traditions*, 176.
5. Miles, *Image as Insight*, 12.
6. I again credit Judith Brin Ingber for bringing the Miriam pictures to my attention, and sharing with me how she read the paintings and how she looked for suggested motions in the figures. With the insights she provided, I was able to examine these images and compare them with written texts.
7. Kealiinohomoku, "Dance Culture," 99.
8. Ibid., 99–100.
9. Metzger and Metzger, *Jewish Life*, 216; Narkiss, *Spanish and Portuguese Manuscripts*, pt. 1, 216, 42–43; Gutmann, *Hebrew Manuscript Painting*, 69.
10. Metzger and Metzger, *Jewish Life*, 217.
11. Schechner, "From Ritual to Theater and Back," esp. 75.
12. Ivanova, *Dance in Spain*, 44.
13. Ibid., 42–43.
14. Metzger and Metzger, *Jewish Life*, 146–47.
15. Hanna, *To Dance Is Human*, 126–27.
16. See Ivanova, *Dance in Spain*, 43.
17. Narkiss, *Spanish and Portuguese Manuscripts*, 77–78.
18. Ivanova, *Dance in Spain*, 54.

19. Ibid., 55.

20. Royce, *Anthropology of Dance*, 32–37.

21. Ibid., 94.

22. Ibid., 94–95.

23. Ibid., 35.

24. Narkiss, *Spanish and Portuguese Manuscripts*, 45.

25. Meyers, "Drum-Dance-Song Ensemble," 60–61.

26. Ibid., 64–66.

27. Pardes, *Countertraditions*, 90–93. According to the hymn Pardes provides, Isis's role was "creating breath with her wings," to bring Osiris back to life. This scene was also depicted in many Egyptian works of art (90). Lincoln Kirstein also notes that "wall reliefs at Gizeh . . . show girls posturing with tambourines, clacking castanets curved and carved to form conventionalized fingers"; *Dance*, 12.

28. Kirstein, *Dance*, 10–13.

29. Grossman, "Women and the Jerusalem Temple," 19.

30. Ibid.

31. Sendrey, *Music in Ancient Israel*, 520–21.

32. Grossman, "Women and the Jerusalem Temple," 22–24.

33. Patai, *Hebrew Goddess*, 85. Patai lists his source as M. Sukka 5:1. If you understand evidence to say that belly dances were used for Goddess/fertility rituals in the Near East, then the dancing for *Sukkot* may have included a women's *machol* dance. I discuss this issue in "Searching for Biblical Roots of Belly Dance."

34. Brooten, "Women Leaders"; Safrai, "Women and the Ancient Synagogue," 41–42.

35. Ibid., 43.

36. See Shiloah, *Jewish Musical Traditions*, 73–76.

37. Doug Adams provides a study of this discussion in *Congregational Dancing*, 99–101. He refers to R. Judah ben Zebna, Sotah 12a, the Talmud, and Nashim VI. See also Kethuboth 1:17a for a discussion on dance for weddings. For an example of how voice and rhythm instruments were used for Sabbath dancing, see Bahat and Bahat, "Jewish Yemenite Songs from the Diwan."

38. Epstein, trans., *The Babylonian Talmud*, 95.

39. Taitz, "Women's Voices, Women's Prayers," 61.

40. Haut, "Women's Prayer Groups," 137, 141.

41. Shiloah, *Jewish Musical Traditions*, 85.

42. See Ashtor, *Jews of Moslem Spain*, esp. 1:400–2, 3:162–64. Raymond Scheindlin, *Wine, Women and Death*, presents the poetry and culture of the *zambra* parties. Composed by noted medieval Jewish poets, the sensual poetry evokes images similar to those found in the Zohar.

43. Shiloah, *Jewish Musical Traditions*, 212–13.

44. Seroussi, "De-gendering Jewish Music."

45. See Schechner, *Essays*, 106–52. There were exceptions, and life passage events provide details of situations that were more like what Schechner describes as a braiding of cultural and religious performance.

46. Shiloah, *Jewish Musical Traditions*, 136.

47. Ibid., 137.

48. Ibid., 135–36, 146.

49. Ibid., 145.

50. Haut, "Women's Prayer Groups," 144–45.

51. Ibid., 156 n. 40.

52. Adams, *Congregational Dancing,* 89–94. Biblical passages he refers to are Exodus 15:20, Psalms 30:11, I Samuel 18:6, and Jeremiah 31:13. Talmudic references include Gemara Kethuboth 17a, Nashim III, Mishnah Sukkah 51a–b, Gemara Sukkah, and Mo'ed VI.

53. Rabbi Lynn Gottlieb brings out this point in *She Who Dwells Within.*

54. Haut, "Women's Prayer Groups," 155 n. 37. The NEV translates this passage as "The basin and its stand of bronze he made out of the bronze mirrors of the women who were on duty at the entrance to the Tent of the Presence."

55. Significantly, Ibn Ezra traveled widely around the Mediterranean and Arabic world. He is known for his meticulous attention to grammar. His translations were not always in keeping with rabbinic tradition, but neither were they kabbalistic.

56. Reguer, "Women and the Synagogue," 51–56, quote from 54.

57. Grossman, *Pious and Rebellious,* 154–55, 160–61, 186–87.

58. Shaye Cohen, "Purity and Piety," 104–13, 104; Grossman, *Pious and Rebellious,* 182–83.

59. Shaye Cohen, "Purity and Piety," 109–10.

60. Ashtor, *Jews of Moslem Spain,* 3:139–40. In comparison, Yitzhak Baer's information on education in Spain under the *Reconquista* does not comment directly on women, but he does note that there was a general problem of "illiteracy," even among men in ruling positions. Baer, *History of the Jews,* 1:432.

61. Sered, "Synagogue as a Sacred Space," 209.

62. See Joann Kealiinohomoku, "Hopi Social Dance," 36–37.

63. Baer, *History of the Jews,* 1:267. There is almost a paradox of information in this, as the kabbalistic imagery is of the courts. Again, there is an idealization factor involved. As a practical point of history, Ivanova says that the dances of the lower classes would not have differed much from that of the court, as mentioned above.

Chapter 4: Miriam at the Wedding Celebration

1. References to dates of performance are supplied in this and the following chapter when available. Of the reports I offer without a specific date, most were documented in the early twentieth century, from Israel post-1950 and looking back on the past, or reports of events that stem from practices dating back to at least the late nineteenth century. Ben-Zaken presents a typical example. She interviewed her grandmother in Israel. Her grandmother's recollection was of music and dance performed in Turkey in previous centuries, although she had nothing more specific in dating. Other sources have several differences; see, for example, http://www.cervantesvirtual.com/servlet/SirveObras/13583830989825832754491/p0000002.htm and María Eugenia Góngora, *Antología de poesía medieval* (Santiago: Bello, 1986).

2. Díaz-Mas, *Sephardim,* 30. The original Ladino reads: "A la salida del banyo se komia kozas se orno i se bevia raki en kantando i baylando en el hamam. En vezes esta seremoniya del banyo tomava lugar un dia antes de la boda . . . i se puede

dizir ke ere una fyesta de mujeres i de grande emportansa." Benbassa-Dudonney, "El Kazamyento de los djudyos-espanyoles," 34.

3. Citing Clifford Geertz, Margaret Miles reminds us that "It is not necessary to be theologically self-conscious to be religiously sophisticated." Miles, *Image as Insight*, 27.

4. Sered, *Women as Ritual Experts*, 104–6.

5. Shiloah, *Jewish Musical Traditions*, 174; see also Biale, *Eros and the Jews*, 127–28; for an Indian comparison, see Jacobson, "Marriage."

6. Stefani Levi, personal interview, October 2009.

7. Dobrinsky, *Treasury*, 48–49.

8. Ibid., 50.

9. Ibid., 56–57.

10. Ibid., 55–56.

11. Díaz-Mas, *Sephardim*, 29. Díaz-Mas cites Larrea Palacín, *Canciones rituales*, 14–15.

12. Díaz-Mas, *Sephardim*, 31, citing Benbassa-Dudonney, "El Kazamyento de los djudyos-espanyoles," 36.

13. In *Judeo-Spanish Moroccan Songs*, Weich-Shahak focuses primarily on women's singing, and there are many musical transcriptions of songs that were sung for different components of the wedding event. Judith Cohen and Oro Anahory-Librowicz have also made a detailed study of Sephardic women's wedding songs; some of their findings are included in the last part of this chapter.

14. Díaz-Mas, *Sephardim*, 30.

15. Shiloah, *Jewish Musical Traditions*, 49.

16. Ibid., 51.

17. Ibid., 51–53. Shiloah quotes from Dumas's book *Le Véloce: Ou Tanger, Alger et Tunis* (Brussels: El Gil Kaíammin, 1849), 79–93.

18. Ibid., 53.

19. Hanna, *Dance, Sex, and Gender*, 52–53. According to Anahory-Librowicz, wedding dances in Morocco were the same for Jews as for Muslims, except that the Jewish women could dance in front of the men. Interview with independent scholar Jaime Cader, March 1998.

20. Hanna, *Dance, Sex, and Gender*, 48–49.

21. Dance customs differed in the various communities, generally following the practices of their immediate neighbors. In general, rabbinic authority set restrictions on Jewish women's dance.

22. Shiloah, *Jewish Musical Traditions*, 175.

23. Ibid., 177. When I attended a Jewish wedding dance seminar, two Persian women described their henna ceremonies with similar detail. One said that she wiped off the henna paste so that she could get up and dance with the others. The dance manner was demonstrated, and followed a Persian–Middle Eastern styling.

24. Weich-Shahak, *Judeo-Spanish Moroccan Songs*, 11–12.

25. Ibid.

26. Larrea Palacín, *Canciones rituales*, 16. In Spanish, the report reads: "Al llegar a casa de la novia, las mujeres casadas de la familia del prometido le ponen los: una prenda cada una de ellas de esta guida: la chialdeta, o falda; el cazoto, o chaleco; el cazoto, o chaleco; la punta, o peto; las mangas; la ukaya que es una

faje de seda roja con franja de or que se colocas detras de las falda; la cuchaca, o cenidor, y las crinches, o madejas de hile negro que se le poned como postizo de cabellos."

27. Ibid., 16. In Spanish, the report reads: "Luego otras familares toman el retoñoy con el lian a la voia cinco vuelta en el cuello ye sobre los peches, con un nudo en cada vuelta."

28. According to Larrea Palacín, the ritual requirement for pure water was not enforced for the *lavado chiquita*. Ibid., 16–17.

29. Ibid., 16–17. In Spanish, the report reads:

> En el agua que sirvio para el lavado chiquito se derramo auea de rosas y disolvia azumbe, piedra olorosa; no era costumbre perfumar le del ban~o proque esta purification ritual se cumple en la tevila, piscina cuyas medidas y normas estan establecidas por preceptros religiouses. La madre del novio entrega la novia completamente desnuda a la bañera, o mujer encargada de asistra, la cual entra con aquella en el baño y cuida de que el agua la cubre por completo, de que no roce su cuerpo con los muros de la piscina y de rezar las oraciones de la purification . . .
>
> Es la madere del del novia quien viste la camis a la novia, ye las demas mujeres de la familia del desposado las demas prendas, que han de ser blancas para que lavida que va a comenzar sia clara y alegrea.

Translation in Díaz-Maz, *Sephardim*, 32.

30. According to Larrea Palacín, these items of clothing were wrapped around the bride.

31. See Rosenzweig, *The Star of Redemption*, chap. 2. Rosenzweig offers dance as the bridge between silence and the spoken word. He discusses dance as an art form (pt. 2, books 2 and 3), then comments on movement in Jewish worship in a separate section of the book (pt. 3, book 2).

32. Benbassa-Dudonney, "El Kazamyento de los djudyos-espanyoles," 36.

33. Steele, "The Bride Unveiled." "Ecstatic" is a word that conveys many meanings regarding a change in consciousness. In the more extreme sense, ecstatic dance may refer to trance dances such as those induced in *zar* and *vodoun* ceremonies. Other examples might include the Sufi whirling dervishes and Hasidic dancing in Judaism. I use the term in a more generic sense, recognizing that dance, drumming, and music will transform mood and activity.

34. Ibid.

35. Dobrinsky, *Treasury*, 48–49; Díaz-Mas, *Sephardim*, 29.

36. The types of lyrics for the wedding songs and their nature will be discussed below. Anahory-Librowicz mentions the risqué lyrics in "Expressive Modes," 285ff.

37. Sered, *Priestess, Mother, Sacred Sister*, 138–39.

38. Ibid., 128.

39. Northup, *Ritualizing Women*, 51.

40. Steele, "The Bride Unveiled."

41. Dosick, *Living Judaism*, 298.

42. Ibid., 296–98.

43. Díaz-Mas, *Sephardim*, 31; Dobrinsky, *Treasury*, 52, 57–58.

44. Hanna, *Dance, Sex, and Gender*, 22–23.

45. Kethuboth 1:17a; Nashim III:92–93, cited in Adams, *Congregational Dancing*, 93, 101. The house of Hillel stressed that it is important to rejoice at a wedding, and therefore one should dance for the bride.

46. Unterman, *Dictionary*, 118.

47. See Biale, *Eros and the Jews*, 110.

48. Patai, *Hebrew Goddess*, 268. Patai also details how the Matronit is derived from Near Eastern images of goddesses; ibid., 138–60.

49. Bohlman, "The Shechinah."

50. Sered, *Women as Ritual Experts*, 79. Sered also mentions women in male-dominated societies who emphasize or make their own use of parts of established practices (9).

51. Weich-Shahak, *Judeo-Spanish Moroccan Songs*, 50.

52. Shiloah, *Jewish Musical Traditions*, 193.

53. Larrea Palacín, *Canciones rituales*, 21–22.

54. Díaz-Mas, *Sephardim*, 119.

55. Díaz-Mas, *Sephardim*, 126; Larrea Palacín, *Canciones rituales*, 21–22. In Ladino, the last lines read "para ponerte la tu camiza/para meterte en el agua fria" and "para ponerte la tu delgada/para meterte en el auga clare."

56. Stotesbury, "Songs of Life," 11. Stotesbury shares her observations of a recording of the tune by Judy Frankel on her album *Silver & Gold*.

57. Anahory-Librowicz, "Expressive Modes," 285.

58. Ibid., 286, 288.

59. Ibid., 287, 289.

60. See Friedhaber, "Dance among the Jews."

61. Recording from Weich-Shahak, *Judeo-Spanish Moroccan Songs*, book 50, for musical transcription of audio recording.

62. Driver, *Magic of Ritual*, 30.

63. I say "Jewishness" understanding that Turner's description of the ritualization of the liminal is a temporary state, allowing for group expression, before returning to regulated society. In this case, the regulated society is a male-dominated Jewish community.

64. Driver, *Magic of Ritual*, 16.

65. Translation by Ben-Zaken, from *The Bride Unfastens Her Braids*.

66. Weich-Shahak, *Judeo-Spanish Moroccan Songs*, 77–78. In an interview, dance researcher Jaime Cader told of hearing about this dance from Oro Anahory-Librowicz, who said that it was done at the sea. So the lyrics might be taken literally.

67. Larrea Palacín, *Canciones rituales*, 92, 21.

68. Sered, *Women as Ritual Experts*, 102.

69. See Weissler, "The Tkhines."

70. Gottlieb, *She Who Dwells Within*, 137.

71. For more information on Jewish use and transformation of Goddess worship, see Frymer-Kensky, *In the Wake*, for a cogent and detailed argument.

72. Lévy and Lévy Zumwalt, *Ritual Medical Lore*, 159.

73. Ibid., 179–80.

74. Schechner, *Performance Theory*, 120.

75. Hanna, *To Dance Is Human*, 238.

76. Gottlieb, *She Who Dwells Within*, 116.

77. Ibid., 116–17, 130.

Chapter 5: The Rachel Tradition

1. Pohren, *The Art of Flamenco*, 144.
2. "Solea My Madre," written by Mari Elena, "La Cordobesa," recorded on Davies, *Paths of Convergence*.
3. In Ladino, the lyrics are "Ya crecen las hierbas / y dan de color, / y este, mi corazon, / vive con dolor. / Ya creceb kas guerbas / y dan de amarillo, / y este mi corazon / viva de suspiro."
4. In modern Spanish, *duende* means goblin. As used in flamenco, it appears to be related to the word *doler*, meaning grief, sorrow, and mourning.
5. See Amnon Shiloah on the *tanyaderas* in *Jewish Musical Traditions*; see also Novick, "History of Rosh Chodesh," 17.
6. Sered, *Priestess, Mother, Sacred Sister*, 130–33. See also the information below on Whyte, *Dance of Death*, as well as accounts given by Alvar in *Endechas*.
7. Shiloah, *Jewish Musical Traditions*, 178.
8. Ashtor, *Jews of Moslem Spain*, 3:115–21.
9. Baer, *History of the Jews*, 1:31, 444 fn.
10. Metzger and Metzger, *Jewish Life*, 154, 234.
11. Díaz-Mas, *Sephardim*, 32–33.
12. Dobrinsky, *Treasury*, 71, 69–109.
13. Alvar, *Endechas*, 26. Alvar cites Manuel L. Ortega in *Los hebreos en Marruecos: Estudio histórico, político y social*, 4th ed. (Madrid: Ed. Nuestra Raza, 1934). In Spanish, the quote reads: "Antes, y aun hoy en algunas ciudades, existian plañideras mercenarias que recitaban versos en la casa mortuoria y saltaban en lugubres danzas como poseidas, mesandose los cabellos, arañandose el rostro y lanzando macabros laments. Ya esta costumbre, que quiza fuera importada de Espana, va desaparciendo."
14. Ibid., 26.
15. Whyte, *Dance of Death*, 56–58. It should be noted that while Whyte's dissertation contains valuable material, it reflects antisemitic attitudes and displays a lack of knowledge about the positive multicultural life of medieval Spain. For instance, she calls the "Oriental" influence of the laments a result of "long contact with the alien races."
16. Ibid., 47–48.
17. Backman, *Religious Dances*, 140–42.
18. Ibid., 155–56.
19. Ibid.; my emphasis.
20. Ibid., 158.
21. Alvar, *Endechas*, 14–22.
22. Shiloah, *Jewish Musical Traditions*, 112.
23. Weich-Shahak, *Judeo-Spanish Moroccan Songs*, 12; see also Alvar, *Endechas*, 22–35.
24. *Saetas* are a flamenco *cante* of deep *duende*. Their origin in Jewish ritual laments is fairly well accepted.
25. Frymer-Kensky, *In the Wake*, 105.
26. Ibid., 166–68.
27. Ibid., 116.
28. Ibid., 36, 37.

29. Ibid.

30. Ibid., 38.

31. Frymer-Kensky comments on this at the end of *In the Wake of the Goddesses* and, perhaps unfortunately, attributes the loss of women's role within Judaism to Greek thought. Greek mythology and tradition also had an established pattern of death dances, some of which also stemmed from the Near East and Asia Minor. Furthermore, later Greek Neo-Platonic interpretations had a definite influence on the Spanish kabbalists, who regarded a feminine, earth-centered aspect of God as extremely important.

32. See Avenary "Flutes for a Bride or a Dead Man," 10–11.

33. Ibid., 15.

34. Ibid., 21. See the Talmud, Sukkah 51a–b, Mo'ed VI. It is striking that the fertility/*machol*-related flute was played in the Temple, and that the associated dance activity occurred within the Temple courts in mixed company, at least originally. The ceremony was tied to local fertility customs, but was used in the rabbinic period to celebrate the life and death cycle in nature.

35. Sendrey notes that in verse 17 of this passage, the wailing women are not simply *qinot*. Here they are described as *hakamot*—wise women. *Music in Ancient Israel*, 168. In the Talmud, Mo'ed Ketan 3:8D–E, 3:9, the rabbis first question what a dirge might be. The answer is that it is a mourning song of call and response. Women lead the dirge, teaching it to the mourners.

36. Sendrey, *Music in Ancient Israel*, 471, 473.

37. Gruber, "Ten Dance-Derived Expressions," 48–59. Gruber is citing W. O. E. Oesterley, *The Sacred Dance*, 44.

38. Sendrey, *Music in Ancient Israel*, 471–73.

39. A messianic hope of and belief in bodily resurrection was a living theology for the Jewish community of medieval Spain. Here I refer merely to the difference in understanding of a life and death cycle. Baer has quite a bit of information about this topic in *History of the Jews*, 2:159–62 (on messianic hope); "Destruction and Conversion," 2:95–169.

40. Mitchell, *Flamenco Deep Song*, 127.

41. See Pohren, *Art of Flamenco*, 39–40. In discussing these theories, Pohren draws from the classical flamenco studies of Manuel García Matos, Anselmo González Climent, Ricardo Molina and Antonio Mairena, Hipólito Rossy, and Manuel Ríos Ruiz.

42. Ibid. See also Miriam Sarada Phillips, "Both Sides of the Veil: A Comparative Analysis of Kathak and Flamenco Dance" (master's thesis, University of California, Los Angeles, 1991), 46, citing Mitchell on flamenco origins.

43. Pohren, *Art of Flamenco*, 41, 102, 154.

44. Ibid., 41, 53.

45. Mitchell, *Flamenco Deep Song*, 53.

46. Pohren, *Art of Flamenco*, 134.

47. Flamenco dance patterns do change over time. However, the overall pattern and especially the tone of the dances have remained consistent. *Soleares* is a good example. An art historian I talked to who studies flamenco history reminded me that it was not actually danced until the late nineteenth century, but agreed that visual information does seem to indicate that the typical patterns and tone of movement were consistent with the *endechas*.

48. Jiménez, *La otra historia,* 18–20, 104–5.

49. Ibid., 104–5.

50. Leah Novick describes customs of Jewish women for *Rosh Chodesh* in "History of Rosh Chodesh," 13–21.

51. Buxbaum, *Jewish Spiritual Practices,* 584.

52. Elijah de Vidas, quoted in ibid., 584–85.

53. Ibid., 575.

54. Northup, *Ritualizing Women,* 51, quoting Caroline Walker Bynum, "Complexity of Symbols," in Caroline Walker Bynum, Stevan Harrell, and Paula Richman, *Gender and Religion: On the Complexity of Symbols* (Boston: Beacon Press, 1986), 13.

55. Sered quoted in Berrin, *Celebrating the New Moon,* 79.

56. See Frymer-Kensky, *In the Wake,* 36–37.

Conclusion

1. Adler, *Engendering Judaism,* 37.

2. Ibid.

BIBLIOGRAPHY

Abrahams, Israel. *Jewish Life in the Middle Ages.* New York: Atheneum, 1981.
Adams, Doug. *Congregational Dancing in Christian Worship.* Rev. ed. Austin, Tex.: Sharing Co., 1980.
——. "Theological Expressions through Visual Art Forms." In *Art, Creativity, and the Sacred: An Anthology in Religion and Art,* edited by Diane Apostolos-Cappadona, 311–18. New York: Crossroad, 1988.
Adelman, Penina V. *Miriam's Well: Rituals for Jewish Women around the Year.* 2nd ed. New York: Biblio Press, 1990.
Adler, Rachel. *Engendering Judaism: An Inclusive Theology and Ethics.* Philadelphia: Jewish Publication Society, 1998.
Aguilar, Manuel, and Ian Robertson. *Jewish Spain: A Guide.* Madrid: Altalena, 1984.
"Al-Andalus: Where Three Worlds Met." *Unesco Courier,* December 1991, 14–44.
Alpert, Rebecca. "Our Lives Are the Text: Exploring Jewish Women's Rituals." *Bridges* 2, no. 1 (Spring 1991): 66–80.
Alter, Robert. *The Art of Biblical Narrative.* New York: Basic Books, 1983.
Alvar, Manuel. *Endechas judeo-españolas.* Granada: University of Granada, 1953.
Anahory-Librowicz, Oro. "Expressive Modes in the Judeo-Spanish Wedding Song." In *New Horizons in Sephardic Studies,* edited by Yedida K. Stillman and George K. Zucker, 285–96. Albany: State University of New York Press, 1993.
Ann, Martha, and Dorothy Myers Imel, eds. *Goddesses in World Mythology.* Santa Barbara, Calif.: ABC-CLIO, 1993.
Apffel-Marglin, Frédérique. "Female Sexuality in the Hindu World." In *Immaculate and Powerful: The Female in Sacred Image and Social Reality,* edited by Clarissa W. Atkinson, Constance H. Buchanan, and Margaret R. Miles, 39–59. Boston: Beacon Press, 1985.
——. *Wives of the God-King: The Rituals of the Devadasis of Puri.* Oxford: Oxford University Press, 1985.
Apostolos-Cappadona, Diane, and Doug Adams, eds. *Dance as Religious Studies.* New York: Crossroad, 1990.
Aranov, Saul I. *A Descriptive Catalogue of the Bension Collection of Sephardic Manuscripts and Texts.* Edmonton: University of Alberta Press, 1979.
Ariel, David S. *The Mystic Quest: An Introduction to Jewish Mysticism.* Northvale, N.J.: Jason Aronson, 1988.
Armistead, Samuel G. *El romancero judeo-español en el Archivo Menéndez Pidal:*

Catálogo-índice de romances y canciones. Madrid: Catédra-Seminario Menéndez Pidal, 1978.

Asad, Talal. *Genealogies of Religion: Discipline and Reasons of Power in Christianity and Islam.* Baltimore: Johns Hopkins University Press, 1993.

Ashtor, Eliyahu. *The Jews of Moslem Spain.* Translated from the Hebrew by Aaron Klein and Jenny Machlowitz Klein. 3 vols. Philadelphia: Jewish Publication Society of America, 1973.

Avenary, Hanoch. *Encounters of East and West in Music: Selected Writings.* Tel Aviv: Tel Aviv University, 1979.

———. "Flutes for a Bride or a Dead Man: The Symbolism of the Flute According to Hebrew Sources." *Orbis Musicae: Studies in Musicology* 1, no 1 (1971): 10–24.

Backman, E. Louis. *Religious Dances in the Christian Church and in Popular Medicine.* Translated by E. Classen. London: Allen and Unwin, 1952.

Baer, Yitzhak. *A History of the Jews in Christian Spain.* Translated from the Hebrew by Louis Schoffman. 2 vols. Philadelphia: Jewish Publication Society of America, 1966.

Bahat, Naomi, and Avner Bahat. "Jewish Yemenite Songs from the Diwan." Notes to *Jewish Yemenite Songs from the Diwan (Recordings and Commentaries),* AMTI 8201. Jerusalem: Hebrew University, 1982.

Barryte, Marcia Aron. "Dance among the Sephardic Jews from Rhodes Living in Los Angeles." Master's thesis, University of California, Los Angeles, 1984.

Bartenieff, Irmgard, and Martha Davis. *Effort-Shape Analysis of Movement: The Unity of Expression and Function.* 1965. Reprinted in Martha Davis, advisory ed., *Research Approaches to Movement and Personality.* New York: Arno Press, 1972.

Baskin, Judith R. "Jewish Women in the Middle Ages." In J*ewish Women in Historical Perspective,* edited by Judith R. Baskin, 94–114. Detroit: Wayne State University Press, 1991.

Beinart, Haim, ed. *The Sephardi Legacy.* 2 vols. Vol. 1. Jerusalem: Magnes Press, 1992.

Bell, Catherine. *Ritual: Perspectives and Dimensions.* Oxford: Oxford University Press, 1997.

———. *Ritual Theory, Ritual Practice.* Oxford: Oxford University Press, 1992.

Benbassa-Dudonney, Esther. "El Kazamyento de los djudyos-espanyoles en Turkiya a la fin del dizimueven siglo." In *Actas de las Jornadas de Estudios Sefardíes,* edited by Antonio Viudas Camarasa, 31–37. Cáceres: University of Extremadura, 1981.

Berk, Fred. *The Chasidic Dance.* New York: American Zionist Youth Foundation, 1975.

———. *Ha-Rikud: The Jewish Dance.* New York: American Zionist Youth Foundation, 1972.

Berrin, Susan, ed. *Celebrating the New Moon: A Rosh Chodesh Anthology.* Northvale, N.J.: Jason Aronson, 1996.

Biale, David. *Eros and the Jews: From Biblical Israel to Contemporary America.* New York: BasicBooks, 1992.

———. *Gershom Scholem: Kabbalah and Counter-History.* 2nd ed. Cambridge, Mass.: Harvard University Press, 1982.

Biale, Rachel. *Women and Jewish Law: An Exploration of Women's Issues in Halakhic Sources.* New York: Schocken Books, 1984.

Bialer, Yehuda L., and Estelle Fink. *Jewish Life in Art and Tradition.* Photographs by David Harris. London: Weidenfeld & Nicholson, 1976.

Bohlman, Philip V. "The Shechinah, or the Feminine Sacred in the Musics of the Jewish Mediterranean." *Music & Anthropology: Journal of Musical Anthropology of the Mediterranean,* no. 3 (1998), http://www.umbc.edu/MA/index/number3/bohlman/bohl_0.htm (accessed February 26, 2010).

Borg, Marcus J. *Reading the Bible Again for the First Time: Taking the Bible Seriously but Not Literally.* San Francisco: HarperOne, 2001.

Borowitz, Eugene B. *Choices in Modern Jewish Thought: A Partisan Guide.* New York: Behrman House, 1983.

Boyarin, Daniel. *Intertextuality and the Reading of Midrash.* Bloomington: Indiana University Press, 1994.

Brooks, Lynn Matluck. *The Dances of the Processions of Seville in Spain's Golden Age.* Kassel: Reichenberger, 1988.

Brooten, Bernadette. "Women Leaders in the Ancient Synagogue." In Grossman and Haut, *Daughters of the King.*

Bunis, David M. *Sephardic Studies: A Research Bibliography Incorporating Judezmo Language, Literature and Folklore, and Historical Background.* New York: Garland, 1981.

Buonaventura, Wendy. *Serpent of the Nile: Women and Dance in the Arab World.* New York: Interlink, 1989.

Butler, Judith. *Gender Trouble: Feminism and the Subversion of Identity.* New York: Routledge, 1990.

Buxbaum, Yitzhak. *Jewish Spiritual Practices.* Northvale, N.J.: Jason Aronson, 1994.

Cader, Jaime. "A Sefardi Woman from the Island of Rhodes." *Habibi* 16, no. 1 (Winter 1997): 13.

Cain, Kathleen. *Luna: Myth and Mystery.* Boulder, Colo.: Johnson Books, 1991.

Castel, Nico. *The Nico Castel Ladino Song Book.* Arranged by Richard J. Neumann. Cedarhurst, N.Y.: Tara Publications, 1981.

Chill, Abraham. *The Minhagim: The Customs and Ceremonies of Judaism, Their Origins and Rationale.* New York: Sepher-Hermon Press, 1979.

Christ, Carol P., and Judith Plaskow, eds. *Womanspirit Rising: A Feminist Reader in Religion.* San Francisco: HarperSanFrancisco, 1979.

Cohen, Judith R. "The Music of the Songs: Musical Transcriptions and Commentary of the Songs Discussed by Oro Anahory-Librowicz in 'Expressive Modes in the Judeo-Spanish Wedding Song.'" In *New Horizons in Sephardic Studies,* edited by Yedida K. Stillman and George K. Zucker, 297–304. Albany: State University of New York Press, 1993.

———. "'Ya Salió de le Mar': Judeo-Spanish Wedding Songs among Moroccan Jews in Canada." In *Women and Music in Cross-Cultural Perspective,* edited by Ellen Koskoff, 55–68. New York: Greenwood Press, 1987.

Collingwood, R. G. *The Principles of Art.* Oxford: Clarendon Press, 1938.

Cooey, Paula M. *Religious Imagination and the Body: A Feminist Analysis.* Oxford: Oxford University Press, 1994.

Dalglish, Cass. *Nin.* Duluth: Spinsters Ink, 2000.

———. "Skipping, Jumping, Twisting and Untwisting: Reading the Oldest and Newest of Writing Styles." *Enculturation* 1, no. 1 (Spring 1997). http:// enculturation.gmu.edu/1_1/dalglish.html (accessed April 23, 2010).

Danforth, Loring M., and Alexander Tsiaras. *The Death Rituals of Rural Greece.* Princeton, N.J.: Princeton University Press, 1982.

Davidman, Lynn, and Shelly Tenenbaum, eds. *Feminist Perspectives on Jewish Studies.* New Haven, Conn.: Yale University Press, 1994.

Davis, Martha, advisory ed. *Research Approaches to Movement and Personality.* New York: Arno Press, 1972.

Desmond, Jane C., ed. *Meaning in Motion: New Cultural Studies of Dance.* Durham, N.C.: Duke University Press, 1997.

Díaz-Mas, Paloma. *Sephardim: The Jews from Spain.* Translated by George K. Zucker. Chicago: University of Chicago Press, 1992.

Dobrinsky, Rabbi Herbert C. *A Treasury of Sephardic Laws and Customs: The Ritual Practices of Syrian, Moroccan, Judeo-Spanish and Spanish and Portuguese Jews of North America.* Hoboken, N.J.: Ktav, 1986.

Donaldson, Laura E., and Kwok Pui-lan. *Postcolonialism, Feminism, and Religious Discourse.* New York: Routledge, 2001.

Dosick, Rabbi Wayne. *Living Judaism: The Complete Guide to Jewish Belief, Tradition, and Practice.* San Francisco: HarperSanFrancisco, 1995.

Drinker, Sophie. *Music and Women: The Story of Women in Their Relation to Music.* New York: Feminist Press at CUNY, 1995.

Driver, Tom F. *The Magic of Ritual: Our Need for Liberating Rites That Transform Our Lives and Our Communities.* San Francisco: HarperSanFrancisco, 1991.

Eichenbaum, Rose. "A Comparative Study of the Liturgical Practices and Accompanying Dance and Ritualized Movement Behavior of the Ashkenazic and Sephardic Jews Living in Los Angeles." Master's thesis, University of California, Los Angeles, 1980.

Eilberg-Schwartz, Howard, ed. *People of the Body: Jews and Judaism from an Embodied Perspective.* Albany: State University of New York Press, 1992.

———. *The Savage in Judaism: An Anthropology of Israelite Religion and Ancient Judaism.* Bloomington: Indiana University Press, 1990.

Elazar, Daniel J. *The Other Jews: The Sephardim Today.* New York: Basic Books, 1989.

Eliade, Mircea. *The Sacred and the Profane: The Nature of Religion.* Translated from the French by Willard R. Trask. New York: Harcourt, Brace and Co., 1959.

Elwell, Sue Levi. "Reclaiming Jewish Women's Oral Tradition? An Analysis of Rosh Hodesh." In *Women at Worship: Interpretations of North American Diversity,* edited by Marjorie Procter-Smith and Janet R. Walton, 111–26. Louisville, Ky.: Westminster/John Knox Press, 1993.

Epstein, I. *The Babylonian Talmud.* London: Soncino Press, 1938.

———. *The Responsa of Rabbi Simon b. Zemah Duran, as a Source of the History of the Jews in North Africa.* Greenwich, Conn.: New York Graphic Society, 1971.

———. *The Responsa of Rabbi Solomon ben Adreth of Barcelona, 1235–1310 as a Source of the History of Spain: Studies in the Communal Life of the Jews in Spain as Reflected in the Responsa.* Greenwich, Conn.: New York Graphic Society, 1971.

Espenak, Liljan. *Dance Therapy: Theory and Application.* Springfield, Ill.: Thomas, 1981.

———. "A New Non-Verbal Approach to Personality Evaluation." Paper presented at the American Association on Mental Deficiency, Region 10, Conference at Provincetown, Mass., September 27–29, 1970.

al Faruqi, Lois Ibsen. "Dance as an Expression of Islamic Culture." *Dance Research Journal* 10, no. 2 (Spring–Summer 1978): 6–13.

———. "Dances of the Muslim People." *Dancescope* 11, no. 1 (1976): 43–51.

Fiorenza, Elisabeth Schüssler. *In Memory of Her: A Feminist Theological Reconstruction of Christian Origins.* New York: Crossroad, 1985.

Firestone, Tirzah. *The Receiving: Reclaiming Jewish Women's Wisdom.* San Francisco: HarperSanFrancisco, 2003.

Fisdel, Steven A. *The Practice of Kabbalah: Meditation in Judaism.* Northvale, N J.: Jason Aronson, 1995.

Fletcher, Richard. *Moorish Spain.* New York: H. Holt, 1992.

Flood, Gavin. *An Introduction to Hinduism.* New York: Cambridge University Press, 1996.

Friedhaber, Debbi. *From the Dance Customs of Kurdish Jews.* Haifa: Jewish Dance Archives, 1974.

Friedhaber, Zvi. "Bibliographic Sources in Research of Dance among the Jews." *Israel Dance Annual* (Tel Aviv), 1986, 31–34.

———. "Dance among the Jews in the Middle Ages and the Renaissance." *Israel Dance Annual* (Tel Aviv), 1984, 5–9.

———. "The Dance in the Jewish-Mediterranean Communities, since the Expulsion from Spain until the Beginning of the 19th Century." Ph.D. thesis, Hebrew University, 1986.

———. "Jewish Dance Tradition, Part 2: Dance in the Jewish Communities in Italy during and after the Renaissance." *Israel Dance Quarterly* (Tel Aviv), October 1994, 116–17.

Frymer-Kensky, Tikva. *In the Wake of the Goddesses: Women, Culture, and the Biblical Transformation of Pagan Myth.* New York: Fawcett Columbine, 1992.

———. *Reading the Women of the Bible: A New Interpretation of Their Stories.* New York: Schocken, 2002.

Gaster, Moses. *Daily and Occasional Prayers.* Vol. 1 of *The Book of Prayer and Order of Service: According to the Custom of the Spanish and Portuguese Jews.* London, 1901.

———. *Jewish Folk-Lore in the Middle Ages.* London: Jewish Chronicle, 1887.

Geertz, Clifford. *The Interpretation of Cultures: Selected Essays.* New York: Basic Books, 1973.

Gerber, Jane S. *The Jews of Spain: A History of the Sephardic Experience.* New York: Free Press, 1992.

Gerson-Kiwi, Edith. *Migrations and Mutations of the Music in East and West: Selected Writings.* Tel Aviv: Tel Aviv University, 1980.

———. "On the Musical Sources of the Judaeo-Hispanic *Romance.*" *Musica Quarterly* 50, no. 1 (1964): 31–43.

Giller, Pinchas. *Reading the Zohar: The Sacred Text of the Kabbalah.* Oxford: Oxford University Press, 2001.

Ginio, Alisa Meyuhas. *Jews, Christians, and Muslims in the Mediterranean World after 1492.* London: Frank Cass and Co., 1992.

Ginzberg, Louis. *The Legends of the Jews.* Translated from the German manuscript by Henrietta Szold. Philadelphia: Jewish Publication Society of America, 1909–38.

Goellner, Ellen W., and Jacqueline Shea Murphy. *Bodies of the Text: Dance as Theory, Literature as Dance.* New Brunswick, N.J.: Rutgers University Press, 1995.

Goitein, S. D. *A Mediterranean Society: The Jewish Communities of the Arab World as Portrayed in the Documents of the Cairo Geniza.* 6 vols. Berkeley: University of California Press, 1967.

Goldstein, David. *Hebrew Manuscript Painting.* London: British Library, 1985.

Gottlieb, Lynn. *She Who Dwells Within: A Feminist Vision of a Renewed Judaism.* New York: HarperCollins, 1995.

Green, Arthur, ed. *Jewish Spirituality: From the Bible through the Middle Ages.* New York: Crossroad, 1986.

Greenberg, Yudit Kornberg. *Better Than Wine: Love, Poetry, and Prayer in the Thought of Franz Rosenzweig.* Atlanta: Scholars Press, 1996.

Grimes, Ronald L. *Beginnings in Ritual Studies.* Rev. ed. Columbia: University of South Carolina Press, 1995.

———. *Deeply into the Bone: Re-inventing Rites of Passage.* Berkeley: University of California Press, 2000.

———. *Ritual Criticism: Case Studies in Its Practice, Essays on Its Theory.* Columbia: University of South Carolina Press, 1990.

Grossman, Avraham. *Pious and Rebellious: Jewish Women in Medieval Europe.* Waltham, Mass.: Brandeis University Press, 2004.

Grossman, Susan. "Women and the Jerusalem Temple." In *Daughters of the King: Women and the Synagogue,* edited by Susan Grossman and Rivka Haut, 15–37. Philadelphia: Jewish Publication Society, 1997.

Grossman, Susan, and Rivka Haut, eds. *Daughters of the King: Women and the Synagogue.* Philadelphia: Jewish Publication Society, 1997.

Grosz, Elizabeth. *Volatile Bodies: Toward a Corporeal Feminism.* Bloomington: Indiana University Press, 1994.

Gruber, Mayer I. *Aspects of Nonverbal Communication in the Ancient Near East.* Rome: Biblical Institute Press, 1980.

———. "Ten Dance-Derived Expressions in the Hebrew Bible." In *Dance as Religious Studies,* edited by Diane Apostolos-Cappadona and Doug Adams, 48–66. New York: Crossroad, 1990.

Gupta, Roxanne Kamayani. *A Yoga of Classical Indian Dance: The Yogini's Mirror.* Rochester, Vt.: Inner Traditions, 2000.

Gutmann, Joseph. *Hebrew Manuscript Painting.* New York: George Braziller, 1978.

Hacohen, Dvora, and Menachem Hacohen. *One People: The Story of the Eastern Jews.* Rev. ed. New York: Adama Books, 1986.

Hanna, Judith Lynne. *Dance, Sex, and Gender: Signs of Identity, Dominance, Defiance, and Desire.* Chicago: University of Chicago Press, 1988.

———. *To Dance Is Human: A Theory of Nonverbal Communication.* Chicago: University of Chicago Press, 1979.

Harding, M. Esther. *Women's Mysteries, Ancient and Modern: A Psychological Interpretation of the Feminine Principle as Portrayed in Myth, Story, and Dreams.* New York: Harper Colophon, 1976.

Haut, Rivka. "Women's Prayer Groups and the Orthodox Synagogue." In *Daughters of the King: Women and the Synagogue*, edited by Susan Grossman and Rivka Haut, 135–58. Philadelphia: Jewish Publication Society, 1997.

Heschel, Susannah. *On Being a Jewish Feminist: A Reader*. New York: Schocken, 1983.

Heskes, Irene. "Miriam's Sisters: Jewish Women and Liturgical Music." *Notes* 48, no. 4 (June 1992): 1193–1202.

Hoffman, Lawrence A. *Beyond the Text: A Holistic Approach to Liturgy*. Bloomington: Indiana University Press, 1987.

———. *The Canonization of the Synagogue Service*. Notre Dame, Ind.: University of Notre Dame Press, 1979.

Idel, Moshe. *Enchanted Chains: Techniques and Rituals in Jewish Mysticism*. Los Angeles: Cherub Press, 2005.

———. "Jewish Thought in Medieval Spain." In *The Sephardi Legacy*, edited by Haim Beinart, 1:261–81. Jerusalem: Magnes Press, 1992.

———. *Kabbalah: New Perspectives*. New Haven, Conn.: Yale University Press, 1996.

Ingber, Judith Brin, ed. "Dancing into Marriage: Collected Papers on Jewish Wedding Dances." *Dance Research Journal* 17, no. 1 and 18, no. 2 (Fall 1985–Spring 1986): 49–86.

———. *Dancing into Marriage: Two-Day Conference on Jewish Wedding Dance*. Minneapolis: Jewish Research Center of Greater Minneapolis, 1982.

———. *Seeing Israeli and Jewish Dance*. Detroit: Wayne State University Press, forthcoming.

———. *Shorashim: The Roots of Israeli Folk Dance*. New York: Dance Perspectives Foundation, 1974.

———. *Victory Dances: The Story of Fred Berk, a Modern Day Jewish Dancing Master*. Tel Aviv: Israel Dance Library, 1985.

Ivanova, Anna. *The Dance in Spain*. New York: Praeger Publishers, 1970.

Jacobson, Doranne. "Marriage: Women in India." In *The Life of Hinduism*, edited by John Stratton Hawley and Vasudha Narayanan, 63–75. Berkeley: University of California Press, 2006.

Jagoda, Flory. *The Flory Jagoda Songbook: Memories of Sarajevo*. Cedarhurst, N.Y.: Tara Publications, 1993.

Jiménez, José Romero. *La otra historia del flamenco: La tradición semetico musical andaluza*. Seville: Junta de Andalucía, Consejería de Cultura, Centro Andaluz de Flamenco, 1997.

Kadmon, Gurit. *'Am Roked* [A People Dance]. Tel Aviv: Shoken, 1969.

Kaplan, Aryeh. *Meditation and Kabbalah*. Northvale, N.J.: Jason Aronson, 1995.

Katz, Israel. "The Musical Legacy of the Judeo-Spanish Romancero." In *Hispania Judaica: Studies on the History, Language, and Literature of the Jews in the Hispanic World*, edited by Josep M. Solà-Solé, Samuel G. Armistead, and Joseph H. Silverman, 2:45–58. Barcelona: Puvill, 1980.

———. "The 'Myth' of the Sephardic Musical Legacy from Spain." In *Proceedings of the Fifth World Congress of Jewish Studies*, edited by Pinchas Peli, 4:237–43. Jerusalem: World Union of Jewish Studies, 1973.

Kealiinohomoku, Joann. "Dance Culture as a Microcosm of Holistic Culture." In *New Dimensions in Dance Research: Anthropology and Dance—The American*

Indian, edited by Tamara Comstock, 99–106. Tucson: University of Arizona, 1974.

———. "Hopi Social Dance as a Means for Maintaining Homeostasis." In *Hopi Music and Dance,* by Robert Rhodes. Tsaile, Ariz.: Navaho Community College Press, 1977.

Kedourie, Elie, ed. *The Jewish World: History and Culture of the Jewish People.* New York: Henry N. Abrams, 1979.

———. *Spain and the Jews: The Sephardi Experience, 1492 and After.* London: Thames and Hudson, 1992.

Kilmer, Anne Draffkorn. "Music and Dance in Ancient Western Asia." In *Civilizations of the Ancient Near East,* edited by Jack M. Sasson, 4:2601–13. New York: Charles Scribner's Sons.

King, Richard. *Orientalism and Religion: Postcolonial Theory, India and "the Mystic East."* New York: Routledge, 1999.

Kinkelday, Otto. *A Jewish Dancing Master of the Renaissance: Guglielmo Ebreo.* New York: Dance Horizons, 1929.

Kirstein, Lincoln. *Dance: A Short History of Classic Theatrical Dancing.* Princeton, N.J.: Princeton Book Co., 1987.

Kitov, Eliyahu. *The Book of Our Heritage: The Jewish Year and Its Days of Significance.* 3 vols. New York: Feldheim, 1978.

Laban, Rudolf von. *Laban's Principles of Dance and Movement Notation.* 2nd ed. Boston: Plays, inc., 1975.

Lakoff, George, and Mark Johnson. *Metaphors We Live By.* Chicago: University of Chicago Press, 1980.

———. *Philosophy in the Flesh: The Embodied Mind and Its Challenge to Western Thought.* New York: Basic Books, 1999.

Langer, Robert, Dorothea Lüddeckens, Kerstin Radde, and Jan Snoek. "Transfer of Ritual." *Journal of Ritual Studies,* 20, no. 1 (2006): 1–10.

Lapson, Dvora. "Dance." In *The Universal Jewish Encyclopedia,* 3:455–63. New York: Universal Jewish Encyclopedia Co., 1939.

Larrea Palacín, Arcadio de. *Canciones rituales hispano-judias: Celebraciones familiares de tránsito y ciclo festivo anual.* Madrid: Instituto de Estudios Africanos, 1954.

Lawler, Lillian B. *The Dance in Ancient Greece.* Middletown, Conn.: Wesleyan University Press, 1978.

Levy, Fran J. *Dance/Movement Therapy: A Healing Art.* Rev. ed. Reston, Va.: National Dance Association, American Alliance for Health, Physical Education, Recreation and Dance, 1992.

Lévy, Isaac Jack, and Rosemary Lévy Zumwalt. *Ritual Medical Lore of Sephardic Women: Sweetening the Spirits, Healing the Sick.* Urbana: University of Illinois Press, 2002.

Maimonides, Moses. *Kovets teshuvot ha-Rambam ve-igrotav.* Leipzig: Ba-defus shel H. L. Shnoys, 1859.

Markus, Jacob R. *The Jew in the Medieval World: A Source Book, 315–1791.* Cincinnati: Sinai Press, 1938.

Martin, Randy. *Critical Moves: Dance Studies in Theory and Politics.* Durham, N.C.: Duke University Press, 1998.

Matt, Daniel C. *The Essential Kabbalah: The Heart of Jewish Mysticism.* San Francisco: HarperSanFrancisco, 1996.

———. *Zohar: The Book of Enlightenment.* New York: Paulist Press, 1983.

———. *The Zohar: Pritzker Edition.* 5 vols. Stanford, Calif.: Stanford University Press, 2003–2009. Aramaic text and online resources, http://www.sup.org/zohar/ (accessed April 23, 2010).

Merrill-Mirsky, Carol. "Judeo-Spanish Song from the Island of Rhodes: A Musical Tradition in Los Angeles." Master's thesis, University of California, Los Angeles, 1984.

Metzger, Thérèse, and Mendel Metzger. *Jewish Life in the Middle Ages: Illuminated Hebrew Manuscripts of the Thirteenth to the Sixteenth Centuries.* New York: Alpine Fine Arts Collection, 1982.

Meyers, Carol. "The Drum-Dance-Song Ensemble: Women's Performance in Biblical Israel." In *Rediscovering the Muses: Women's Musical Traditions,* edited by Kimberly Marshall, 49–67. Boston: Northeastern University Press, 1993.

Miles, Margaret R. *Image as Insight: Visual Understanding in Western Christianity and Secular Culture.* Boston: Beacon Press, 1985.

Millgram, Abraham E. *Jewish Worship.* 2nd ed. Philadelphia: Jewish Publication Society of America, 1975.

Mitchell, Timothy. *Flamenco Deep Song.* New Haven, Conn.: Yale University Press, 1994.

———. *Passional Culture: Emotion, Religion, and Society in Southern Spain.* Philadelphia: University of Pennsylvania Press, 1990.

Moscona, Isak. "Rituals and Customs of the Bulgarian Jews in the Past." *Social, Cultural and Educational Association of the Jews in the People's Republic of Bulgaria, Central Board: Annual* (Sofia) 7 (1972): 173–95.

Mutius, Hans-Georg von. *Rechtsentscheide jüdischer aus dem maurischen Cordoba.* Frankfurt am Main: Peter Lang, 1990.

Narkiss, Bezalel. *The Spanish and Portuguese Manuscripts.* Vol. 1 of *Hebrew Illuminated Manuscripts in the British Isles.* Part 1: Text. Part 2: Plates. Jerusalem: Oxford University Press for the Israel Academy of Sciences and Humanities and the British Academy, 1982.

Neuman, Abraham A. *The Jews in Spain: Their Social, Political and Cultural Life during the Middle Ages.* 2 vols. Philadelphia: Jewish Publication Society of America, 1942.

Neusner, Jacob. *A History of the Mishnaic Law of Women.* 5 vols. Leiden: Brill, 1980.

———. *The Talmud of Babylonia.* Atlanta: Scholars Press, 1996.

Northup, Lesley A. *Ritualizing Women: Patterns of Spirituality.* Cleveland, Ohio: Pilgrim Press, 1997.

Novick, Leah. "The History of Rosh Chodesh and Its Evolution as a Woman's Holiday." In *Celebrating the New Moon: A Rosh Chodesh Anthology,* edited by Susan Berrin, 13–22. Northvale, N.J.: Jason Aronson, 1996.

Oesterley, W. O. E. *The Sacred Dance: A Study in Comparative Folklore.* New York: Cambridge University Press, 1923.

Pardes, Ilana. *Countertraditions in the Bible: A Feminist Approach.* Cambridge, Mass.: Harvard University Press, 1992.

Patai, Raphael. *The Hebrew Goddess.* 3rd enl. ed. Detroit: Wayne State University Press, 1990.

———. *On Jewish Folklore.* Detroit: Wayne State University Press, 1983.

Pérez, Joseph. *History of a Tragedy: The Expulsion of the Jews from Spain.* Translated from the Spanish by Lysa Hochroth. Urbana: University of Illinois Press, 2007.

Peskowitz, Miriam, and Laura Levitt, eds. *Judaism since Gender.* New York: Routledge, 1997.

Plaskow, Judith. "Embodiment, Elimination, and the Role of Toilets in Struggles for Social Justice." Paper presented at the American Academy of Religion Conference, November 2007, San Diego, Calif.

———. "Embodiment, Elimination, and the Role of Toilets in Struggles for Social Justice." *CrossCurrents: The Journal of Addiction and Mental Health* 58, no. 1 (2008): 51–64.

———. *Standing Again at Sinai: Judaism from a Feminist Perspective.* San Francisco: Harper and Row, 1990.

Plaskow, Judith, and Carol P. Christ, eds. *Weaving the Visions: New Patterns in Feminist Spirituality.* San Francisco: HarperSanFrancisco, 1989.

Pohren, D. E. *The Art of Flamenco.* Madrid: Society of Spanish Studies, 1990.

Raphael, Chaim. *The Road from Babylon: The Story of Sephardi and Oriental Jews.* New York: Harper & Row, 1985.

———. *The Sephardi Story: A Celebration of Jewish History.* London: Vallentine Mitchell, 1991.

Redfern, Betty. *Introducing Laban Art of Movement.* London. MacDonald & Evans, 1965.

Reguer, Sara. "Women and the Synagogue in Medieval Cairo." In *Daughters of the King: Women and the Synagogue,* edited by Susan Grossman and Rivka Haut, 51–57. Philadelphia: Jewish Publication Society, 1997.

Rhodes, Robert. *Hopi Music and Dance.* Tsaile, Ariz.: Navaho Community College Press, 1977.

Rosenberg, Roy A. *The Anatomy of God: The Book of Concealment, the Great Holy Assembly and the Lesser Holy Assembly of the Zohar, with the Assembly of the Tabernacle.* New York: Ktav, 1973.

Rosenzweig, Franz. *The Star of Redemption.* New York: Holt, Rinehart and Winston, 1971.

Roth, Cecil. *Doña Gracia of the House of Nasi.* Philadelphia: Jewish Publication Society of America, 1977.

———. *The Jews in the Renaissance.* Philadelphia: Jewish Publication Society of America, 1959.

Royce, Anya Peterson. *The Anthropology of Dance.* Bloomington: Indiana University Press, 1977.

Rush, Anne Kent. *Moon, Moon.* New York: Random House, 1976.

Sachar, Howard M. *Farewell España: The World of the Sephardim Remembered.* New York: Knopf, 1994.

Sachs, Curt. *A World History of the Dance.* Translated by Bessie Schönberg. New York: Bonanza Books, 1937.

Sacks, Maurie, ed. *Active Voices: Women in Jewish Culture.* Urbana: University of Illinois Press, 1995.

Safrai, Hannah. "Women and the Ancient Synagogue." In *Daughters of the King: Women and the Synagogue,* edited by Susan Grossman and Rivka Haut, 39–49. Philadelphia: Jewish Publication Society, 1997.

Satlow, Michael L. *Creating Judaism: History, Tradition, Practice.* New York: Columbia University Press, 2006.

Sautter, Cynthia. "Searching for Biblical Roots of Belly Dance." *Habibi* 16, no. 1 (Winter 1997): 8–9, 23.

Schechner, Richard. *Between Theater and Anthropology.* Philadelphia: University of Pennsylvania Press, 1985.

———. *Essays on Performance Theory, 1970–1976.* New York: Drama Book Specialists, 1997.

———. "From Ritual to Theater and Back: The Structure/Process of the Efficacy-Entertainment Braid." In *Essays on Performance Theory, 1970–1976,* 63–98. New York: Drama Book Specialists, 1997.

———. *The Future of Ritual: Writings on Culture and Performance.* New York: Routledge, 1993.

———. *Performance Theory.* Rev. and expanded ed. New York: Routledge, 1988.

Schechner, Richard, and Mady Schuman, eds. *Ritual, Play, and Performance: Readings in the Social Sciences/Theatre.* New York: Seabury Press, 1976.

Scheindlin, Raymond P. *The Gazelle: Medieval Hebrew Poems on God, Israel, and the Soul.* Philadelphia: Jewish Publication Society, 1991.

———. *Wine, Women, and Death: Medieval Hebrew Poems on the Good Life.* Philadelphia: Jewish Publication Society, 1986.

Scholem, Gershom. *Kabbalah.* Jerusalem: Keter, 1974.

———. *Major Trends in Jewish Mysticism.* New York: Schocken, 1941.

———. *Zohar: The Book of Splendor.* New York: Schocken, 1963.

Sendrey, Alfred. *Music in Ancient Israel.* New York: Philosophical Library, 1969.

Sered, Susan Starr. *Priestess, Mother, Sacred Sister: Religions Dominated by Women.* New York: Oxford University Press, 1994.

———. "The Synagogue as a Sacred Space for the Elderly Oriental Women of Jerusalem." In *Daughters of the King: Women and the Synagogue,* edited by Susan Grossman and Rivka Haut, 205–16. Philadelphia: Jewish Publication Society, 1997.

———. *Women as Ritual Experts: The Religious Lives of Elderly Jewish Women in Jerusalem.* New York: Oxford University Press, 1992.

Seroussi, Edwin. "De-gendering Jewish Music: The Survival of the Judeo-Spanish Folk Song Revisited." *Journal of Musical Anthropology of the Mediterranean* 3 (November 1998). http://www.muspe.unibo.it/period/ma/index/number3/seroussi/ser_o.htm (accessed April 23, 2010).

Shaye Cohen, D. J. "Purity and Piety: The Separation of Menstruants from the Sancta." In *Daughters of the King: Women and the Synagogue,* edited by Susan Grossman and Rivka Haut, 103–15. Philadelphia: Jewish Publication Society, 1997.

Shiloah, Amnon. *Jewish Musical Traditions.* Detroit: Wayne State University Press, 1992.

———. "The Ritual and Music of the Synagogue." In *The Jewish World: Revelation, Prophecy and History,* edited by Kedourie Elie, 120–27. New York: H. N. Abrams, 1979.

Silberman, Neil Asher. *Heavenly Powers: Unraveling the Secret History of the Kabbalah.* Edison, N.J.: Castle Books, 1998.

Slingerland, Edward. *What Science Offers the Humanities: Integrating Body and Culture.* New York: Cambridge University Press, 2008.

Smith, Jonathan Z. *Imagining Religion: From Babylon to Jonestown.* Chicago: University of Chicago Press, 1982.

Spector, Johann. "Bridal Songs and Ceremonies from Sana'a." In *Studies in Biblical and Jewish Folklore,* edited by Raphael Patai, Francis Lee Utley, and Dov Noy, 255–84. Bloomington: Indiana University Press, 1960.

Spencer, Paul, ed. *Society and the Dance: The Social Anthropology of Process and Performance.* New York: Cambridge University Press, 1985.

Sperling, Harry, and Maurice Simon, trans. *The Zohar.* London: Soncino Press, 1931.

Steele, Mike. "The Bride Unveiled." *Minneapolis Star Tribune,* July 5, 1998, F1, F5.

Steinsaltz, Adin. *The Talmud: The Steinsaltz Edition.* Vol. 7: *Tractate Ketubot, Pt. 1.* New York: Random House, 1989.

Stevenson, Robert. *Spanish Music in the Age of Columbus.* The Hague: M. Nijhoff, 1960.

Stillman, Norman A. *The Jews of Arab Lands: A History and Source Book.* Philadelphia: Jewish Publication Society of America, 1979.

Stillman, Yedida. "The Art of Women Singing in Morocco." In *African Jewry in the Nineteenth and Twentieth Centuries,* edited by Mikhael Avitbol, 163–71. Jerusalem: Ben Zvi Institute, 1980. (English/Spanish/Hebrew)

Stone, Merlin. *Ancient Mirrors of Womanhood: A Treasury of Goddess and Heroine Lore from around the World.* Boston: Beacon Press, 1979.

Stotesbury, Vivian J. "Songs of Life: Music of the Sephardim." *Habibi* 16, no. 1 (Winter 1997): 10–12.

Suarès, Carlo. *The Song of Songs: The Canonical Song of Solomon Deciphered According to the Original Code of the Qabala.* Berkeley, Calif.: Shambala, 1972.

Taitz, Emily. "Women's Voices, Women's Prayers: The European Synagogues of the Middle Ages." In *Daughters of the King: Women and the Synagogue,* edited by Susan Grossman and Rivka Haut, 59–71. Philadelphia: Jewish Publication Society, 1997.

Tishby, Isaiah. "The Doctrine of Man in the Zohar." In *Essential Papers on Kabbalah,* edited by Lawrence Fine, 109–53. New York: New York University Press, 1995.

———. "Prayer and Devotion in the Zohar." In *Essential Papers on Kabbalah,* edited by Lawrence Fine, 341–99. New York: New York University Press, 1995.

———, ed. *The Wisdom of the Zohar.* 3 vols. Oxford: Oxford University Press, 1989.

Trachtenberg, Joshua. *Jewish Magic and Superstition: A Study in Folk Religion.* New York: Atheneum, 1977.

Tsoffar, Ruth. *The Stains of Culture: An Ethno-Reading of Karaite Jewish Women.* Detroit: Wayne State University Press, 2006.

Turner, Victor W. *The Ritual Process: Structure and Anti-Structure.* Baltimore: Penguin Books, 1969.

Twersky, Isadore, ed. *Rabbi Moses Nahmanides (Ramban): Explorations in His Religious and Literary Virtuosity.* Cambridge, Mass.: Harvard University Press, 1983.

———. *Studies in Medieval Jewish History and Literature.* Cambridge, Mass.: Harvard University Press, 1979.

Umansky, Ellen M. "Creating a Jewish Feminist Theology: Problems and Possibilities." In *Weaving the Visions: New Patterns in Feminist Spirituality,* edited by Judith Plaskow and Carol P. Christ, 187–98. San Francisco: HarperSanFrancisco, 1989.

———. "Finding God: Women in the Jewish Tradition." *Cross Currents* 41, no. 4 (Winter 1991): 521–37.

———. "Special Section on Appropriation and Reciprocity in Womanist/Mujerista/Feminist Work: Respondents." *Journal of Feminist Studies in Religion* 8, no. 2 (Fall 1992): 120–22.

Unterman, Alan. *Dictionary of Jewish Lore and Legend.* London: Thames and Hudson, 1991.

Van der Leeuw, G. *Religion in Essence and Manifestation.* Tübingen: J. C. B. Mohr, 1977.

———. *Sacred and Profane Beauty: The Holy in Art.* New York: Holt, Rinehart and Winston, 1963.

Weich-Shahak, Susana. *Judeo-Spanish Moroccan Songs for the Life Cycle/Cantares judeo españoles de Marruecos para el ciclo de la vida.* Jerusalem: Jewish Music Research Centre, Hebrew University of Jerusalem, 1989.

———. "Structural Phenomena in the Wedding Songs of Bulgarian Sephardic Jews." In *The Sephardi and Oriental Jewish Heritage: Studies,* edited by Issachar Ben-Ami, 413–20. Jerusalem: Magnes Press, 1982.

———. "The Wedding Songs of the Bulgarian-Sephardi Jews." *Orbis Musicae* 7 (1979): 81–107.

Weissler, Chava. "The Tkhines and Women's Prayer." *CCAR Journal* 40 (Fall 1993): 75–88.

Whyte, Florence. *The Dance of Death in Spain and Catalonia.* Baltimore: Waverly Press, 1931.

Winkler, Gershon. *Magic of the Ordinary: Recovering the Shamanic in Judaism.* Berkeley, Calif.: North Atlantic Books, 2003.

Wolfson, Elliot R. "The Body in the Text: A Kabbalistic Theory of Embodiment." *Jewish Quarterly Review* 95, no. 3 (2005): 479–500.

———. *Circle in the Square: Studies in the Use of Gender in Kabbalistic Symbolism.* Albany: State University of New York Press, 1995.

Discography

Altramar Medieval Music Ensemble. *Iberian Garden: Jewish, Christian, and Muslim Music in Medieval Spain.* Vol. 2. Troy, N.Y.: Dorian Discovery, 1998.

Anahory-Librowicz, Oro. *Cancionero séphardi du Québec* (recording and video). Montreal: Collège du Vieux Montréal, 1988.

Ben-Zaken, Eti. *The Bride Unfastens Her Braids, the Groom Faints: Ladino Love Songs.* San Francisco: New Albion Records, 1999.

Canto Antiguo. *Musical Traditions of the Sephardim: A Mediaeval View of Judeo-Spanish Song.* Somerville, Mass.: Titanic Records, 1993.

Davies, Scott Mateo. *Paths of Convergence.* Minneapolis: Robbins Music Corporation, 1995.

Frankel, Judy. *Sephardic Songs of Love and Hope (Canticas Sephardis de amor y esperansa).* New York: Global Village Music, 1992.

———. *Silver & Gold (Pata y oro)*. San Francisco: Judy Frankel, 1997.

Jagoda, Flory. *The Grandmother Sings (La nona kanta)*. New York: Global Village Music, 1992.

———. *Memories of Sarajevo*. New York: Global Village Music, 1991.

———. *Songs of My Grandmother (Kantikas di mi nona)*. New York: Global Village Music, 1989.

La Rondinella. *A Song of David: Music of the Sephardim and Renaissance Spain*. Troy, N.Y.: Dorian Discovery, 1995.

———. *Songs of the Sephardim: Traditional Music of the Spanish Jews*. Troy, N.Y.: Dorian Discovery, 1993.

Levy, Gloria. *Sephardic Folk Songs*. New York: Folkways Records, 1958.

Voice of the Turtle. *Bridges of Song: Music of the Spanish Jews of Morocco*. Somerville, Mass.: Titanic Records, 1990.

Yurchenco, Henrietta. *Ballads, Wedding Songs, and Piyyutim of the Sephardic Jews of Tetuan and Tangier, Morocco*. New York: Folkways, 1983.

INDEX

Biblical Passages Cited

Talmud Passages Cited